Paying Calls in Shangri-La

ADST·DACOR Diplomats and Diplomacy Series

Series Editor: MARGERY BOICHEL THOMPSON

Since 1776, extraordinary men and women have represented the United States abroad under widely varying circumstances. What they did and how and why they did it remain little known to their compatriots. In 1995, the Association for Diplomatic Studies and Training (ADST) and DACOR, an organization of foreign affairs professionals, created the Diplomats and Diplomacy book series to increase public knowledge and appreciation of the professionalism of American diplomats and their involvement in world history. JUDITH HEIMANN's portrait of a tandem couple's diplomatic career is the 60th volume in the series.

Paying Calls in Shangri-La

Scenes from a Woman's Life
in American Diplomacy

• • • • • • • • • • • •

JUDITH M. HEIMANN

AN ADST-DACOR DIPLOMATS AND DIPLOMACY BOOK
OHIO UNIVERSITY PRESS • ATHENS

Ohio University Press, Athens, Ohio 45701
ohioswallow.com

Printed in the United States of America
Ohio University Press books are printed on acid-free paper ⊗ ™

26 25 24 23 22 21 20 19 18 17 16   5 4 3 2 1

Library of Congress Cataloging-in-Publication Data

Names: Heimann, Judith M., author.
Title: Paying calls in Shangri-La : scenes from a woman's life in American diplomacy / Judith M. Heimann.
Description: Athens : Ohio University Press, 2016. | Series: An ADST-DACOR diplomats and diplomacy book | Includes bibliographical references and index.
Identifiers: LCCN 2016024896 | ISBN 9780821422328 (hardcover : acid-free paper) | ISBN 9780821422335 (paperback : acid-free paper) | ISBN 9780821445785 (electronic)
Subjects: LCSH: Heimann, Judith M. | Women diplomats—United States—Biography. | Diplomats—United States—Biography. | Diplomats' spouses—United States—Biography. | Diplomacy—Social aspects—History—20th century. | United States. Foreign Service—Officials and employees—Biography. | United States—Foreign relations—1945—1989. | BISAC: BIOGRAPHY & AUTOBIOGRAPHY / Women. | BIOGRAPHY & AUTOBIOGRAPHY / Personal Memoirs. | POLITICAL SCIENCE / International Relations / Diplomacy.
Classification: LCC E840.8.H436 A3 2016 | DDC 327.730092 [B] —dc23
LC record available at https://lccn.loc.gov/2016024896

Dedicated to my late husband, my son,

my grandson, my daughter and daughter-in-law,

and all daughters finding their way in an ever-new world

*All that I hope to say
in books, all that I
ever hope to say, is
that I love the world.*

—*E. B. White*

Contents

• • • • • •

Illustrations

• • • • • • •

Following page 110

Prologue

• • • • • •

Memory is a funny thing. I cannot remember where I left my keys an hour ago. But, if I concentrate, I can clearly remember me at seventeen, standing next to the Christmas tree in our comfortably shabby sixth-floor walk-up apartment on York Avenue in Manhattan. I was standing perfectly still, better to observe my wonderful mother look at twenty-year-old John Heimann. John was a Harvard classmate I had met that fall, and I already suspected he would be my life's companion.

My mother, a tall, good-looking, clever, and worldly woman, had sought divorce (when I was eight years old) despite what she knew would be our consequent straitened circumstances. She had found she preferred having lovers she could send home, rather than continue being the wife of my father, Warren Moscow. He was a man she liked and respected as a talented journalist, but after years of trying, she found she could not love him enough to give away her independence.

By now (1953), I had long been the person she cared most about in the world. And I could see she was looking at John as someone who very likely would marry me in the next few years. He had made no secret of his plan to take me away to the ends of the earth, as he pursued his dream career as an American diplomat, beginning right after college.

I could read her expressions so well that it was almost as if she said out loud: "This young man is going to take Judy away into worlds where I cannot follow. But he is going to make her happy. It would be wrong for me to try to hold her back." She looked over at me, and our eyes locked. My gratitude for her generous spirit brought me almost to tears. I promised myself then that I would—at least in letters—let her know, as truthfully as I could, everything that mattered in my life, a life that would be lived so far from hers.

I wrote those letters, and she kept them all; they were returned to me after her death. They form the chief backing for what I describe in this book. They are supplemented by my peculiarly powerful oral memory, which includes conversations from many decades ago, and also poems and hundreds of songs (down through the fifth verse) that I learned, starting before I could read. Undoubtedly, there are misrememberings mixed among my recollections, but I have tried my best to tell the truth as I know it.

My desire, in writing this book—which covers more than a half-century as a diplomat's wife, career diplomat myself, and rehired retired diplomat—is to let you, the reader, share my discoveries as I made them. I want to let you experience what it was like—and to some extent still is—to go out into the world as a career diplomat or as part of a diplomatic family. I often arrived in the new place with little preparation for living and working there. If, at the start of a chapter, you wonder what was really going on in the place I was living, that is because so was I at the time.

When, after fifteen years as a diplomat's spouse, I became a diplomat myself, I soon learned that what a career diplomat is supposed to do was something I already loved doing. For me it was a joy to live in a foreign country and get to know many people there. As a career diplomat, I would especially seek out opinion-makers and people who could help me in my efforts to devote serious and sustained attention to what this host country cared about. That way, I could maybe help find a fit with what my country wanted from the host country. Such work is best done out of the glare of the public spotlight, and, if done right, it does not make headlines. But when it is well done, it provides a long-term sense of complicity, even affection, between diplomats like me and our counterparts in the host country. It also can produce a warm feeling that our successors on both sides can draw upon.

Although women have come late to the field, I think many women are well suited to this work. I confess that I have adventurous women especially in mind as I present these memoirs to the reading public. For the reader who wants to know where John and I were and when in our Foreign Service career, I recommend consulting the Appendix on our Foreign Service posts.

I start this memoir with a chapter out of chronological sequence because it shows me making a crucial friendship with an important opinion-maker in his country and on his terms. This man taught me perhaps my single most important lessons about how to be a woman diplomat.

Chapter 1
Political Apprenticeship in Africa

• • • • • • • • • • • • • • • • • •

DIPLOMATS ASSIGNED TO A NEW
post often have strong preconceptions about it and clear expectations of what
it will be like. I had very strong views and expectations about Kinshasa, and
virtually all of them proved to be wrong.

After six years in Belgium, the first place where I was not only my diplomat husband's wife but a diplomat in my own right, in 1978 we received
orders for home leave and transfer. Our new post was Kinshasa, capital
of Zaire (the name President-for-life Mobutu had given to the ex-Belgian
Congo, now known as the Democratic Republic of the Congo).

Just then, news was breaking of the taking as hostages of some three
thousand foreigners, mostly Europeans, in Kolwezi. This was a place in the
Congo's southeast, and further news told of the murder there of more than
two hundred of those hostages by an armed rebel Congolese group with
the aid of some Cuban and East German military officers. We spent a lot of
our home leave in the summer of 1978 explaining to family and friends that
Kolwezi was a thousand miles away from Kinshasa.

Yet even before the Kolwezi incident, the ex-Belgian Congo was known
to be unsafe, uncomfortable, and expensive, and home to terrifying diseases
like Ebola and a fatal wasting disease that was later identified as AIDS.
(We were grateful that our kids were safely home in college and boarding
school, respectively.)

My Kinshasa job would not be available for months after we got there.
I had pleaded for a house with a swimming pool, which I had been told
was typical housing in Kinshasa for someone of John's rank. I argued that I
was being forced to be on leave without pay; at least I could work on my tan.

But word came back that we would have an apartment—without swimming pool—right in the middle of town.

Having arrived in Kinshasa—which looked to be as dispiriting a place to live in as I had been warned—I asked the embassy personnel officer, "Couldn't I go somewhere else in Africa on temporary duty for some of the time until my job here comes free in late November?" Well, yes, I could.

The Department promptly offered me a job in Nairobi, Kenya, as acting chief of the consular section. It was enormous fun while it lasted, but within a few months I was back in Kinshasa, ready to report for work as "protocol officer" in the political section. I was not really looking forward to it.

I had by then become comfortable doing consular work, first in Brussels and then in Nairobi, and felt competent at it. But now, I realized, as a new, untrained political officer, I was back in kindergarten again. This is not an unusual experience for junior and mid-level career diplomats, I would learn. In the late 1950s, when John started his diplomatic career, Foreign Service officers usually received language and area training for their new assignments, sometimes including a year of graduate school at a top university. The officer was then expected to hone that expertise during the bulk of what remained of his or her career. But by the time I joined, fifteen years later, in the Kissinger era, that policy had changed somewhat.

The new rules were that officers should expect at least once every eight or so years to be uprooted from a place where they had expertise and made to serve somewhere else. The theory was that this would keep us from becoming too emotionally committed to a favorite area or country and would also give diplomats serving in hardship posts a fairer share of life in the fleshpots of Europe.

I felt ready to kick and scream like a spoiled child at what I saw as a squandering of our hard-won knowledge and contacts. If they had wanted us to leave Europe after six straight years, fair enough. But why (I wondered aloud) couldn't the State Department have sent us back to Southeast Asia? John had been a diplomat there while I had been his wife and diplomatic hostess during six fascinating years. We both spoke Indonesian and Malay and were more than willing to learn Thai or even Burmese.

Still, I had to concede in fairness to the State Department, we had always said our highest priority as a "tandem" couple was to be assigned together.

And State had managed—just—to find jobs for both of us in Kinshasa. Although Kinshasa was then often referred to as the second worst "hell hole" in Africa (after Lagos, Nigeria), John would have a good job there. He would be counselor for economic affairs, at a time when Zaire's economy was a basket case being kept on life support by the IMF and the Paris Club. John's new job, one of the top three or four in a big embassy, was sure to get him noticed by the powers-that-be in Washington. My job, however, was an entry-level job, two grades *below* my then low rank; it was not even in my career specialty, consular work.

My new job's title was Protocol Officer and, recalling that protocol had been only a small part of John's political officer duties years ago in Jakarta, I asked my new boss, Political Counselor Bob Remole, what my job would entail. "Not much," he said frankly. "Basically, the protocol job here amounts to carrying the ambassador's briefcase at meetings, if he lets you go along, and meeting his flights—usually in the middle of the night, given the international plane schedules. You then get to carry his suitcase to and from the airplane."

I felt my worst fears for this assignment had been confirmed. Trying not to sound too negative, I asked if there was anything else I could do. He paused and then said, "John tells me you can write. The person you are replacing, a very nice young man, cannot. Maybe you could already help by turning his newest effort at drafting a cable into something we can send to Washington." John had always claimed to me that my writing would be an asset in diplomacy. Well, now I would see if it was.

I said I would try, but wished I hadn't when I looked at the draft. There was no way I could edit this in a quick and discreet way so as not to embarrass the drafter—who *was* a nice young man of considerable cultivation, despite his awkwardness with a pen. It was clear that he had spent many hours on this long, convoluted message, with lots of repeated bits. It was as if (which seemed likely) he had tried putting sentences and the odd paragraph first in one place and then in another, and forgot to remove them from their earlier position. In the privacy of the file room, taking scissors, I cut the cable into several segments and removed the redundant text. After putting the stray sentences into what looked to be the right paragraphs, and the paragraphs into an order that seemed to make sense, I retyped them in that order. I edited, as I went, conserving as much of his wording as I could. Seeing the horrified look on his face when he picked up the new draft, I hastened to say: "You remember those hilarious advertisements for cheap records of the classics? The ones that promised you all nine Beethoven symphonies on two LPs with 'all the unnecessary repetitions left out'? Well, that is all I did here. This is still your text, your cable."

At this point fate intervened in the form of a wonderfully helpful colleague, Harlan "Robby" Robinson. Robby was the number two of the section, a civil servant who was on loan from the Africa Office of the State Department's Bureau of Intelligence and Research. Unlike most of the rest of us, including me, Robby spoke flawless French. He also knew a lot about Africa, including the Congo, from previous study. Also, he had already been in this job for two years and had extended for a third year. He came over and said, "Judy, if you have nothing better to do, I suggest you accompany a friend of mine, David Gould, who has just turned up. He's a famous academic on the Congo; he's the man who first used the term *kleptocracy* to describe the Mobutu regime. He is going out to the University of Kinshasa where he has lots of interesting Congolese friends on the faculty you could meet."

I wondered if our boss would let me be away from the office on my second day at work in his section, but Remole said, "Oh yes, that's a good idea of Robby's! I should have thought of it myself. Go ahead!" (Given the much stronger centripetal forces in embassies nowadays, I doubt that any boss now would have let me out of the embassy in the company of somebody not on his staff on my second day in the office.)

As it happened, nothing could have been a better introduction for me to some of the smartest and kindest Congolese in Kinshasa than being passed on to them by Professor Gould. Gould was a man they all admired (and whom they would mourn when, some years later, he was killed in the Lockerbie air crash tragedy). After a day in the professor's company, during which his Congolese academic friends and their wives included me in their (literally) warm embrace—because it looked odd to be hugging him and not me—I invited these academics to a buffet supper at our apartment. I already knew that the Zairian government (their employer) tried to discourage contacts with American diplomats. For this reason, some of my embassy colleagues tried to prepare me for a disappointing turnout at my party, but almost all the professors and wives I invited came.

I began to realize how fortunate it was that our apartment was situated on the eleventh floor of one of Kinshasa's few attractive modern buildings. Our guests enjoyed the spectacular view from our terrace of the widest part of the Congo River, just where the rapids start to push the river 850 feet downward and nearly a hundred miles westward to the Atlantic Ocean. I came to realize only later, when my work portfolio changed, that one of the biggest pluses of where John and I lived was that it was in a big apartment building occupied by many Congolese and other VIPs. From outside, Mobutu's intelligence services could not guess whose apartment a visitor was coming to.

I was finding to my surprise and delight that being a woman was not a handicap to being a diplomat in the Congo. One of my new Congolese friends pointed out that people could recognize me because I was wearing a skirt, whereas many Congolese had difficulty distinguishing one white face from another. Indeed, the only problems I had as a woman diplomat in the Congo came from within my own embassy. A few weeks into my new job in Kinshasa, I was still waiting to be called to meet the ambassador's plane and carry his bags when I found to my chagrin that he was calling on my more senior colleagues in the political section to do what was clearly my job as protocol officer. I finally got up the nerve to go see the ambassador and ask him straight out why he wasn't letting me do my protocol job.

The ambassador was a career officer but a rather conventional kind of man and had evidently not been raised by a mother like mine. He grudgingly confessed that he felt uncomfortable about having the wife of his economic counselor getting up in the middle of the night to meet his plane and carry his suitcases. Knowing that John did not share his views, I had my answer ready: "How do you think it makes me feel—or, for that matter, the poor guy who has to get up in the night to do my job—that you are not letting me do what I am assigned to do?"

Taken aback, he said, "I never thought of that."

"Well, sir," I said, "I am asking you to think of it from now on."

Fortunately, I got on well with my boss, Bob Remole, who came from the mountains of the Far West and was more devoted to Save the Planet, World Wildlife Fund, and Amnesty International issues than to the conduct of traditional foreign policy. Dismayed at how little room there was in the State Department's realpolitik foreign policy for someone with his priorities, he was planning to retire at the end of this tour.

Remole was upset that our government was, for Cold War reasons, on such supportive terms with President Mobutu, a half-educated, charismatic African dictator. Mobutu's chief virtue for us was that he was not a communist and he allowed us to use staging places in his country to support rebels in neighboring communist-led Angola. (I did not then know—though I suspected—the big role of the CIA in putting him in power and keeping him there.)

Mobutu was notorious for his own corrupt acts and for encouraging corruption by his government. The rot ran from the top ministers on down to the cop on the beat, the soldier on patrol, even the prison guard. In recent years Mobutu had presented himself as a nearly God-like figure in his television broadcasts and had bestowed on himself ever more high-flown titles, one of his more modest being that of Zaire's *Guide Eclairé* (enlightened guide).

My boss passed on to me the useful fact that Dean Hinton, our current ambassador's predecessor, had been declared persona non grata (PNG) and expelled by Mobutu, allegedly for having shown disdain for the Enlightened Guide of Zaire by arriving one weekend afternoon at the official presidential residence in his tennis shorts to deliver an urgent message to Mobutu from Washington. According to Remole, our current ambassador lived in terror of being PNG'd himself. The barely hidden, though unspoken, moral of this story went: It would be best to avoid doing things that would anger Mobutu, because the ambassador would probably not back you up.

I occasionally had more substantive work to do than meeting my ambassador's plane. In November 1978, soon after I came officially onto Kinshasa's payroll, I was assigned to make my first demarche. As I explained in a letter to my mother: "This is where I go to the Foreign Ministry and say (in French) that 'my government has instructed me to say . . . .' And then I listen with yogic concentration while the man in charge of—in this case—United Nations affairs replies. I then make notes the moment I escape from his office and send a cable to Washington telling his part of it."

I enjoyed doing it. I went over without phoning ahead because, as often happened, neither our phones nor theirs were working. When I finally took the elevator to an upper floor where he had his office, he was out, and I waited fully an hour for him to return. He turned out to be an extremely pleasant Congolese in his midthirties who spoke good French and was able to cope on the spot with the subject, saying nicely quotable things in reply to my demarche. I left his room, but by then the elevator had conked out and I had to descend the six flights to the accompaniment of cries of "*Bon courage, Madame*" at each landing, down to my waiting embassy driver and Land Rover.

Back at the office, I wrote up my message. Remole made a few sensible changes to my draft, and I got it typed on cable stationery by our secretary. Remole told me to take it along to the deputy chief of mission (DCM) and duck, because the DCM was a nitpicker. The DCM read it immediately, found the one typographical error, fixed it, signed off and said, "Congratulations on your first message from Kinshasa."

Remole was a thoroughly decent guy, but was so offended by our policy toward Mobutu that he could not keep his views to himself when speaking to his boss, DCM Alan Davis. Davis (also an honorable man) had come to dread being lectured by his subordinate. When Remole found that I got on well with Davis, he took to using me as his messenger to the front office, where the DCM sat.

It got a bit awkward for me one day when my boss wrote a cable in which he used a bit of ironic humor. I read it before bringing it up to Davis to sign off on. I said to Remole that I thought ironic humor was always tricky when written down; it could so easily be misunderstood in Washington. Remole was rather proud of his clever remark and told me to take the cable along to the DCM. I did, but Davis sent it back to be retyped with a red line through the humorous bit. Remole showed me the mutilated cable and, with his hand shaking, said something to the effect of, "Nobody seems to want to know my views, but can't I even make a little joke once in a while?"

I felt sorry for both him and the DCM, and a little anxious not to be caught in the middle of a battle between them. And then I remembered a quotation I had read from the great eighteenth-century wit, Dr. Samuel Johnson, who once recalled that an old tutor had said: "Read over your compositions, and wherever you meet with a passage you think is particularly fine, strike it out." I typed it out and put it on my boss's desk after he had left for the day.

The next morning Remole was in his cubicle when I came in, and I found my note back on my desk. He had scratched out "strike it out" and replaced it with, "cut it in half." I laughed out loud, because, as anyone who reads my written work knows, I am addicted to overlong sentences. When Remole came back to his cubicle after lunch, the paper was back in front of him with my one-word comment: "*Touché.*" I heard him guffaw.

I hoped to have more demarches to make, but few came my way, and I began to wonder again what my job would amount to. The ambassador was still not using me to meet his plane or carry his bag. Fortunately, about then I acquired a new item in my portfolio that would gradually take up much of my time and even more of my interest. Robby, who was trying to pass on some of his work as he prepared to leave that summer, got the idea of passing on his entire contact list of interesting Congolese dissidents to me.

That is why, in January 1979, I found myself one afternoon taking a car ride alone with a total stranger, a tough-looking young Congolese, to an unknown destination. That car ride brought me to what turned out to be one of the most useful learning experiences of my diplomatic career.

The Shah of Iran had just fallen, and the State Department stood accused of not having prepared for his fall by troubling to get to know the people who might take over after him. So the word had gone out to the political sections of overseas posts such as the US Embassy in Kinshasa, where we were for Cold War reasons on close terms with President-for-life Mobutu, that *someone* should cultivate the dissidents, the people who, without promoting violence, opposed the country's dictator. In my embassy, thanks to Robby's introductions, I was that someone.

What made me the ideal choice was that I was the officer least likely to worry President Mobutu's secret intelligence chief; I was the junior-most officer in the political section and a woman. Also, although I had been a diplomat's wife more than twenty years by then, I had been a diplomat myself less than seven years. I was officially in the consular career track, not political. Everyone knew that the only reason I had a job in Kinshasa's political section was because the embassy wanted John as its economic counselor and his price for going there had been a job for me.

A barrier to my getting to know the political dissidents was that members of the country's parliament were not permitted to go to a foreign diplomat's house without the prior permission of the head of Mobutu's secret intelligence service. This was a limitation that no diplomat from a free country can accept, but it was imperative that, if we met with these politicians, we did so in a way that would not put them in danger.

Moreover, it soon became obvious to me that the people of the Congo were unaccustomed to dealing with a Western woman who was not a missionary, a nun, or the wife of a *bwana* (the Swahili term for a white man, usually a colonial boss). Of the politicians I needed to get to know, few of them had wives with even a high school education, and still fewer of these men had any experience dealing with a woman diplomat.

I had discreetly invited some dissident members of parliament—chosen by Robby because of the high regard their colleagues had for them—to dinner at John's and my apartment. The dinner party took place, and several of the dissidents came (leaving their wives at home), but the leading politician among them simply did not appear. We all felt his absence. I thought he might be understandably cautious about breaking the rule on going to a diplomat's home without informing the secret police, but still I was disappointed. He was the one the others most respected; I doubted the others would come again to see me, given the risk, if he did not show that he was willing to do so.

It was now the afternoon of the next day and, at the embassy, our secretary said I had a visitor. I went downstairs to the lobby and was handed an unsigned handwritten note delivered by a tough-looking young Congolese. I guessed that the note was probably from my missing guest; it said I should go with the messenger in his car.

The thought crossed my mind that this might be a risky thing to do. The Congo was a dangerous place then; the Kolwezi massacre in which hundreds of Europeans had been murdered had happened the year before.

But then I thought: If the note really came from my missing guest, it would be worth my taking a chance to talk to the country's leading nonviolent dissident politician.

The messenger drove to an unfamiliar part of the city, where my being white made me stand out. There were few traffic lights, and Congolese men, women, and children were dodging traffic every few yards to try to cross the wide road. The road had potholes everywhere. Of the cars parked alongside, most lacked hubcaps and windshield wipers and some were without tires. Although in Kinshasa it rained most days, there seemed to be dust everywhere. Overhead above the road were cement and metal pedestrian walkways that were missing stairs up to them or were broken off halfway across their arc. They looked to have been abandoned in mid-construction years earlier.

The driver parked the car on the sidewalk, and we entered a dusty, dimly lighted café. The furniture looked shabby and dirty. The only contrast to this dismal scene came from a radio, which was blasting forth the vibrant Congolese popular music of the day. A pair of big, well-built young men, who were seated at a table, I presumed to be bodyguards. Behind them in a corner was seated the "no-show" of my dinner party. The driver made a gesture to point him out to me and went outside to wait to drive me back.

The man stood up—he was a very big, tall man—and indicated that I sit on the wooden chair across from him. We both sat down. There was no offer to buy me a drink and the conversation (in French) was brief.

He: "You invited me to dinner at your place last night."

I: "Yes, I did."

He: "I didn't come."

I: "I noticed."

He: "I didn't know what rules you play by."

It was then that I realized that he had no precedents, no rules, for his dealings with me—a woman and a diplomat—and that he had sent the ball into my court. Suddenly aware that a lot could hinge on how I handled this moment, I sent the ball back to him by saying: "What rules do *you* play by?"

He: "I don't want anybody else who is there to be uncomfortable about my being there. And I don't want to be surprised about anybody else who is there. Also, I don't ever want to be quoted to another African."

By then I had lived in both Asia and Europe, and so I blessed the fact that, apparently, in Africa people would say what they meant a lot sooner than would any Asian or most Europeans I had met. "Those are my rules, too," I said, realizing how sensible they were. "I never quote anybody in the host country to some other person of the host country." "And," I added, "just to make sure that you are happy with the guest list, from now on I will show it to you first, before I invite anyone else. You can then cross out—or add to—the names on the list."

He stood up to indicate that our meeting was over—and, for the first time, he smiled. It was not just his giant size that was impressive. He had the presence of a leader. From then on, we trusted each other, and through him I was able to learn a lot about what was going on in the dissident camp and report it by confidential cable to the State Department. Anxious to protect my dissident sources, I got permission to use pseudonyms in cables and in vouchers seeking reimbursement for dinners I hosted for them. Only my bosses in Kinshasa knew the real names.

Since I was the "dissidents" officer, the ambassador eventually asked my views, among others, on whether to stick with Mobutu or to encourage the dissidents to take over. I pleaded for the dissidents to be given a chance on the grounds that if we waited until, inevitably, Mobutu lost power, the dissidents—who included virtually the only people in the country who had had access to a decent education and who for the most part had a commitment to democratic principles—would probably be too old to take power. And the Congo would then go the way of too many former colonies around the world, with their educated potential leaders killed or jailed, and ending up headed by near-illiterate charismatic but bloodthirsty bullies.

To my sorrow, the decision was made to stick with Mobutu, which even I had to concede was a reasonable decision, given that there were large stretches of the country where the dissidents commanded little or no support.

Yet, though I had to come to terms personally with the tragedy that I could see lying ahead for a country I had come to care about, thanks to my giant friend and the dissidents I met through him, my whole career path had changed. I was no longer regarded at the embassy as a "token" female. I ended my tour there promoted to the next higher grade and was invited to move to the political career track, which was better suited to my penchant for reporting and making contact with politicians than would have been remaining a consular officer.

The rules my friend taught me turned out to be sound rules for maintaining a dialogue with important contacts, regardless of country. But more important was the way in this brief exchange we had established that our relationship would be led by him. I was not the bwana's wife or a nun or a teacher to whom he would have been expected to humble himself in the old colonial days. This was his place, not mine, and, by sending the ball back into his court, I had acknowledged that he had the right to make the rules. New as I was, I realized that this man, by reaching out to me and talking straight, was trusting me literally with his life. Together with me, he was inventing a way to deal with a kind of diplomat new to him—a female. I am forever in his debt.

. . . .

John was greatly tickled at the thought of my being allowed—even encouraged—to cultivate the most interesting people in the country and to be the chief link between the legal opposition and the US government. It was a far cry from the banal world of protocol duties to which I had been originally assigned. John found being present at those dinners—at which Robby was usually also present until he and his family left later that year— made up for his having to spend time dealing with Mobutu's very corrupt and often boring commercial cronies. My dissident contacts liked John a lot. They trusted him to give them a good sense of what support they could expect from Uncle Sam.

Robby, who still had too much to do, also offered me the human rights dossier. Being the human rights officer at our embassy to Zaire meant following what was happening for good or ill as regards human rights in the host country and then writing a report. The report would be published, after editing back in Washington, as a chapter in the State Department's annual assessment of human rights in all the countries we recognize.

It was in that connection that I got involved in the effort to get a pardon for prisoners. I was working with a Congolese man Robby admired and had nominated for an International Visitor's grant to the United States. After coming back, the man—who was now my friend, too—had been appointed to a position high up in the Ministry of Justice. One of his first acts in the new job was to visit as many as he could of the country's prisons; he was appalled by what he found there.

Together, he and I drafted a pardon for some of these prisoners, over a series of breakfast meetings at my apartment. (We had noticed that Mobutu's secret police were not early risers.) My new friend's idea was that the pardon should apply to those who had been in jail for two or more years without being charged, or who had less than two years to serve to complete their sentence. After consulting with me, and my checking with my bosses, my friend told his minister that these prisoners were by and large not troublemakers but that, unless released soon, most of them were likely to die of starvation, leading to headlines abroad that could keep Mobutu from getting in to see President Carter at the White House.

Mobutu signed the pardon in May or June of 1980, and somewhere close to 40,000 people were set free. I felt absurdly proud when our new career ambassador, Robert Oakley, asked my friend whether the pardon was due to the just concluded visit of Pope John Paul II. My friend smiled and pointed at me, saying, "*Voici le Pape.*" It wasn't me, of course. It had only happened because the US government was then believed by Mobutu and his advisers to care about human rights. I think of this pardon when politically fashionable people of various nations pooh-pooh the effectiveness of human rights policies like Carter's. But looking back now, I realize that the benefits of this human rights coup cut two ways. Yes, it saved tens of thousands of lives, but it also made it easier for the United States to defend its continued support of a dictator who had allowed prisoners to starve to death in jail.

Chapter 2

Paying Calls

• • • • • • • •

IN NOVEMBER 1958, LONG BEFORE the State Department allowed spouses to take the Foreign Service exam, long before John and I became one of the first so-called tandem couples, I left my country for the first time.

I was accompanying John to his first post: the American Embassy in Jakarta, Indonesia. There he was assigned to be an officer in the political section. We both had graduated from college the year before but, unlike John, I was not officially a diplomat and had received no State Department training. I arrived in Jakarta almost totally ignorant of the place where I was going to live for the next three years or why Uncle Sam was sending us there.

In those days before we were all tethered to the Internet, diplomatic pouches sent once in six weeks by sea were our only route for getting personal mail, and international phone calls were out of the question. So I knew I would have to come to terms with what was—like it or not—our new home. The first impression of this new home was not altogether encouraging.

"SEATO Hands off Indonesia" read some of the signs on the trees lining the road from Kemayoran Airport into town. Other signs showed President-for-life Sukarno giving a big kick to a supine Uncle Sam. There seemed to be similar signs and slogans on every spare space on fences and walls along our route.

Looking beyond the lurid posters, I could see in the putrid water of Jakarta's roadside canals golden-skinned naked women and children bathing downstream from where men were squatting to defecate. I told myself I could not have asked for a greater contrast to the genteel streets of

Northwest Washington, D.C.—which I, as a New Yorker, had found a little too tame. Well, I thought, at least Jakarta won't be too tame.

. . . .

U p until a few months earlier, we had assumed we would be sent to Malaya. John and I had met as freshmen and married just after our junior year at college—he at Harvard and I at Radcliffe (which had all its classes except freshman gym with and at Harvard). John had dreamed of being an American diplomat, ideally in Asia, since he was a child; he had dedicated his senior honors thesis, "The Independence Movement in Malaya," "To my wife Judy who will share the world with me."

John started his diplomatic orientation course at the State Department the day after we graduated from college. After that, he had volunteered for nine months of Indonesian language training because he knew that the same language was spoken in Malaya. Malaya in those days was a relatively safe, comfortable place where English was widely used. It was a good place, he must have thought, to introduce his wife to living abroad.

Then word came that we were going instead to Jakarta, capital of Indonesia, a disease-ridden, uncomfortable country where little English was spoken and several bloody rebellions were going on. I tried to soften John's possible disappointment by saying cheerily: "That will be great. I can learn to speak decent French there," having somehow got Indonesia and French Indochina mixed up in my head. I saw John's face grow pale. Although he used to joke about the limited horizons of English majors like me, I think it was only at that moment that he realized how truly ignorant of the outside world I was.

Now we were in Indonesia, and John was sitting beside me in the back-seat as we were driven in from Kemayoran Airport; he seemed to be taking in everything he saw. I guessed that Jakarta, with its many Chinese shop signs, reminded him of the Shanghai he had known as an eight-year-old in 1940–41, a time when that part of China was not yet in Japanese hands. By now I knew that John's Shanghai year included the happiest memories of his life with his mother.

His mother, Doris Olsen, was the daughter of a Danish immigrant civil engineer and a no-nonsense Yankee housewife who stayed at home, cooked, sewed, and raised her three girls—of whom Doris was the parents' favorite. But Doris had scandalized her family by marrying a New York Jew. This was almost as bad as a cousin who married a Boston Irish Catholic. So nobody was terribly shocked when in 1940, nearly a decade later, Doris again threw convention aside. This time it was to accept the invitation from a Chinese actor named Yao, who was her lover at the time, to go back to Shanghai with him and teach English there for a year. She left John's physician father, Harry Heimann, at home in New York City and took their only child, seven-year-old John, with her.

John had loved his time in China, especially the food. To the end of his life, he preferred a meal based on a bowl of rice to anything else. He also loved having the sense of being inside a brand new world, which Shanghai was in those days—thanks in part to his mother's dashing friend Yao. Yao was one of the pioneers in bringing Western theater there.

Most of all, I guess, John had loved that, during that time, his mother had seemed happy and fulfilled as he had never seen her before or since. Yao and his modernist friends treated her like a grown-up person and a smart one. But when the Japanese moved to take over Shanghai in 1941, his mother took John home again, on the last American President Line passenger ship not to be torpedoed by the Japanese Imperial Navy.

They returned to John's patiently waiting father. He loved this brilliant, adventurous woman but did not know how to make her happy. Doris had been one of the first women to pass the Massachusetts bar exam in the early 1930s. But she could not get a law firm to treat her other than as what would now be called a "paralegal." Fed up, she had quit her job at the law firm and married John's handsome father Harry. Harry was the son of poor East European immigrants, and had started out at a Hebrew Yeshiva and gone on to do brilliantly at New York City College's tuition-free medical school. Doris had met him when he was starting his residency at Mass General in Boston. A pioneering scientist of occupational health, but awkward socially, Harry never figured out how to help his wife fulfill her potential in that sexist era.

Unlike me, John was not one to parade his feelings, but it was clear—from the bits of information about his mother he provided me during three years of courtship and two of marriage thus far—that he worshipped her. His worldliness, his sense of what was done and not done in fashionable circles, which served him well at Harvard and beyond, evidently came from things Doris had told him or showed him, even though she was not herself a member of that world. I deduced that she must have been an acute outside observer, a trait her son had inherited. But it would take me decades to realize how much John's life with his mother would influence his life with me.

Fresh out of the army at age nineteen, John had been spending a year in India with his parents before starting college, when his mother died in Delhi of the long-term effects of alcoholism. His father by then was a Public Health Service officer on loan to the American Embassy to advise the Indian government on health risks to mica miners. Harry had then married a nice widow, the sister of a diplomat at the embassy. In the summer of 1953, John, his father, and his stepmother had sailed back home, crossing the Atlantic on the *United States*. John (age twenty) and I (seventeen) would meet a month or so later during our first week at college—and fall in love.

. . . .

Now, in 1958, five years after that first meeting, the street scene around us after we left Jakarta's Kemayoran Airport may have reminded John of China and India, but it was brand new to me. We inched along potholed streets that were jammed with vehicles of every description, from oxcarts and horse-drawn carriages to shiny black limousines with license plates showing they were embassy vehicles, such as the car that had collected us. There seemed to be dozens of bicycle rickshaws that John called *becaks* (pronounced *bechaks*), with the passenger seated on a bench facing forward, sometimes under a shabby but garishly colored awning, while the barefoot driver sat on a bicycle seat behind, and pedaled.

Slowed to a snail's pace as they approached the city, all the car drivers were leaning on their horns while the becak drivers rang their tinkling bells. Workmen and peddlers walked calmly down the middle of the crowded street with a long pole balanced on a shoulder or across the back. Each end of the pole was bent down by the weight of a load of rice or fish or raw rubber or small electrical appliances or lumber or firewood.

John's experience of life overseas and his diplomatic aspirations fascinated me. By age sixteen, I had already known I wanted to be part of a bigger world than I could find within my own country. It must have been already obvious to my New York City high school classmates, who chose for my senior yearbook a verse by Edna St. Vincent Millay to go under my picture: "The world is mine. A gateless garden, and an open path / My feet to follow and my heart to hold." And then, during my first week at Radcliffe, I met John, fresh from India.

Until the plane trip that brought us to Jakarta by way of Tokyo, Hong Kong, and Singapore, I had never been on a ship or an airplane, much less abroad. But I had lived in Poe's and Hemingway's Paris and Conrad's Africa, Dickens's England, Eric Ambler's Eastern Europe and Levant, Somerset Maugham's Southeast Asia, and Kipling's India. Those places were as real to me as anything I had seen myself. Looking back on our contemporaries in the Foreign Service of those days, I think we were typical: the husband long interested in a career in diplomacy or foreign policy, the wife ready to go where her husband took her, both of them well-educated and eager for adventure.

When we finally got to the middle of town, the view out the window changed: we were now among nineteenth-century colonial houses in a scene straight out of the stories of Somerset Maugham. I began to be intrigued.

That first day, we were given lunch and much good advice by John's boss, John Henderson, and his wife, Hester, in their lovely old Dutch colonial house in town, set in a tropical garden. The house had marble floors and massive rooms with high ceilings from which hung 1930s ceiling fans. Hester explained that the old-fashioned charm of the house helped compensate for unreliable electricity, no air-conditioning in the public rooms, and no hot water. She said that less than a year earlier, in December 1957, President Sukarno had expelled the tens of thousands of Dutch who had been living in Indonesia up to then, in her house and others like it.

After lunch, we were driven home—a trip that could take anywhere from a half hour to an hour and a half, depending on the traffic—to one of a row of eight embassy-owned prefabs that had been designed for northern climes. Were it not for the palm trees and the tropical vines that clung to the wire fences, our street could have been in an American postwar mass-produced suburb, such as Levittown outside New York City.

I could reach up and lay my hand against the ceiling of the tiny rooms under a flat, black, tarred roof that absorbed heat when the sun shone and leaked when it rained. The kitchen, with its white enamel kerosene stove and fridge and wooden-faced built-in cabinets, looked almost American. But our embassy guide explained that there was not enough electricity to run a stove or fridge. Thus the need for kerosene.

Fortunately, there was enough power (from a noisy generator next door to our house) to allow all eight prefabs to run a window air-conditioner in the master bedroom. We were advised to keep anything leather in that room. "Otherwise, in three days in this humidity, mold will turn your shoes into blotting paper." All the windows had screens, shutters, and crisscross security bars as well as venetian blinds, making us feel a bit as if we were living in a miniature fortress.

We were introduced to what seemed to be a lot of servants, mostly inherited from our predecessors, and we changed out of our wilted clothes into fresh ones.

I quickly learned that diplomats in Indonesia in the late 1950s, in addition to having a big domestic staff, were exposed to a variety of dangerous diseases. Chief among these were amoebic and bacillary dysentery, malaria, typhoid, and dengue fever, and, more rarely, polio and tuberculosis. Entertainment consisted of lunches, dinners, and teas at people's houses. One communicated with friends chiefly by hand-delivered notes. There were occasional engraved invitations to formal dinners and balls on gilded, embossed cards. Even the most informal notes inviting people to supper arrived on folded "informal" cream or white stationery with the hostess's married name engraved (never printed) in black on the top page. The whole scene seemed vaguely familiar to me, striking a chord in my English-major brain. And then I realized what living as a diplomat's wife in Jakarta in those days most resembled. It was not so much the 1930s exotic, colonial world of Somerset Maugham as it was the earlier, smaller, class- and caste-ridden world of Jane Austen's rural England.

The squirearchy that ran our little social world was headed by our ambassador and his wife. Important secondary roles were played by the deputy chief of mission (DCM) and his wife and, in our case, the political counselor and his wife.

International diplomatic etiquette—which had been transmitted without change from the nineteenth century—required that I pay calls on the wives of all the officers at the embassy senior to John, beginning at the top, and then call on the wives of John's counterparts in other embassies in town. (Whatever their country or language, John's counterparts at the different embassies in town and their wives had also all been taught to pay and receive calls.)

My first protocol call took place in the Puncak (pronounced *poon-chak*), a retreat in the mountains, where the air was cooler. The Puncak was two hours away by road from Jakarta, southeast on the road past Bogor toward Bandung. John's boss, Political Counselor John Henderson, and his wife, Hester, had invited us for our first weekend to go there with them.

On the drive up through lush tropical and semitropical scenery, the first stretch of green we had seen since arriving at Kemayoran Airport, John Henderson explained that their weekend house was on a few acres belonging to the representative of the American motion picture industry, Billy Palmer. Billy was an old Southeast Asia hand, he added, and was said to have grown up at the palace of the Thai king. Billy had had a "good war" during World War II in Southeast Asia working for one of the clandestine services.

From the front porch of the Hendersons' mountain bungalow, our hosts pointed out to us Billy's swimming pool, Ambassador and Mrs. Jones's cottage down the hill, and the low green bushes of the surrounding tea plantation. The horizon consisted of tall, blue, cone-shaped volcanic mountains. In the valley just below, among patchwork squares colored rich gold, brilliant green, and silver, barefoot farmers were guiding big, gray, docile water buffalo to plow terraced fields for another rice crop.

American and European diplomats and businesspeople and their families were sitting or standing around Billy's swimming pool. The adults mostly were red-faced, slightly overweight, dressed in faded cotton shirts and shorts or sagging bathing suits. (Elastic was usually the first casualty from the effects of scrubbing laundry on rocks or wooden washboards.)

Sprinkled through the crowd around the pool were honey-colored, crisply uniformed Indonesian Army officers in sunglasses, and their elegantly saronged wives, whose thick blue-black hair was caught up in elaborate chignons.

It seemed like one big house party, with swimming, drinking, card playing, and gossiping. This hum of conversation was punctuated occasionally by the sound of a J. Arthur Rank–style gong at one end of the pool, being struck by a manservant in a batik sarong draped below a white drill fitted jacket, to announce meals. Cut off from the heat and squalor of the plains where Jakarta was, this mountain resort seemed to me more like Shangri-La than like a real place in a real country.

At night after dinner, a movie screen was set out on the grass in front of a roofed terrace. Billy's dozens of guests sat on the terrace to watch the latest film from Hollywood or a cinema classic. Villagers from miles around watched from mats spread out on the grass. Peddlers selling refreshments and curios set up their portable stalls and stoves in front of the terrace and did a lively trade on all sides.

John had once said to me that Asia grows magical after dark—and that was certainly the case here. It was a clear night, and the moon and stars seemed so much closer, with no city lights to dim their brightness. There were also little scraps of light scattered through the grass, from charcoal grills, oil lamps, and anti-mosquito coils. Zippo lighters passed hand to hand as people lighted their cigarettes before the movie began.

It was a classic film: *Sergeant York* (1941) with a young and handsome Gary Cooper in the leading role of a good country boy who did not like violence but became the most decorated American soldier of World War I. It was based on a true story, and it was easy for us Americans there to feel proud of a country that could produce such a man. I sensed that Billy Palmer's handpicked Indonesian military guests could share our feelings. The social atmosphere here among these high-level Indonesians made me hopeful that John and I would find Indonesian friends, despite the ugly posters and graffiti that had greeted us in Jakarta. None of us Americans knew then that these pro-Western military men would a few years later save their country, the most populous Muslim country in the world, from falling into the hands of supporters of Mao's Chinese Communist Party.

We were told that the Palmer estate and the tea plantation around it were surrounded by territory riddled with Darul Islam (Islamic extremist) rebels who were engaged in episodic armed combat against the religiously tolerant central government. The Darul Islam held sway after dark on the mountain road connecting Billy's estate and Jakarta to the north and Bandung to the south. A couple of years earlier, John Henderson told us, one of his best journalist friends and another American he was traveling with had been flagged down and killed by the Darul Islam on that West Java road. Outsiders like us had no way of telling who was Darul Islam and who was not.

The word was out, however, that Billy Palmer had made a deal with the rebels that they could attend the film showings so long as they maintained a truce while on his property. Billy, who seemed to be the consummate insider, was widely rumored to be the CIA's chief agent in Indonesia (though I doubt this was the case). But he had clearly learned from his days in World War II special operations how to build up trust and fruitful relations with all sorts of people.

John was invited after the movie to play poker with the big boys—the deputy chief of mission and John Henderson, among others—in Billy Palmer's bungalow. I waited for him before going to bed, and overheard bits of the conversations around me—some of it apparently in Dutch—among the elegant Indonesian women guests whose high bosoms were visible through their tight-fitting sheer blouses above waistlines that Scarlett O'Hara would have envied. Most of the Western women had already retired for the night.

Sitting there in a bamboo lounge chair and looking up at a blanket of stars, I could hardly believe I was in such an exotic place among such exotic people. I thought if I dozed off and woke up, I might find myself back in Kansas, like Dorothy in *The Wizard of Oz*. When John turned up and we went off to our neat, sparsely furnished little bedroom, I told him I was glad we had started off our Foreign Service life in Indonesia. No place else could be so foreign and such a mixture of the wonderful and the terrible.

In the morning, Hester Henderson took me to pay my first protocol call, on Mary Lou Jones, the ambassador's wife. A tall, rangy woman who looked to be in her late fifties, Mrs. Jones wore a faded cotton dress and no makeup. She was down to earth in her manner, despite her husband's rank as head of our diplomatic community. The Joneses were now on their second tour in Indonesia and must have had many stories to tell, but I could sense that Mrs. Jones, although courteous to me, was a very private person who would have preferred her weekends to be a respite from protocol.

My call on Mrs. Jones approached its conclusion, and Hester, who had kept the conversation going, rifled through my calling cards and pointed out that I should give Mrs. Jones two of John's cards and one of mine or, alternatively, I could give her one Mr. and Mrs. card and an extra one of John's. That was because I was supposed to leave John's cards on both the husband and wife, since men could call on both men and women, but women were only supposed to call on women. In fact, as was usual during formal calls, neither of the men was present. Odder still, according to Hester, if Mrs. Jones had not been home, I should have turned down a corner of one of the cards and maybe written a note on it—in pencil, not ink. That was because, back in the days when the rules were made, there were no portable pens and thus a pencil showed you had come yourself.

It is easy to laugh at the absurdity of this kind of paying formal calls, but it helped us women feel that we were part of our country's representation abroad. Since the other diplomats' wives, regardless of nationality, were operating from the same set of archaic rules, it gave us all a quick and fairly efficient way to meet the other diplomatic families in our own and other embassies. In a secretive dictatorship like Indonesia, our diplomats could sometimes learn what was happening within Sukarno's inner circle from foreign diplomatic colleagues.

When we got back to Jakarta at the end of the weekend, I was no longer in Shangri-La, but back in Jane Austen country. I spent most mornings of my first month in Jakarta—wearing a dress or skirt and blouse, plus a hat, nylons, and short white cotton gloves and armed with the right calling cards—calling upon the other twenty-eight (yes, twenty-eight) wives of John's more senior embassy colleagues. Some of these women seemed worth knowing better, and many of their houses were handsome and well arranged, perhaps because these women had more experience of furnishing houses in the tropics than I did. Indeed, they had more experience, period.

Some of these women, however, had become visibly fed up with a life that—in the Jakarta diplomatic setting—made it nearly impossible to exercise their skills, whether professional work of some kind or even cooking and childcare, which were done chiefly by servants.

In those days, wives of American diplomats were often commandeered for various unpaid jobs by the embassy. There was even space in our husbands' annual performance evaluations for their supervisor to comment on how well the wife entertained and in other ways contributed positively to the mission's goals. (Nowadays, many more Foreign Service officers are women, and many more wives are either officers themselves or able to work in the local economy, thanks to the tireless efforts of the State Department to obtain reciprocity on work permits for diplomatic spouses abroad.)

· · · · · · · · · · · · · · · · · ·

John would chat with these world-weary women on the cocktail circuit. Remembering how at seventeen he had welcomed the National Guard call-up that let him escape from a home then dominated by his mother's drinking, he seemed to understand where these women's low spirits were coming from. He would later occasionally say to me of some woman he met who seemed to have once had a spark that "she had died in the war." I sometimes wondered if that would be my fate, too, after the novelty of being a diplomat's wife wore off.

American diplomats' wives are no longer obliged to pay calls or to participate in any way in their husband's social duties. But in quite a few countries they still have no right to a work permit and can only hope to occupy themselves in volunteer work, social clubs, a job at the American embassy, or perhaps in an American-funded school or business. Given the current climate of opinion regarding women's roles, no boss's wife would dare to try to teach subordinate spouses what is expected of them, the way Hester taught me. Yet the wives are still expected to know.

I found calls on foreigners more interesting than calls on other Americans, but they were more complicated, as often the person I called on and I had no more than a few words in a common language. But one Pakistani wife who spoke fluent English was especially cordial to me, expressing gratitude for the American diplomats at her husband's last post, in Saudi Arabia, where the only chance she had to leave the house and be out of doors unveiled had been when invited to picnics by her husband's American colleagues. Muslim she might be, but Pakistan in her day was a place (like Indonesia) where an educated Muslim woman enjoyed much more freedom than in the Arab world.

Most of my diplomatic calls were pretty tame affairs. Coffee or tea or orange squash was served, along with something to nibble on, a brief polite conversation took place, and I was expected to leave within the half hour. But not all calls were like that. It is not really stretching a point to say that Barbara Benson's call on the wife of one of her husband's Indonesian contacts changed the course of history between our two countries.

Barbara was the wife of Assistant Military Attaché Major George Benson, and was a registered nurse. And when she paid a call on the wife of a highly placed army colonel named Yani, who lived a short walk from the Bensons' house, she found Mrs. Yani writhing with labor pains; Barbara stayed and helped the midwife deliver the baby.

From then on, the Bensons and the Yanis were closer than family, and the Bensons' adventurous four-year-old son, Dukie, would sometimes escape his out-of-breath baby amah to wander over to the Yanis' front porch. Dukie's father, George, perhaps the most charming Irish American Jakarta had ever known, would routinely walk over to reclaim his son after he came home from work. One evening he found not only Dukie but much of the top brass of the Indonesian army sitting around Yani's table in front of maps of a part of Sumatra that contained a rebel stronghold. George Benson, having been well trained at West Point, and recognizing the people sitting around the table, immediately understood what was going on. And he could not keep from pointing out to Yani and his colleagues a better way to invade Sumatra and defeat the rebels. They took his advice and it worked, thereby further cementing his good relations with the anticommunist Indonesian Army leadership. (Benson would be called back again and again in future years to work at our Jakarta embassy when someone was needed who knew everyone that mattered.)

The irony was that Benson was not privy to the then closely held secret that the CIA under its director Allen Dulles, abetted by Dulles's brother, Secretary of State John Foster Dulles, and with the approval of President

Dwight D. Eisenhower, was supporting the Sumatran rebels and other rebels in Indonesian islands northeast of Java. The Dulles brothers encouraged the rebels and armed them with cash, weapons, logistics, and mercenaries, in the hopes of toppling what they believed to be the dangerously pro-communist Sukarno regime.

A fairly typical Cold War gambit for that era, this covert effort at subverting a country with which we were in theory enjoying friendly relations was so clumsy and inept that the Indonesian government easily uncovered it. Had it not been for the help provided by Major Benson and the near infinite patience and tact of our ambassador to Indonesia Howard P. Jones (who was also at least partly out of the Dulles loop), it is probable that Sukarno would have publicly exposed the plot and used it as a pretext to sever relations with the West and move his country firmly into the Eastern bloc.[1]

The lesson I drew from that incident was that there are times—fortunately rare—when diplomats on the ground have both the obligation and capability to save our country from the consequences of mistakes made by our bosses at home.

Though I never paid a call that turned out to be half as momentous as Barbara Benson's, I found there were occasional glamorous moments in diplomacy, such as the annual Queen's Birthday Ball held (where else?) at the British Cricket Club, better known as "the Box." While our furniture was in storage in America, I had had shipped out with our most essential belongings my only ball gown. This was a white lace confection made by Worth of Paris—straight out of an Edith Wharton novel. John had insisted we buy it at Bonwit's in Boston in a wildly extravagant moment, for me to wear to the Harvard senior prom. I had no idea, then, how much use I would get out of such a ball gown over the years.

At the ball a Viennese waltz was played, of course. David Goodall, John's counterpart at the British embassy, stood to help me from my chair onto the dance floor, and said, "I feel I must warn you, I don't reverse!" A happy but very dizzy young woman in white lace was returned to her seat

---

1. For more about this failed attempt at regime change, read *Subversion as Foreign Policy: The Secret Eisenhower and Dulles Debacle in Indonesia,* by Indonesia scholars Audrey Kahin and George McT. Kahin, published by New Press in 1995 and based on declassified official US government sources.

afterward, to drink champagne and to feel that the diplomatic life was, every once in a while, precisely what one imagined it should be. David, almost intimidatingly well educated, remained one of our closest friends ever after. He became a consummate British diplomat, and over the years that brought him ever better jobs and higher honors, we stayed in touch. During those years, David taught John and me a lot about what good diplomats do and, also, how differently our closest allies can sometimes approach the same issues our government faces.

I learned another, more painful lesson about dealing with British diplomats during that first year in Jakarta. Through David Goodall, John and I met an absolutely charming and original poet and British council member named Henry, who came from a very modest family background and whose excellent education had been entirely the product of his good brain and hard work. Also through David, we were later introduced to a new, very upper-class British couple at his embassy, whom I shall call Hermione and Alec. Just for fun, we invited Hermione and Alec to our house for dinner, the only other guest being Henry. While we watched helplessly, the couple put Henry through a thorough examination of his background: where had he gone to school? Oxford, ah yes, but they meant *school*, and Henry was obliged to name the state-financed grammar school he had attended, not a famous so-called public school like Eton or Harrow. And who were his friends? Alec and Hermione didn't know them. And where did his parents live? And on and on, while John and I cringed with embarrassment at having exposed poor Henry to this onslaught—to which I must confess Henry seemed more inured than John or I were.

The worst came when Henry got to ask them where *their* parents lived. At the mention of a village somewhere near Bath, Henry said with a twinkle in his eye, "Ah yes, I rather think my father passed through there during the Jarrow Hunger March of '36."

I still shudder when I think of that evening. The lesson I drew was never to invite British people to the same small occasion unless I was sure they were from the same class. It would take me longer to learn (from my Congolese giant friend) that I needed to compose every dinner party carefully to make sure all our guests would be comfortable with one another.

I was almost finished with my protocol calls when Hester Henderson, her heart in the right place, over dinner with her husband and John and me, tried to involve me in a Women's International Club sewing circle. The ladies' project, she explained, was to make stuffed animals out of cotton felt, as toys for Indonesian children. My own view (which even I knew enough to keep to myself) was that the children would probably prefer a new white blouse or shirt for school. In any case, the prospect of my spending hours each week, sitting around with the club's ladies sewing, filled me with dread. John, seeing my face, said bravely: "You know, Hester, some people don't drink and some don't smoke—and my wife doesn't sew." I would have married him again for that alone.

Undaunted, Hester next inveigled me into becoming the treasurer of the Women's International Club, but I couldn't get into the club's postal bank account without bribing the clerk—which John wisely discouraged me from attempting, so I had to resign. Eventually Hester found for me a class of Indonesian women who spoke English and were looking for a native English speaker to help them learn how to give public speeches, since they were seeking to participate in international conferences. Teaching that weekly class of a dozen enterprising women soon became my favorite activity.

Looking back on my introduction to being a diplomat's wife, I am struck by the almost infinite effort made by the wife of my husband's boss to help me fit in and find satisfying ways to occupy my time. In those days in our Foreign Service, the boss's wife was often regarded as a dragon needing to be placated for fear she might breathe fire and destroy one's husband's career. Hester probably *was* a dragon in the sense that she wanted me to learn to do things "the right way," but I thank her for taking the trouble to teach me what I needed to know.

Chapter 3

Party Magic

• • • • • • • •

During those early diplomatic days in Jakarta, there was one job I was assigned by my dragon lady boss's wife that I bet few other wives were ever asked to do. And yet, in that time and context, somebody had to do it.

As the lowest-ranking officer in the political section, John's duties included being the embassy's protocol officer. The protocol job came to an annual crescendo of activity in preparation for the Fourth of July reception at the ambassador's residence, the biggest diplomatic reception of the year. John and a cast of thousands—or so it seemed—prepared guest lists, kept track of how many people would attend, and figured out the logistics for such a big event. I was not involved until about a week before the party, when Hester told me that I was responsible for making sure that it did not rain during the reception. How I did it was up to me.

I had reason to take the assignment seriously. By then I knew that Billy Palmer, our Shangri-La weekend host, had been obliged to host a full-blown *selamatan* (a big feast with lots of food, gamelan music, costumed dance and puppet shows, and featuring the efforts of a local sorcerer to placate mischievous spirits) after the third attempt to pour cement for his swimming pool in the hills had failed. As his domestic staff boasted afterward, the fourth pouring went without a hitch.

I went to Chi-chi, our astute one-eyed cook, to get advice on how to prevent rain at the residence on July Fourth. She first suggested a selamatan, but I said that even if we could ignore the ambassador and his wife's strong Christian Science beliefs, I could never get the money for such an enterprise. Nor did we have time to arrange it; the Fourth was just days away.

In that case, her second-best suggestion was for me to do precisely what she now would tell me, at the residence on the day of the party. I nodded. I knew I would have to be at the residence four hours ahead, to handle the receipt of flowers and other gifts, recording who sent what for later thank-you notes (to be drafted by guess who?). I would also be expected to deal with any emergencies that needed to be handled by someone with a better command of Indonesian than Mrs. Jones had.

First, Chi-chi said, I should ask Mrs. Jones for a pair of her underpants, preferably ones that she had worn and that had not yet been laundered.

Gulping, I nodded again.

"Then turn the panties inside out and get them put up on the roof."

Eyes wide, I nodded again.

"Then take four ordinary hot red chili peppers and get the gardener to bury them in the four corners of the part of the lawn where most of the guests will be."

"Anything else?" I asked.

"No," she said. "That should do it."

Midmorning of July Fourth found me already dressed in my best reception-going dress, carrying out my peculiar errand. I had wondered for days how to approach Mrs. Jones with my weird request for her underwear, and finally decided to just play it straight. I need not have worried. She burst out laughing and, with a shrug, asked her *babu cuci* (laundress) to comply, including carrying the item up to the roof and leaving it there while I watched. There followed a quick trip to the kitchen for four red chilies, and to the garden to get them planted in the four corners of the lawn, where a clearly inadequate awning was being installed that might temporarily protect half the expected turnout in case of a quick, light shower. (There were no *light* showers at that time of year.) Without hesitation, the gardener planted the chilies.

From then on, I had merely to help receive the flowers and the gifts and, during the party, join the officer and spouse workforce whose job was, more or less politely, to move the reception along, through and past the receiving line and into the garden. If I could spot VIPs who needed to be plucked from the line and brought directly to Ambassador and Mrs. Jones, so much the better.

It was only after the last straggling guest had downed his last gimlet that I took notice of the fact that it had NOT rained on our parade. I asked around, and it turned out—as usual at this time of year—there had been heavy tropical cloudbursts all over town before, during, and after our reception, but none at the residence until well after the awning had been taken down and carted away and our embassy colleagues had started to depart.

When John and I reached home, I burst through the kitchen door to say (in Indonesian), "Chi-chi! You really are wonderful. I did what you said and it worked!"

Looking up at me balefully through her one good eye, she said, "What are you talking about? I have been praying to Allah all afternoon!"

. . . .

That was my first inkling of how complicated religion in Java was. Chi-chi's seamless switch from animistic magic to orthodox Islam rocked me on my heels. Was she joking with me? And if so, which was the joke: The ritual she had me carry out? Or was she joking when she said she had prayed all afternoon? I knew by then that she (like most Javanese in those days) occasionally ate pork, sometimes drank beer, never wore a head-scarf, rarely went to the mosque, and did not fast during the fasting month. Clifford Geertz, an American who was the best anthropologist ever to work on Java, would answer those questions a few years later in his seminal book, *The Religion of Java*.

Until then, much of what John and I knew of the subject was taught us one memorable afternoon shortly after July Fourth. We were picnicking near an emerald-green rice paddy along the north coast road between Central and East Java, and a peasant farmer—upon whose field we were probably trespassing—came up to greet us.

John invited him to join us and, at some point, seeking to try out my still imperfect Indonesian, I asked him a question I almost never ask anyone: "*Pak* [father], what is your religion?"

"I am Javanese," he said.

"Yes, but what I had asked was: 'What is your religion?'"

"I am Javanese; that means I am Muslim."

His words hung in the air until he took pity on me and expanded his answer a bit: "The Javanese are Muslim—but, of course, we have not been Muslim long."

I nodded for him to continue, while absorbing the fact that five centuries did not seem as long to him as it would to a Westerner like me.

"And"—making hand gestures to indicate descending layers—"before that we were Hindu-Buddhist—or our kings were—but before that, and always, and still now, we are Javanese."

What a country, I thought, where even a subsistence farmer could gracefully take you through a thousand years of religious history in a few sentences: Islam on top from about 1400 CE on; Hindu-Buddhism from the third or fourth to the sixteenth century on Java and still the religion of Bali. And, going back at least as far as the first Neolithic settlements on Java and still now, animism—the placating of local spirits, which is what I had been doing at the ambassador's residence on the Fourth of July.

. . . .

We Western diplomats would have been ill advised to laugh at the natives' "superstition." We were constantly being confronted with evidence that all three religious belief systems still had a hold on the same people—up and down the Indonesian social and educational scale—depending on the circumstance. All Javanese little boys were circumcised according to Muslim rites, and almost all marriages involved dances and puppet shows that were visibly derived from the Hindu-Buddhist court traditions prevailing on Java until the spread of Islam chased the courts eastward to Bali where, for the first time, the court religion became the popular religion too.

In daily life, however, it was animism—called *agama jawa* (Javanese religion)—that seemed to have the most direct hold on the island of Java's more than sixty million people. Westernized Indonesian friends of ours were always holding selamatans or calling in a *dukun* (shaman/sorcerer) to deal with problems attributed to spirits. A young Javanese friend who went on to study international law at Yale was one of the many to warn me, seriously, not to wear green on the southern beaches of Java, for fear that the goddess of the sea there might get jealous and drown me.

Even the embassy had to pay attention when word spread through the politically active community that President Sukarno's mystic invisible bird, which by the 1950s was widely believed to sit on the president's shoulder, a symbol of his divine authority to rule, had not been seen lately. I remember there being rumors sometime in late 1959 or early 1960 that the bird had turned up on the shoulder of Sukarno's most widely respected potential rival, the Sultan of Yogyakarta. John and, no doubt, other junior officers in other embassies in town were assigned to track down where the mystic bird had been sighted most recently. Within a week, John told me it was back on Sukarno's shoulder, and the panicky rumors died down.

. . . .

L earning how modern Javanese men and women thought at that time about religion was perhaps the most useful knowledge I acquired during three years in my first foreign country. It taught me that people of other cultures who seem to think like us actually have all sorts of different thoughts, beliefs, and reactions that are utterly foreign. That discovery would not have come to John and me if we had not been able to communicate with local people in a local language and if we had not had the chance to get to know, at least slightly, a wide variety of local people. Nowadays, for security and other reasons, the United States has reduced the number of diplomats it sends to posts abroad, and fewer still are comfortable speaking the local language. And with reduced staffing at our missions, our diplomats—though they keep on trying—have fewer opportunities to travel about the country where they might get a better sense of how the local people approach their own history, their religion(s), and their national identity.

I find this trend worrisome. I remember reading long ago that the 1857 Indian Sepoy Mutiny, India's first war of independence, was caused by the Indian enlisted men working for the British East India Company believing a rumor that the paper cartridges for their rifles that they would have to bite off before firing their weapons were greased with pork or beef fat. A crucial lesson drawn from that event was that it did not matter if the rumor were true or not, so long as the soldiers and their supporters believed that the company's armed forces were led by men who were so ignorant of Indian religious beliefs that such a gaffe was conceivable.

Chapter 4

Domestic Dramas

• • • • • • • • • • •

AMERICAN DIPLOMATS IN THE Third World often have the help of domestic servants. Those of us unused to having such helpers find them a mixed blessing. Imagine my amazement when I found that at our first overseas home, John and I had been handed a domestic staff of seven: a cook, houseboy (butler), laundress, gardener, day and night watchmen, and a driver! When I protested to Hester that two adults should not need so many helpers, she explained that any Javanese who had a job had at least one relative dependent on him or her and so was anxious to divide the work so that the cousin or sibling could earn a living too. Though there was barely room for John and me to turn around in our little prefab bungalow, there was, under these circumstances, no way we could get by with fewer servants.

Their salaries were negligible at the rate at which we exchanged our dollars at the embassy for rupiahs, but it was a real challenge to supervise so many employees. And, thanks to the State Department in those days banning spouses' access to the nine-month Indonesian language course John was taking, I arrived in Jakarta unable to speak a word of Indonesian. The servants, of course, spoke no English.

This was before two-way radios, much less mobile phones or the Internet, and our home phone (note the singular) was of the old brass and Bakelite type now sold as antiques; it had no dial. You just picked up the big black receiver and prayed for an operator to come on the line. Then, aided by a handwritten glossary of the Indonesian words for zero through nine, you asked the operator to connect you to your party. You could spend half a day trying to make a call before you succeeded or gave up.

That was the main reason for needing a driver. Despite the traffic jams between our suburb and town, our driver Hassim could usually deliver a message far faster than I could reach somebody in town by phone, that is, unless Hassim was waiting in line for hours to get gas for the car or kerosene for the stove and the fridge. The cook and the butler (or "houseboy") shared the honors of standing in line at Chinese shops for soap, rice, flour, sugar, and other rationed or scarce commodities. We had no washing machine or dishwasher, which was just as well since we often went for weeks without electricity, and sometimes without running water.

By now, you have an idea why it was not such a bad idea to have so many helpers. The problem was how to deal with them. My immediate plan was to learn enough Indonesian to be able to address the staff, and most especially Chi-chi, the leader of the pack. She was our petite, middle-aged, one-eyed but clearly intelligent cook, who had previously worked for a series of American embassy people.

Indonesian, fortunately, is one of the world's easiest languages to learn at a basic level, it being perfectly phonetic. It also has no articles, genders, cases, or tenses, and forms the plural by doubling the singular. From my first days and for many months, I spent the hottest part of each weekday being driven in a car with no air-conditioning to and from the embassy for a noon-hour lesson. When I got back home, Chi-chi would be there, waiting to hear what I would say. With the first words out of my mouth, you could almost hear the gears in her brain turn as she reasoned: "She said *berangkat* [to leave]. That's Lesson Three, so she probably also knows the word *berikut* [to follow], which is in one of the sentences in that lesson that she is supposed to learn by heart."

When I finally felt up to talking seriously to the cook and perhaps understanding her replies, I said, "Chi-chi, you no doubt realize I have never had so many people work for me before. Can you help me figure out the best way to do it? Should I put you in charge?"

I have never forgotten Chi-chi's answer: "I am sorry, Madam, but with seven of us, you are just at the limit of how many you must direct yourself. I could try to do it, but they would come to you anyway. If we were nine or ten or more, then everybody would know you cannot be dealing with each alone. But you will have to handle this many by yourself. Keep me informed, and I will help as much as I can."

I later came to realize how right she had been. When I had to supervise embassy or consular colleagues, I found that I could be the head (as I once was) of a staff of a couple of hundred more easily than I could direct the efforts of a group of seven or eight subordinates. With a big staff, they know that you have to delegate. They realize you need to keep free from the day-to-day business to devote your energies to "putting out fires" as necessary. You cannot be in a position where dealing with an emergency means that the ordinary work of the office is neglected or delayed by your absence. With a small staff, however, you simply have to make face time for all of your subordinates, or they will think you don't respect or care about them.

Domestic servants were nearly the only ordinary people of the host country that the wives of diplomats got to see regularly. This was especially true in a Third World country like 1950s Indonesia. And, indeed, the wives often learned more about what local people were thinking and feeling and enduring from their servants than did their husbands, who spent much of every workday in an American, English-speaking office or dealing with very Westernized, English-speaking Indonesian diplomats.

The island of Java, with 1,500 inhabitants per square mile, was then the most densely populated, primarily rural, place for its size on earth. Even with three bountiful rice crops a year (thanks to its soil being enriched by the eruptions of numerous active volcanoes), Java's 50,000 square miles could not produce enough food for the more than sixty million people living there. Now that the Dutch colonial government was no longer around to forbid them leaving the countryside, young job-seeking Javanese were pouring into a handful of cities, such as Jakarta and Surabaya, tripling the island's urban population compared to before World War II, but with no increase in health care facilities, plumbing, electricity, or permanent housing.

On Java, even privileged foreigners like John and me suffered the kind of hardship that friends at home would hardly believe. Our day-to-day existence certainly did not fit our American friends' image of diplomats as cookie pushers who went from one glamorous party to another. Short on foreign exchange, Indonesia could import very few goods. We had no US military commissary or Post Exchange shop. Goods ordered from Singapore were often stolen after arriving at the docks near Jakarta.

We rich foreigners had to manage without fresh pasteurized milk, butter, onions (though there were local shallots), apples, oranges, lemons (though there were less satisfactory tropical citrus fruits), or any nontropical fruits except sometimes strawberries grown in the hills. These berries, unfortunately, were kept fresh en route to market by being sprinkled with parasite-laden water.

By the time we had been in Jakarta a year or so, granulated sugar had disappeared (it now came only as a solid brown mass inside a half coconut shell), as had granulated salt; salt now came in brick-sized gray hunks. Word of toilet paper in one of the half-empty Chinese shops would spread through the foreign community like wildfire.

Meat—other than poultry, which was sold live at the open market, as was fish—came to the door in a tepid tin box on the back of a peddler's bicycle. Chiefly from water buffalo or goat, it was boneless and without fat, making it hard to guess what part of the animal it came from, or how long to cook it. That mattered, because eventually kerosene got very scarce and was saved to run our fridge (electricity being too unreliable), whereas the kerosene stove stood idle and cooking was done on a charcoal hibachi, with little Chi-chi climbing up on a ladder every rainy evening to wipe the black smoke stains off the kitchen ceiling.

There was also galloping inflation. We American embassy people were lucky that we could legally exchange our dollars at the black-market rate. We used the rupiahs the embassy held as "counterpart funds" (the virtually worthless local currency provided by the Indonesian government to "pay" for our gifts of surplus agricultural products). Other foreigners were forced to use the black market, and ordinary Indonesians, lacking foreign currency, had to go outside the law just to survive. One morning we heard that the lawn of one of our neighboring prefab houses had been stolen overnight. We thought the story must be a joke. It wasn't.

When we had been in Jakarta less than a year, President Sukarno, in an anti-hoarding effort, moved the decimal point on the value of all large bills and froze the assets in all bank accounts. From then on, people went shopping carrying heavy, greasy bundles of one rupiah bills, each bill worth a diminishing fraction of a US cent. Barter became more prevalent. You could not buy local beer (one of the few local goods that still maintained some of its previous quality) without giving the seller an equivalent number of empty bottles, because the ingredients to make the bottles were now so scarce.

This gave rise to a popular story we heard about the good brother and the bad brother. The good brother worked hard and saved his money and put it in the bank, while the other one spent his money on beer and sat on his front porch drinking, and throwing the empties over his shoulder into the back. Eventually, the good brother went bankrupt, but the bad brother had a fortune in empty bottles in his back yard.

. . . .

*I*ndonesia lacked many things we were used to and yearned for. I remember frequently complaining about the things it didn't have when talking with American and expat friends. Yet it had some things no other place did.

"*Nyonya mau?*" (Madam would like?), our driver Hassim asked me, when he turned up one afternoon at the kitchen door with a little fuzzy ball lying on his open hand. I peered down into the face of a little feline creature with tawny, spotted fur, round ears and big, round, pale green eyes set close to its little nose. Except for its tiny size, it could have been a leopard—and who knows?—it might be one. I had never seen a newborn leopard and this creature was probably only a day or two old.

"Yes," I said, "Madam WOULD like!"

Hassim said its mother had been killed inadvertently by his brother, driving down a road through a jungle west of Jakarta. His brother had then stopped the car and, seeing that the dead mother had enlarged teats, had looked for and found this infant by the roadside. Hassim said that it was a *kucing hutan* (jungle cat) but was also known as a *macan tutul* (spotted panther). He set it down on my open palm and it stayed where its body could feel the warmth from mine for the next several days. Hassim guessed it was male, and so I called it Mathew—from its spotted panther name (*ma-can tu-tul*)—and John and I became besotted by its beauty.

I asked Chi-chi if it would be all right for us to keep Mathew and con-fessed that I did not know how big he might get. She said we could worry about that when it happened, but clearly Mathew charmed her and the other servants, too.

At first, Mathew slept in the crook of my arm at night and would wake me with a sound rather like a bird chirp. That was to tell me he wanted an-other eyedropper or two full of a mixture I made up for him of canned milk mixed with a raw egg. Nobody at the Jakarta zoo knew what to feed such a creature; their efforts to raise them had always ended badly. For a time, though, Mathew thrived. I loved to watch him teach himself the things his mother should have taught him. For example, he would spend hours leaping up onto ever higher rungs of our dining chairs, to practice climbing.

John had always loved cats and usually they loved him too, but this creature had an increasing aversion to all males, though Mathew treated me as his mother and would allow other women to stroke him. I recall one day walking home from around the corner, and hearing a sound like a roaring lion. I got home to find our houseboy standing in the doorway between the kitchen and the living room, leaning forward and saying, "*Bagus, bagus*" (good, beautiful). From the far side of the room, Mathew—now almost his full size (that of a slender domestic cat)—roared at him not to take another step into his domain.

By then Mathew was starting to have digestion problems as we tried, under the vet's instructions, one diet after another. The little cat also got feline distemper or something similar which temporarily paralyzed his hind quarters, but we nursed him successfully back to health. One day, Mathew went for a daylong checkup to see if he was completely cured of his distem-per. When the vet was finished, some mindless assistant put the animal in a plastic Pan Am bag and zipped the zipper all the way closed. When I went to fetch Mathew, his body was still warm, but stiff and dead from asphyxiation.

I could not stop sobbing for days and gave as my excuse that I was thinking that, if this could happen at the vet's, what could happen to my baby when it came? Because by then I knew a baby was on the way.

Meanwhile, I kept looking for worthwhile things to do that would fill my days. This would remain an off and on problem for me for many years, and it is perhaps the biggest hardship a Foreign Service spouse endures. I spent three gratifying months as a substitute teacher of seventh graders at the international school, until they got a permanent teacher; I was sorry to give it up.

. . . .

For the young people streaming out of the Javanese countryside trying to earn enough money to obtain minimal food, clothing, and shelter for themselves and their families, getting a job at a diplomat's home was like winning the lottery. It was, however, a situation that placed a frightening amount of power in the hands of inexperienced housewives like me. A servant could be dismissed on the mere suspicion (sometimes fed by a rival servant looking to find a job for a cousin) that he or she had stolen an item that had merely been mislaid. The dismissed domestic had no recourse. And without a letter of recommendation from previous employers, few former servants could get another job.

John and I felt very lucky in our domestic staff in Jakarta, and when it came time to leave for Surabaya, I realized I would miss the servants more than any other people I knew there; I knew them better. And they all had been so patient with us and ready to help us cope with life in this very foreign place. Where they lived, the walls and fences plastered everywhere with anti-US slogans, it could not have been comfortable to be known as working for American embassy people. They had sympathized with us when our running water stopped flowing or the electricity gave out, without reminding us that they had neither at home.

Hassim, the driver, would be coming to help us out briefly at our next post, Surabaya, at the eastern end of Java, so at least I did not have to think about saying good-bye to him yet. Of those remaining in Jakarta, I knew I would find it especially hard to say good-bye to Iam, our tall, lovely laundress. I remembered that when I had been staying home, anxious about our baby Paul who was born nine weeks early and had spent a month in an incubator in Jakarta's best hospital, Iam would often arrive at siesta time, bringing me a flower arrangement she had just made. She could throw a flowering branch of mauve bougainvillea into a bamboo basket and it became a work of art.

I asked her one afternoon, as I lay there sick with worry, waiting for Paul to come home, where she came from, and she said Cilacap—a town notorious for being at the center of Java's poorest farm district. Most of our servants were very short in stature, indicative (I thought) of poor nutrition in their younger years, and so I asked Iam how she had managed to grow so tall and lovely. She said, "We were so poor that we could find to eat only the roots and the rice husks and vegetable peelings that others threw away. And from those roots"—she added, smiling—"I grew."

. . . .

Our Jakarta driver, Hassim, after driving our car east to Surabaya, stayed on the first month to help us find a new set of servants. We soon had the usual seven or eight, none of whom spoke English. They spoke the lingua franca, Indonesian/Malay, to foreigners such as John and me and Paul, and Javanese to each other. (To make sure we were all dealing with Paul from the same script, John and I also spoke Indonesian to Paul, so that the servants could overhear what we said to him.)

The Surabaya servant I remember best is our baby *amah* (Asian pidgin for maid). Her name was Mina, and she was small and dainty, with a round face and a husky voice. She had never worked as a domestic servant before, but I could see that her heart went out immediately to Paul. She was visibly intelligent and seemed determined to do whatever the job entailed to be with this beautiful child. Paul returned her affection, though he also loved to spend time with Buawi, our wonderful houseboy. Paul also adored being carried around in the late afternoons by our new driver, so that he could follow the meanderings along the upper walls of the house of our resident wall lizards—coral-colored chameleons that ate any mosquito or other flying insect foolish enough to venture onto the walls, outdoors or indoors.

I enjoyed sharing Paul with Mina and the others. To fully understand this, you have to know that I had been brought up—both before and after my parents' divorce when I was eight—by my mother (who had to go off to work after the divorce) and my nanny, Louise, whom my mother hired when I was two and who stayed with her for the next fifty years. Louise remained like another parent to me all her life.

In addition, I acquired a charming stepmother, Jean, when my father remarried in 1948 when I was twelve. Jean survived my father and was present at our little ceremony when we were scattering my nanny Louise's ashes in the East River a few years ago and I sang, "Sometimes I feel like a motherless child." Jean corrected me afterward, pointing out that "nobody ever had as many mothers as you did."

Mina and I had a mutual understanding on how to handle Paul from the first day. But I did not know she had children of her own until she had worked for us more than a month. One day she told me that she had two children, and asked if she could bring them to work the next day, so that I could see them.

Intrigued, I agreed, and the next morning she appeared with one little boy who looked to be four or near it and a babe in arms with huge eyes in a head almost as big as his shriveled body. Puzzled and alarmed, I said, "How old is this little one?" "Nearly two," she answered, "but I had to stop nursing him to go look for work, and there was no other food for him."

Rather shaken, I asked our houseboy Buawi to bring coffee for Mina and me, and she told me her story. Her husband had left her while she was pregnant with the younger child. Although she lived with her parents, they were poor too, and had recently moved to town. There was not enough money or other resources to feed the family. Mina had calculated that if she tried to feed both children, she would risk being too weak herself to find a job and then they would all die. The only logical solution seemed to be to feed herself and the older boy, who had a better chance of surviving than did the baby. Now, with this job, she could also feed the baby, but maybe it was too late? Unspoken was the fact that she had waited weeks before telling me about the problem for fear of losing her job with us.

When people talk about poverty and how smart people can work their way out of it, I think of Mina. Fortunately, we had found for Paul a fine Indonesian pediatrician in Surabaya, and I took Mina and her children to him the next day. Over the next months, the little one was nursed back to something like health, though I do not know to what extent his later physical and mental development was affected.

Before we left Surabaya, we racked our brains for months trying to come up with gifts for the servants that would not melt away with inflation or risk being stolen by the unpaid soldiers or police who wandered about the city's streets, fully armed but underfed. John finally had a brain wave: dental care for our staff and their families. At least their teeth could not be stolen from them!

....

Our most memorable domestic servant, Ah Fong, did not enter our lives until some years later when we were living in Kuching, in the state of Sarawak, in Malaysian Borneo. Getting to know Ah Fong and her situation taught me a lot about what it was like to be an overseas Chinese in Southeast Asia.

Bob Duemling, John's predecessor as consul for East Malaysia and Brunei, resident in Kuching, had brought Ah Fong over from Kuala Lumpur; she was what was known as a "black-and-white" amah and was said to be a pearl beyond price. I had written Bob to ask him to ask Ah Fong if she would be willing to stay on in Borneo to work for us. I promised that if either side was not happy by the end of the first month, we would pay her trip back home to Kuala Lumpur. She had agreed.

I already knew that black-and-white amahs (named for their long white starched cotton tunics over wide-legged black satin trousers) were famous throughout Singapore, Hong Kong, and Malaysia for being the best domestic servants you could hope to hire. They were unattached Cantonese women (often widows or runaway wives, escaping from life as near-slaves to their in-laws) who, upon leaving China, had joined together in what in Chinese coastal pidgin was called a *kong-si* and is best described as an organization halfway between a sorority and a trade union. At their kong-si headquarters in Kuala Lumpur, Hong Kong (under the British), and Singapore, these women honed their skills as cooks and housekeepers and found jobs for one another, looked after each other, and set up group homes where they could retire in old age.

Our new black-and-white amah, Ah Fong, was tiny and neat as a pin. With her still black hair coiled tightly in a bun and a single jade circlet around her dainty wrist, she was as lovely as a costume doll. And, though probably about sixty, she had lots of energy and verve. A wonderful cook and cleaner and a gracious greeter of guests, she had the kind of personal authority I associate with Mary Poppins. Our six-year-old boy and four-year-old girl had fallen immediately under her spell, and she gave every impression of enjoying their company and being pleased to work for us.

The month's trial I had set in motion by writing to her former boss was almost up when we received word that President Johnson was coming to West Malaysia and that not only John but I as well would be required to help with the presidential visit.

I liked the idea of going back, all expenses paid, to Kuala Lumpur for a brief visit, although it was a little soon to be leaving the children with a stranger, even one they liked as well as they did Ah Fong. I was sure, though, that she was equal to the task. And so, when I told her that I needed to leave her in charge of the children while John and I went back to West Malaysia for a week—to which she readily agreed—I also mentioned that our month's trial was approaching its end. I said I hoped that she was as happy to stay on in Kuching as we were to have her.

There was a longish pause that set me back on my heels before she said, "Madam, would it be all right if I gave you my answer when you return?" Feeling a bit like a lover afraid of being jilted, I could hardly say anything but yes.

An hour or so later, Ah Fong reappeared with a box wrapped in brown paper and string—the Mary Poppins touch. She looked up into my face very earnestly and asked (in pidgin English), "Madam, would you take this package to a house in downtown Kuala Lumpur? I mean would YOU bring it yourself?"

Once again, there was no way I felt I could say no. I wondered fleetingly if this box could contain drugs or other contraband. But then I said to myself that she came highly recommended and John's and my instinct told us to trust her with our children, so it was highly unlikely that there would be anything wrong with the contents of the package.

John and I flew back to Kuala Lumpur, where it seemed as if the entire city were involved in what seemed to be an imperial visit by President Johnson. John was assigned to develop a "rainy day alternative" at the prestigious Rubber Research Institute. His program came to involve hundreds of Malaysian schoolchildren with little American and Malaysian flags lining the route to a building Johnson never entered—because it did not rain on the preferred site. (I shudder to think of how many families Johnson offended by not turning up after all these children had stood for hours under the hot sun waiting for him.) My job was to help set up and run a souvenir stand at the ambassador's residence, on the off chance that our president or members of his party might want to buy examples of Malaysian art or crafts. (To the best of my knowledge, there were no sales.)

Within a day or two, I found time to take Ah Fong's package to its destination. Transport was no problem; in preparation for the Johnson visit, the embassy had simply rented for the week every taxi and car-for-hire in the city. I soon was in the back seat of a rented Bentley limousine with a smartly uniformed driver who drew us up to the faded painted door of a two-story shop house in the Chinese part of town. Dangling the package by its string, I rang the bell, and a few minutes later an elderly Chinese woman dressed similarly to Ah Fong let me in. Silently, she led me upstairs where, displayed on high walls around the central staircase, was a row of portrait scrolls of dour, elderly Chinese women. They looked to be the older generation of the women standing to greet me, all in white tunics above black trousers.

I was relieved of my package, which was taken away unopened. There was a wooden kitchen chair in the midst of these standing women where I was asked to sit. Unusually for Malaysia, I was not even offered a cup of tea. Standing over me, one woman who spoke pretty fair Malay began asking me questions while the others looked on attentively; they occasionally made hissing sounds in response to my answers, like a gaggle of geese. How big was my family in Sarawak? How big was the house? How old were the children? Were they well behaved? How long was their school day? How many hours did Ah Fong work a week? How often did we give dinner parties? Was Ah Fong free to go out on her free days and could she entertain friends at home in her quarters? Were there other Cantonese amahs she saw there?

Eventually the interrogation came to an end and I was free to go, having promised to pass on their greetings to Ah Fong.

Back home in Borneo later that week, I duly conveyed the ladies' greetings to Ah Fong. She asked no questions, and I volunteered nothing further about my errand.

A few days later, though, Ah Fong came bounding into the living room carrying in her hand an open blue air letter folded into narrow vertical strips the way the Chinese did in those days to help them write their ideograms in columns. She said, "Madam, about the month's trial: I would like to stay on, if you agree."

I could not help it, I laughed out loud. "So I passed the test, did I?"

"Yes," she said primly and padded away in her black felt slippers to make dinner.

I sometimes wondered what was in the box I had carried. It was probably empty; its purpose presumably was just to get me to the kong-si. But then, who knows? In Asia there are always little unresolved mysteries.

Chapter 5

Diplomacy at the Dining Table

· · · · · · · · · · · · · · · · · · ·

IF ASKED TO PICTURE A TYPICAL diplomatic event, other than an embassy cocktail reception, most people think of a formal dinner party: everybody dressed to the nines and seated in front of serried ranks of crystal, silver, and china illuminated by chandeliers and candles—and they wouldn't be wrong. The dining table is often the locus for diplomatic talks to begin or continue. Career diplomats throughout the world know how to give and behave at diplomatic dinners, and the host and hostess try hard to play by the rules, seating people by their protocol rank. To violate that order with serving diplomats of the host or other countries is an insult that—at least as recently as twenty years ago—might have obliged the wronged guest to get up and leave, because it was his country's honor that was being offended.

Once at table, the host and hostess each divide their attention between the person on their right and on their left. Clever hosts and hostesses alert their guests ahead of time who the guests will be sitting next to, so the guests don't squander their conversational gems on their eventual dinner partners ahead of time—during the cocktail or aperitif hour.

Nobody is born knowing how to give or attend such formal occasions. I certainly didn't know, and I did not learn how in Jakarta. Then, after eighteen months in Jakarta, we were sent for another eighteen months to the other end of Java. There, John became the senior vice consul at our consulate in Surabaya, a decaying port that had been the commercial capital of Indonesia when Indonesia had been the Netherlands East Indies.

John had attended several formal diplomatic dinners in New Delhi when his father was on the embassy staff there. He thought that while we were in Surabaya, with a nice house and excellent household staff, would be a good time for us to learn how to host such an event.

Another reason why it seemed the perfect time for us to learn how to host such a dinner is that we had the perfect houseguests: a young French-woman, Anita, and her American anthropologist husband, Clark Cunningham. (They remained our very close friends for the rest of our lives.) We had earlier invited this couple to stay with us while Anita gave birth to her first baby, Nathalie. Clark was a Rhodes scholar doing fieldwork for a doctorate on the ex-headhunters of the remote Indonesian island of Timor. And when we heard that his eighteen-year-old wife Anita was pregnant in such a primitive place—they were living in a sago pith hut where she cooked on three stones—we had invited them to have their baby in Surabaya and lodge at our house. We urged them to come well ahead and stay well after the birth, before returning to Timor.

A strikingly lovely girl, Anita seemed to be able to speak all languages. She had native French and Spanish, having been born of French parents in South America, and had since acquired nearly flawless English while an au pair in Oxford (where she met Clark) and later good Indonesian and fluent Atoni, the language of their Timorese hosts. Her last diploma had been from her French junior high school in Buenos Aires, but she was very intelligent and seemed to take in information and to learn new skills in many fields at an astounding rate.

More important, she had learned from her wonderful French grand-mother how to cook, and she was ready to teach me: French vinaigrette salad dressing, hollandaise and béarnaise sauces, chocolate mousse, duck with olives, boeuf à la mode, profiteroles, French crepes. . . . In Surabaya, unlike Jakarta, we had a source of pasteurized milk and cream (an Armenian dairy farmer and family who had somehow washed up on these shores). So there was nothing Anita and I couldn't do—that is, until the flour gave out.

We learned about this new shortage after our cook had come home from the market very pleased because she had found flour with no weevils. (Sifting the weevils out was my one use for nylon stockings, once I had escaped from Jakarta and its insistence on nylons when we paid formal calls.) The evening of the clean flour purchase, I tried to make a roux to build up a sauce for shrimp Newburg, but it didn't look right. I tasted it and made a face: ground pumice stone! No wonder the weevils weren't attracted to it! No matter, we could still make duck with olives, although the ducks were terribly tough and scrawny.

Eventually, after many wonderful days and evenings with Clark and Anita, many of these evenings shared with our close British Council friends Joan and Peter Martin and other friends, John and I said a tearful farewell to Clark and Anita and their enchanting little six-week-old Nathalie and could hardly wait for them to come again for a visit, which they promised to do soon.

They did come back, some six months later, by which time Nathalie was a real companion for Paul in the wading pool, under Mina's supervision. Anita and I would also jump in, after having baked bread in our bathing suits, using flour that John had had the foresight to import—in beautiful big metal canisters—from Singapore.

John decided that now was the time for us to learn how to give a proper formal diplomatic dinner, in preparation for some future time when John's rank might require it. We got out the protocol books from the consulate library and learned what glasses and knives and forks went where, what was the correct protocol order of seating for such a dinner party, and that each place should have its name card and, if possible, there should be a menu, in French, between every two place settings.

Anita and I both did the cooking, the cook cleaning up behind us, and Anita wrote out the French menus. We had invited Joan and Peter and told them to wear dinner dress (white tuxedo for the man and a long dress for the woman, not too bare on top). We also invited Alan Stevens, another stray American anthropologist living in Surabaya, and loaned him an old white tuxedo of John's that was too big around for Alan and not long enough in the sleeve, but no matter. We also invited a young English sugar estate manager, who, like Anita, happened to have been born in Uruguay and had a serviceable dinner jacket. We gave as our pretext for the party that it was (as it happened) Uruguayan National Day.

I loaned two pairs of my short white cotton gloves to Buawi and our former gardener, who was now Joan and Peter's houseboy. To have enough dishes and glasses and silverware, we were eating off not only our own plates but also Joan and Peter's. Thanks to our Hong Kong purchases years earlier en route to Jakarta, we had lots of big, white, embroidered linen dinner napkins.

It was a marvelous party. We played it straight, toasting Uruguay, Indonesia, and the United States. Since almost all of us were on the closest of terms, the occasion had none of the stiffness sometimes to be found at formal dinners, but it had all the glamor. The table looked beautiful, we women (especially Anita) looked our best, and the food was marvelous—or it seemed so in comparison with what one usually could find to eat in that town in those days.

I was greatly tickled to learn afterward that our Anglo-Uruguayan dinner guest was telling others, "You know, there is no reason to let the side down the way so many do here. Take the Heimanns, for example. They do things right!"

. . . .

Few other formal diplomatic dinner parties that we attended or hosted over the years equaled that first one for lively conversation and sparkle. Our next such dinner was in The Hague, hosted by our next ambassador, a nice, quiet political appointee who was a former treasurer of the Pennsylvania Democratic Party, and who had little in common with the wives of senior Dutch officials seated to his left and right. His apparent lack of ease cast something of a pall on the evening, although the table was beautifully set with flowers and crystal and silver, and the ladies' silk and satin dinner dresses and their jewels sparkling in the candlelight were a delight to the eye.

In time, I came to attend many similar dinners at our ambassador's residence in Brussels, and most of them were more like those in The Hague than like our own maiden effort in Surabaya. The most memorable conversation I ever had at such a dinner at the ambassador's residence in Brussels was when I was seated next to a very handsome Italian a few years older than I, perhaps in his forties. Typically for an American woman, I asked him what he did.

"I'm a banker."

"Oh, where is that?"

"In Zurich, in Switzerland."

"Oh, is that interesting work?"

"No, it's a dead bore."

"Well then, what do you do for fun?"

"Have affairs."

Hardly daring to believe my ears, I could not resist asking: "With whom?"

"With the wives of my colleagues," he said, adding plaintively, "There's nobody else around!"

Years later, when I was consul general in Bordeaux, I remember hearing my ambassador in Paris complain that he hated the interminable formal dinners he was expected to host at his residence. For him, they were a waste of time because he was always seated next to the wife of the person he wanted to talk to, while the man he wanted to speak with was way across the table, next to the ambassador's wife.

When I became a woman officer, my situation was different. As consul general in Bordeaux, I could—like my ambassador in Paris—entertain easily and relatively cheaply at my Bordeaux residence, thanks to the excellent staff Uncle Sam paid for. But unlike at our ambassador's residence, at mine, the senior male guest was always—because protocol demanded it—seated at my right, and the next most senior man was seated at my left. That meant that I could be gracious to the wives before and after dinner, and accomplish my diplomatic business at table. It seems almost unfair for women to have this advantage over their male counterparts. But my feeling is that, so long as we have it, it's a crime not to use it.

If I were a man, I would be inclined to follow the practice of one of my favorite Belgian ambassadors to the United States: keep the numbers down to ten at table and announce to your guests your desire that there be one general conversation. To make that work, you need to choose guests with at least some interests in common, and use a rectangular table or, better still a square, and avoid round tables (whose diameters often make cross-table conversation impossible).

I often thought of my Congolese friend when I was working up a guest list for a dinner in Bordeaux. The need to have the right people with the right people was just as important in Bordeaux as it had been in Kinshasa—but how to know who to invite with whom?

My wine merchant was one of the people who came to my rescue. I would take him the list of proposed guests and ask him what wine to serve. (In Bordeaux, wine was the most important item on the table.) I knew I could get away with serving American wine, if I could find it, but should avoid serving Burgundy—Bordeaux's biggest rival in France. When choosing among Bordeaux wines, my merchant would look at my guest list and say that it was better not to serve Château such-and-such, because the owners have a lawsuit against this guest. Or, another time, he might say that the owner of this château had had an affair with the wife of the owner of that château. So, unlike anywhere else I was assigned, in Bordeaux I chose the wine to go with the guests, and then my cook chose the food to go with the wine.

Gradually, going beyond the wine trade, my wine merchant could be drawn out on what social and political lines were best not crossed at the same dinner party, and I would edit my guest list accordingly. Many French politicians of national importance spent from Thursday through Monday in their electoral district. In my day, the president, prime minister, and foreign minister were all elected from my consular district, as were a number of interesting and informative members of parliament who were often also mayors of towns in my district. Old hands, such as my wine merchant, telling me who was on what terms with whom, were a big help when I was trying to understand the politics of southwest France or trying to figure out who might be sympathetic to some policy my government was trying to promote. I came to realize that diplomacy is like pairing the right wine with the food. A lot depends on subtle nuances only a professional willing to do the homework would know.

Chapter 6

Learning to Drive a Bargain

· · · · · · · · · · · · · · · · · · ·

WHILE BASED IN SURABAYA FROM
mid-1960 to late 1961, John made a number of trips to other islands; he
reported to Washington on the politics and economic conditions of Eastern
Indonesia, which were for the most part desperate, much worse than on Java.
Even on Java, reliable communications and transport were nonexistent. Food
and other basic commodities were scarce; malaria, cholera, tuberculosis, and
dengue fever were common, and there were several simmering armed rebellions against the Republic of Indonesia. For Cold War reasons, some of these
rebellions were underwritten by Mao's China, others by the United States.

The future of the Republic of Indonesia was a big question mark.
President-for-life Sukarno (who, like many Javanese, had only one name) was
a wonderfully skilled and popular politician, corrupt but not bloodthirsty. As
Ambassador Jones would sometimes remark, Sukarno was the only government leader in history who managed to survive in power for decades without
the reliable support of either the armed forces or a political party.

But the Indonesian economy was in such bad shape, and the people
also, that the question on everyone's lips was not *if* there would be a coup
to topple Sukarno, only *when*. And the bigger questions remained: Who
would start it—the Communist Party or the noncommunists in the Armed
Forces? And who would win?

Most knowledgeable Westerners, including America's NATO allies
and many people in the White House, the State Department, and even in
our embassy in Jakarta, thought the coup would be started by the Indonesian Communist Party (the biggest such party outside the Soviet bloc) with
a lot of material and moral support from both the Soviet Union and Mao's

China. And most people thought that, given their seeming broad popularity and good organization, the Reds would most likely end up in power.

Ambassador Jones, who knew Indonesia well, had watched Sukarno *not* avail himself of the excuse to move to the Sino-Soviet bloc when the United States was caught red-handed in armed subversion of his government. Jones thought there was a chance that the good personal relations he had built up with Sukarno, together with Sukarno's instinctive distaste for the humorless, puritanical, intolerant communists at home and abroad, could maybe keep Sukarno from allowing his country to fall under communist control. Jones had helped save Indonesia from the communists once (with help from Major Benson), but—many members of his staff came to feel—he had become blinded by his friendship with Sukarno into thinking he could trust the dictator, in the end, to do the right thing. Now, in the early 1960s, Sukarno, though still a masterful orator and rabble-rouser, was an old man whom the communists knew how to flatter, whereas much of what Sukarno was hearing from our government and our allies, especially the British and the Dutch, was unflattering in the extreme.

Many mornings, when John and I would wake up, one of us would ask the other: "Today the coup?" Meanwhile, throughout the country almost everything that had a Western tinge was being outlawed or made suspect. No more Western tourist ships were allowed entry, and the Rotary, *Time* and *Life* magazines, and noncommunist local newspapers were all banned.

Even the Boy Scouts were disbanded; in Surabaya I saw a bunch of school-age boys in shorts and khaki shirts holding up signs that read (in English, which none of those kids spoke, much less could read) "Stamp Out Baden-Powellism." I stifled my laughter but wished I could send it to the *New Yorker* for its series on "Shouts we doubt ever got shouted."

The sad thing was we had to avoid embarrassing our Indonesian friends by appearing to single them out for friendship. We could invite to our house groups from an organization, such as the Women's International Club, or from a school, or from the local government, but not individual Indonesians just because we liked them.

Nonetheless, our year and a half in Surabaya flew by. Sooner than I could believe possible, we were waiting impatiently for news of our next assignment. If it were to somewhere in the developed world, I would for the first time in three years be able to buy things for a fixed price, rather than having to bargain endlessly for the smallest thing.

Bargaining is a skill that anybody posted to a Third World country needs to acquire, but I always felt awkward doing it. It was obvious that I could afford almost any price, given the exchange rate we had, whereas for many of the Javanese, every rupiah mattered. Nonetheless, my Indonesian friends let me know that if I did not bargain, I just wasn't playing the game and was losing face with the local vendors.

I had bargained, of course, during my nearly three years on Java, but my heart wasn't in it, and I would accede to the vendor's price much too soon. Even I could sense the vendor's disappointment at my cutting short the discussion. John was much better at it and clearly enjoyed his long sessions with the antiques peddlers who would come to the door in the late afternoons. They would set down on the floor small bronze statues of Buddhist and Hindu deities alleged to date from as early as the thirteenth-century in Java and rather lovely Chinese porcelain alleged to date from T'ang, Sung, and Ch'ing dynasties—some of which may have been genuine. (If there were Indonesian laws forbidding the export of antiquities, we were never told of them.)

The peddler would ignore me and go straight for John, who would soon be crouching down on the floor with him, examining one or two of the items laid out on a bamboo mat that caught his fancy. I always knew when the bargaining got serious, because then they would both lower their voices to a whisper. Sometimes the peddler would wrap up his goods again in a worn dish towel or wads of newspaper and come back days later for a fresh round of negotiations. We ended up with a number of little gods and bowls that we treasured ever after—and never dared to check their value.

Thinking I would probably have few chances left to bargain properly in a language both the seller and I spoke, I decided early one morning to go to the Open Market and bargain properly for at least one item.

Despite the frequent anti-West demonstrations on the public streets, I always enjoyed going to the market in Surabaya. I would go by becak, the colorful bicycle rickshaw. Once at the market, my favorite becak driver would wait for me, having turned me over to the care of one of the Madurese basket women. Acting like a human grocery cart, one of these raucous women, coming from a nearby island and seemingly much more volatile than the Javanese, would offer to carry your groceries in the basket on her head. Normally, you told her what you wanted to buy, and she steered you to the stand of the seller whose produce she liked best (or, possibly, the one who gave her the biggest cut).

This time, having got my basic vegetables and fish, I said I wanted to buy some *jeruks* (a citrus fruit which was the tropical substitute for a juice orange). This was the last item on my mental shopping list, and I thought to myself: "Just once before I leave this country I would like to pay the right price for something; why not jeruks?"

Now that there were virtually no Dutch women in town, there were few Western women who went to the market themselves; mostly, they sent their cooks. So I was a bit of a novelty, and my basket lady and I began to attract a small throng of onlookers as we made our way to the part of the market devoted to citrus and other tropical fruits. The man at the jeruk stand addressed me in Indonesian and mentioned a price that even I knew was excessive. I replied in a manner to suggest that I thought he was joking and offered half that price. I could see that the crowd of onlookers was growing, and tried to gauge whether they were with me or with the fruit seller. It might be awkward if there were some local Communist Party leader present who wanted to single me out as a Western capitalist. (Every month or so the rumor of a Communist demonstration against Americans would bring a bunch of Republic of Indonesia soldiers to our house. Their officer would ask permission for them to stay the day on our front porch, and I would take orders for soft drinks for them.)

Fortunately, the jeruk seller expressed amusement and pleasure that I spoke Indonesian well enough for us to converse properly and, eventually, after a bit of backchat on both sides, he offered a price halfway between his first offer and mine. I replied with a price ever so slightly higher than my first offer. By this time, some of the other Madurese basket women and their customers had joined the audience.

After a time, he said—and this was a phrase the bargainers always seemed to say in English—"Last price!" and named a sum that was in the ballpark. I could feel the audience hold its collective breath and then, with some deliberation, I quietly offered a price that was two and a half rupiahs lower than his "last price." (There was a coin called a *ringgit* that was the equivalent to two and a half rupiahs, so it wasn't such a strange sum to use.)

Total silence fell as we all waited for the seller's reply. After a theatrical pause, he grinned at me and said softly: "*Nyonya pinter*" (Madam is clever).

The crowd whooped and shouted and practically carried me on its shoulders, alongside my basket woman, with the pile of orange-green citrus fruit in the basket on top of her head, back to my waiting becak. I paid for the basket (her tip) and prepared to be driven home. It was a triumphant moment, albeit providing strong evidence that this had, indeed, been the only time I paid the right price for anything.

Though, I suspect, security considerations might have made it more difficult for me to be allowed to go off to the market by myself, John and I were convinced that showing ourselves to the public as friendly and unafraid was a much better tactic. It may not have been an accident that, during this tense period in East Java, Communist-led mobs burned down the US Information Service libraries in East Java and threw stones through the glass doors of our consul's residence, but our house was not attacked until the day after we had left the country.

Chapter 7

Girl Talk

• • • • • •

IF ASKED WHAT IS THE SINGLE most useful skill a diplomat and his or her family can acquire for use in a foreign country, I would answer unhesitatingly: knowing the language. The Foreign Service, before we became so short of officers at most overseas posts, used to be more ready to allow the time needed for an officer to learn the language to a truly professional level, usually through full-time language training before arrival at post. Wives were rarely allowed to take language classes, except once at post in one-hour installments. Luckily for me, Indonesian is essentially the same language as Malay (as close as American English is to what Canadians speak). So when, a few years after Indonesia, we were assigned to Malaysia, I arrived able to converse with local people. That led me quickly into an unanticipated intimacy—even more than I'd bargained for—with the wives of John's official contacts. It also revealed that women sometimes have the advantage over men in making friends, especially in traditional societies.

The Malay officials and businesspeople John dealt when he was assistant commercial attaché at our embassy in Kuala Lumpur, West Malaysia— and later as consul for East Malaysia and Brunei—were of an age and a stage in their lives when they were marrying off their children. They often used invitations to a wedding feast to reciprocate hospitality from business contacts like us.

The food was always wonderful. To my mind, Malay food beats Indonesian food every time for flavor. Until recently it was available chiefly in Malay homes, rarely in restaurants. Even in Kuala Lumpur there were virtually no Malay restaurants in our day, so the weddings were a special treat for us gastronomically.

But at a Malay wedding the food was slow in coming, and there was always a long period of waiting on the front veranda for dinner to be served. Meanwhile, the Malay hosts, being stricter Muslims than the Javanese, served no alcohol, but like Indonesians, believed that food that was served really hot or cold was bad for the digestion. They would offer their guests tepid bottled soft drinks, such as orange squash or cream soda.

As the ambient temperature and humidity were never lower than the high 80s, Western male guests sweltered, especially Western men who, like John, had to wear a suit on such occasions. (That was until he was finally able to find batik shirts that were long enough for six-footers like him.) The women were much more comfortably dressed, in loose-fitting overblouses and long skirts in opaque fabrics that could be worn over the minimum of undergarments.

After I had been to a couple of these Malay weddings, I noticed that all the women on the veranda were Westerners or Chinese or Indians. Where were the Malays? Eventually, as it became generally known that I spoke Malay, when I went to one of these parties I would be discreetly led inside the house to a back room off the kitchen. There, sitting on a grass mat floor covering, were the missing Malay ladies, including some of the most senior women, such as wives and daughters of Malay sultans or other senior government officials.

A head taller than most Southeast Asian women, I had learned in Indonesia to lean forward with my knees bent so that I did not loom over the higher-ranking people present. Now, I had to do it sitting on a mat. This involved scrunching down as best I could while making sure that I didn't commit the rudeness of allowing the soles of my feet to face the other women. I found it well worth the bother because the atmosphere was a total contrast to that on the veranda.

On the veranda, poor John would be standing, watching his tepid soft drink lose its fizz, while engaged in stilted conversation in fluent Malay or slowly pronounced English with people who were as bored as he was. Here, seated on the grass mat back near the kitchen, the atmosphere was very informal and the conversation almost giddy, as these women, led by the highest-ranking lady present, recalled their own weddings and those of people they had known in the old days. Their stories, to my amazement, did not stop with the nuptial ceremony or the feast, but continued into the bedroom, in ever-increasing detail. The narrative was accompanied by raucous laughter by these women whom I had not thought to have this Rabelaisian side to them.

They also told stories about friends or famous people they knew who had been divorced by—and then remarried to—the same man. If I understood these ladies correctly, remarriage to the same spouse could not legally occur, according to Islamic law—or maybe it was local customary law—without the woman having an intervening marriage to somebody else. And the intervening marriage had to be confirmed as consummated—leading to the existence of official witnesses of a type I thought had gone out of fashion with the end of the Tudor dynasty.

I'm no prude, but I could feel myself blushing hotly when these ladies turned to me to see if I had a good story or two from my own experience to contribute to the general hilarity. Not knowing what to say, I finally claimed a lack of Malay vocabulary in this field and was let off the hook.

When John and I compared notes after the first time this happened, John was astonished. He said, "To look at those women, I would have thought them so refined that butter would not melt in their mouths."

I began to wonder why they behaved that way on such occasions. Usually, these same ladies were models of decorum. In my reading, I learned that there were three Malay behavioral styles, especially for Malay women: refined, court style, and rough. The refined style usually prevailed when dealing with acquaintances and non-Malays. The court style was only used in the presence of one or more of the several sultans who take turns being Malaysia's sovereign—and few Malays were familiar with it. But the *kasar* (rough, coarse) style was used by people of all social classes among close friends and family, but also with people of demonstrably lower status, such as becak drivers, peddlers, or beggars. A wedding party or any time when women were all together in the kitchen seemed to call for the use of the kasar style, at least among those women guests who were part of the hostess's inner circle.

It may just be that upper-class Malays share with their British counterparts a fondness for racy speech and sexy gossip. I doubt if I shall ever know for certain. But I do know that on these occasions it was much more fun to be a woman than a man.

. . . .

We moved after a year in West Malaysia to Kuching, the biggest town in northern Borneo. There, where John would be based as the American consul for East Malaysia and Brunei, I found again that Malay was the lingua franca, and I soon had the chance to try it out on some "Dayaks," as the Borneo native tribespeople were called.

We had arrived in Kuching—the capital of Sarawak, and a British colony until 1963—on July 3, 1966. At our big July Fourth reception the next day, we met many of the movers and shakers of Sarawak, including many of the British colonial servants who were on their way out. They had just handed over their jobs to local leaders, now that Sarawak had joined the newly independent Federation of Malaysia. Most of the British colonial servants John and I met truly loved Sarawak and its people, and were happy to pass on their fondness for Sarawak to us.

I remember one dear Englishwoman, Margaret Young, whose husband, Bob, had been a powerful figure in the colonial administration of Sarawak. Bob had accepted his golden handshake and was about to leave, when he was asked to stay on a year longer because of the security situation on the border with Indonesian Borneo. After we became friends, Margaret told me that a Sarawak Chinese businessman and politician whom they had always liked had given Bob a little gold necklace for the Youngs' baby daughter. Bob had started to say, "You know I can't accept this," when his Chinese friend put a hand on his arm and said, "Don't be so soft. You aren't anybody anymore. It is we who have the power. Take this for your little girl." And he did.

The humility and the honesty in that story helped me rid myself of some of the anticolonial cant that I had been brought up on. I know there are many true stories of dreadful behavior by colonial officers and their families all over the world, but in my experience, an exception has to be made for Sarawak. (There may be other exceptions I don't know about.)

Sarawak did not become a colony until 1945, having previously been the private estate of members of the Brooke family, the so-called White Rajahs of Sarawak. Post–World War II, under the first British governor general, Malcolm MacDonald, the new colonial regime had by-and-large continued the antiexploitative, anticommercial, and genuinely respectful-of-local-feelings style of the eccentric White Rajahs. The White Rajahs had acquired and ruled Sarawak for a hundred years until they had proved unable to defend their territory from Japanese conquest.

The only awkwardness we had with the departing British civil servants of the ex-colony Sarawak was caused by the desire of some of them that America take on the role of protector of the indigenous people. These departing colonial servants wanted us to continue their efforts to combat what they feared was becoming an excessive Malayization of what had been a deliberately multicultural society.

The three-year-old federal government of Malaysia, headquartered in Kuala Lumpur, still operated on the principle that had long governed the Malay Peninsula, not of multiculturalism but of a plural society of separate ethnic communities, joined together by alliances at the top. The British on the Peninsula had ruled their colony, the Federation of Malaya, indirectly through the inherited aristocracy of the Malay community (Malays being 50 percent of the population), while protecting the commercial and labor rights of the Chinese (33 percent) and Indians (10 percent).

The Cold War political calculus behind the establishment of the new Federation of Malaysia had been that adding the 1.3 million people from the former British colonies of Sabah and Sarawak to the 10 million West Malaysians would guarantee the (anticommunist) Malays—or at least native Muslims—a clear national majority for the foreseeable future. The problem—which was apparent by the time we arrived in Kuching—was that these population estimates were wrong. East Malaysia was only about one-sixth Malay. (By definition, all Malays are Muslim.) East Malaysia was fully one-third Chinese—almost none of them Muslim. And the native tribespeople, the Dayaks, the largest ethnic group in East Malaysia, were almost all either Christian or animist—not Muslim. Nonetheless, the leaders of Malaysia's government in Kuala Lumpur continued to act as if most

East Malaysians were either Muslim or about to become Muslim—and not only Muslim but very similar to the Malays of West Malaysia. This false assumption irritated the tribal people of Sarawak as much as it did the East Malaysian Chinese and infuriated the departing British colonial officers who had worked so hard to maintain Sarawak as a "happy land" of true multiculturalism.

Given the persistent armed efforts by Mao's Communist China and Sukarno's far-Left Indonesia to subvert Malaysia, John's marching orders had been to spread the word in Borneo that the United States was *not* prepared to confront the central government in Kuala Lumpur on behalf of Dayak and other non-Muslim rights. John was supposed to make the case to Malaysian Borneo's local leaders that Sarawak and Sabah would be far better off staying in anticommunist Malaysia than trying to leave the Federation and ending up under the thumb of Sukarno or Mao. This American policy disagreement with some of the departing British colonial officers would lead to an awkward moment for me during my first week in Kuching.

. . . .

A couple of nights after the Fourth of July, John was about to leave Kuching for a swing around northern Borneo. He would be accompanying his predecessor, Bob Duemling, who would be saying his farewells and introducing John to Bob's contacts in Brunei and Sabah. Just then, we learned there was to be a black tie dinner hosted by the governor of Sarawak at his palace while John was away. John was halfway out the door to start his trip when I showed him the formal invitation, embossed with an elaborate Sarawak gold seal on top, which had come for us by messenger.

"You go," John said cheerfully over his shoulder. "You'll have a good time. Everybody will be there: the governor and his wife, the outgoing British colonial officer who used to be permanent secretary running the civil service here, and probably some of the tribal leaders who have now become Sarawak government ministers. I wouldn't be surprised if the Paramount Chief of the Iban—Sarawak's biggest Dayak tribe—is there. He's supposed to be quite a character." The driver closed the office car door and off John and Bob went, leaving me on my own to go through this very public ordeal among the "Wild Men of Borneo."

By then I had been a Foreign Service wife for nine years, but I have to admit to feeling anxious to be attending that dinner alone. If I were to meet one of these wild men, what would I say to him, or he to me? Would we just stare at one another?

A couple of evenings later, leaving the kids at home in the care of Ah Fong, I was driven by road and ferry "across river" to the imposing white bungalow that had been the home of the White Rajahs of Sarawak for a hundred years and was now the Governor's Palace. The governor, a courteous, elderly Sarawak Malay gentleman dressed in a high-collared long-sleeved silk shirt and a beautiful woven silk sarong shot with gold, was there to greet me and the other guests on the veranda. I didn't have to do anything but smile and be glad I had worn a long skirt of Thai silk that did not seem too out of place.

But then we all moved to the dining room.

Above us on the wall hung a portrait of Sir James Brooke, the first White Rajah, a casually but elegantly dressed young English nobleman of the 1840s. The long gleaming mahogany table we sat at was covered with more crystal goblets and silver cutlery than I had ever seen in a place setting before, even at one of our ambassadors' residences. But what really struck me were the people sitting near me. On my right was a man with earlobes like big pink rubber bands that hung nearly to his shoulders and with elaborate spidery black tattooed designs on his throat, wrists, and hands. On the veranda, the governor had explained to me that this man, a Dayak, was the new permanent secretary for administration, replacing the Englishman who would be sitting on my left.

Across from me was a man who had to be the Paramount Chief of the Iban. For, in addition to having more tattoos than the other tattooed men, he was wearing on his head something shaped like a fire chief's hat but in white straw, from the top of which huge black and white hornbill feathers protruded. I had been told that the Iban less than fifty years earlier had been famous as headhunters, and had sought their human prey on land and sea. Looking at this powerfully built, clearly self-confident older man, I could not help wondering whether he had been a headhunter in his youth.

We had barely sat down when the Englishman on my left (the only white person near me) turned to me and said quite distinctly: "So you are the new American consul's wife. Well, if you think I am going to help you, think again!" With that, he abruptly turned his back on me and began to engage the person on his left in quiet conversation.

I looked up at the White Rajah's portrait and had the feeling he was enjoying my discomfiture. John had mentioned briefly that the outgoing permanent secretary for administration had argued fiercely with Bob Duemling about America's unwillingness to stand up to the Malaysian government and fight for the people of Sarawak's cultural rights, but I had not expected the man to take out his irritation on *me*.

From across the table, the Paramount Chief of the Iban had been watching. I knew by then that he was the most powerful leader of the biggest ethnic group in Sarawak. It was clear from the look in his sharp old eyes that, whether or not he spoke English, he was an accurate reader of body language. Instead of talking to the lovely tribeswoman sitting next to him—who had earlobes so long that she could have tied them behind her head—he addressed me in very clear basic Malay.

"Do you speak Iban?" he asked.

"No," I answered in Malay, "but I do speak Malay."

"Oh," he said, "I know a lot of Peace Corps teachers upriver and they all speak Iban."

Another humbling moment for me, but he quickly unbent, his eyes sparkling. "I am going to teach you two Iban words: One is *dik*—it means *child* and that is you. And the other is *Apai*, father, and that is me. From now on, you are my child." I managed to say *"Apai"* back and saw an answering smile, not only from him but also from the other local people sitting around me. I knew enough about traditional Southeast Asian society by then to realize that this was an honor, not a put-down. This Iban aristocrat was adopting me into his family and offering me his protection. And clearly, this was the way the other tribal people round the table saw it.

From that time forward, I received invitations and house calls from the various wives who were at that dinner, and I eventually became part of a small circle of senior local women—tribal, Malay, and Chinese—who took turns teaching each other how to cook one another's dishes. We would pile into each other's kitchens and giggle and gossip while we pounded spices and chopped things small. (The pretty woman from the dinner party did indeed tie her earlobes behind her head when she cooked.) I was later told that this inclusion of the American consul's wife in their circle had not happened before. They also got me into their habit of calling informally at home on one or another of our circle every three to six weeks, just to keep the contact alive. I have tried to phone or email or visit with friends and diplomatic contacts every month or two ever since, and have found it very helpful in maintaining those relationships.

To this day, I bless my irate English dinner partner for having repudiated me so publicly that the local people, out of sympathy for a new arrival and, I think, especially a woman alone, felt inclined to come to my rescue. My being new—and that I spoke enough Malay to be able to grab hold of the lifeline that the chief of the Ibans threw me—turned what might have been a dismal evening that could have embarrassed our hosts into a happy memory.

Chapter 8

Swifts in the Eaves

• • • • • • • • • • •

OUR ARRIVAL IN KUCHING HAD
been almost as unpromising as our arrival eight years earlier in Jakarta. I had
just recovered from three weeks of "sleeping sickness" (mosquito-borne encephalitis), contracted in Kuala Lumpur, and though I was happy to have
recovered with no lasting ill effects, I was a bit nervous about moving to the
wilds of Borneo with two kids aged six and four. I began to grow more
anxious as our ancient Straits Steamship, the *M.V. Kinabalu*—which had
once ferried pilgrims to Mecca and looked just like Jim's ship in Conrad's
Lord Jim—left the South China Sea and chugged its way wearily upriver
through Borneo's coastal mangrove swamp.

Long hours later, our ship came to a stop at a tumbledown dock with
weathered wooden sheds roofed in corrugated iron. A rusty sign read "Pending." John said to the kids and me, "Prepare to disembark. We're here!"

Suddenly appalled, I said, "Is this really IT?"

John, who had paid a flying orientation visit to Kuching a few weeks
earlier, laughed and said, "I'm sorry. I couldn't resist the chance to see your
face when I said that. Pending is as near as this ship gets to Kuching. It
gets its name from being the place where goods waited until released by the
Brooke Rajahs' customs authority. We will be driven to Kuching and our
new home. Don't worry. You'll like it."

We were met by the consulate's car—a modest sedan, driven by a
young Chinese man in uniform—and made our way into town a few miles
away along dusty roads in fair condition. There were few cars on the road
and even fewer traffic lights. John said he had been advised by an old British
colonial officer to wave at everybody going by in a car; if you didn't know
them, you should.

We drove past the Open Market—with its outside row of shops lining the arcaded sidewalk—and came to some handsome nineteenth-century British colonial buildings. The neo-Romanesque courthouse, John explained, had become the home of the Council Negri (Sarawak's parliament). Nearby, there were also the neo-Gothic Square Tower and the grand neoclassical General Post Office with Corinthian columns along its façade.

John asked the driver to take us along the river so that we could see, across the water and atop a hill, a big, very white bungalow under a red tile roof that had been the palace of the White Rajahs. As John explained, the White Rajahs were dashing British baronets of a family named Brooke who had, beginning in the 1800s, managed to induce or compel the Sultan of Brunei to give them rather a lot of his land along the northwest coast of Borneo—where the Malays and Chinese lived—and inland, where the tribal people lived. For more than a hundred years prior to World War II, first James Brooke, the founding White Rajah, then his nephew Charles, and finally his nephew's son had ruled Sarawak as autocrats. Their word was law, but they had not tried to make a lot of money from their holdings. Their only notable interference with local practices had been to bring an end to headhunting among the Dayaks, the tribal people of the interior. The tribal people still remembered the White Rajahs fondly.

Next we drove to what would soon be our house. Like most other houses in Kuching, it was up off the ground on pilings. Knowing that Kuching had an average of 200 inches of rain a year, I understood why.

The house was good-sized and all white except for a big black ironwood front door and black ironwood shutters on all the windows. There were tall handsome fruit trees—mango and rambutan (a delicious tropical fruit similar to a lychee)—scattered about the grounds, and dozens of purple orchids on wooden sticks planted in front.

Although John had said that this was the nicest house available and that our predecessors had been happy here, I had been struck in that initial glance by the heavy spattering of bird excrement on the cement floor the pilings stood on. Looking up under the ironwood eaves, I had noticed a large number of swifts nesting there that had to be responsible for the droppings. In that imperious way one has when just arriving at a new home, I told John that we must get rid of those birds' nests so that we could get rid of the mess below. He promised to see that it was done. It turned out to be a promise John could not keep.

Our Chinese housekeeper, Ah Fong, was the first to object to getting rid of the swifts. She said it would be very bad luck. I was disappointed to find such superstition in the woman to whom we were entrusting the care of our children but wasn't too surprised. She was about sixty years old, after all, and had grown up in prewar Canton Province.

But I heard the same warning from one of my first new friends in Kuching, met the day after we arrived, at the July Fourth party given in the garden of our future home. The new friend, Heidi, was Swiss, and was married to an Iban, whom she had met when they were both university students in New Zealand. The Iban tribe had been the fiercest of the Borneo headhunters but they both seemed to be sensible, modern young people.

As arranged, I was moving us out of the hotel and into our new house while John was being shown around Brunei and Sabah. Soon the neighbors on the opposite hill from our house—Dayaks of whom the husband was now a Sarawak government minister—saw me trying to get our gardener to un-stick the birds' nests from the eaves above the windows. The husband came by in his limo to suggest I would do better to leave the birds' nests alone.

"Okay," I said to myself, feeling besieged on all sides. "What is wrong with this picture?" It was in the early evening of one of our first days after we moved into the new house, and Ah Fong had lighted the table lamps. John was still away, the children were watching her cook dinner, and I was alone, when I noticed that our big living room windows had no glass in them, no screens either—just the ironwood shutters standing open, allowing the bugs to come in. But, in fact, the bugs *weren't* coming in! Why not?

I went to a window and saw that our resident swifts had left their nests and were flying in formation away from the house and intercepting all the flying insects that were headed toward the lights in our living room. It was only then I noticed that there were no cute little coral-colored wall lizards such as we had found in the rooms of our earlier tropical homes.

Finally it sank in: there were no wall lizards inside because there were no bugs for them to eat. Yet there were plenty of lizards on the exterior walls, and my ankles could attest to there being plenty of biting bugs outside in the garden in the early morning and evening. The conclusion was unavoidable: the swifts, those accursed little excrement-dropping creatures, were keeping all the flying bugs out of our house. No wonder houses with swifts in the eaves were supposed to be lucky! No malaria, no dengue fever, no encephalitis for people living in such houses.

It was a humbled Judy who told John the evening he came home—and then the gardener the next morning—they need not bother trying to get rid of the swifts nesting in the eaves. I later learned that, no matter how hard we tried, we would never have been able to get rid of these birds. If you take away their nests, they just rebuild them in the same place. A whole industry of supplying edible nests for the birds' nest soup market (an ancient and still highly lucrative trade between China and Borneo) was built on that fact. Thinking afterward of the "lucky" swifts in the eaves helped remind me that the native inhabitants of a foreign country often have good reasons for what they do—or don't do—that we foreigners would do well to take into consideration.

Chapter 9

Among Ex-Headhunters

• • • • • • • • • • • •

THE DAYAKS WERE THE BIGGEST
ethnic group in Sarawak, and the Iban were the biggest Dayak tribe. It
followed that we could not represent the United States in Sarawak without getting to know the Dayaks—especially the Iban, who were famous
for their self-assurance and their insistence that each man was as good
as the next. The White Rajahs had stated formally that their reign had
as its purpose to serve the people of Sarawak, and the British colonial
government that followed the Rajahs' rule after World War II had the
same expressed aim.

It wasn't just talk. A British attorney general recalls in his memoirs
being sent out to Sarawak by the British Colonial Office in the early 1950s.
The next day he went to the Kuching Court House to pay a call on the high
court judge there (also a British colonial officer). The newly arrived attorney general was asked to wait on a bench outside the judge's office, where
he was obliged to sit next to a near-naked older Dayak in a loincloth, with
tattoos on his arms and shoulders, and with elongated earlobes and what
might be clouded leopard teeth sticking out of his upper ears. After a few
minutes sitting on the bench, the attorney general stood up when the judge
emerged from his chambers. The judge greeted him warmly and shook his
hand before saying, "So glad you have come. I look forward to talking with
you in a little while, but this gentleman [indicating the Dayak by a nod of
his head] was here first."

Especially given that American policy was to try to get the local people of northern Borneo to accept the suzerainty of a Malay-led government that thus far had shown what appeared to be little understanding

or respect for native Sarawak ethnic groups, it was important for John and me to make clear that we, as representatives of the United States, respected the local people of East Malaysia, Dayaks included. We had to show, by word and deed, that our support for Malaysia was not against the rights of Borneo's native people, but against the real and present danger of an armed takeover of Malaysian Borneo by Mao (who was backing a Chinese-led rebellion just over the border in Indonesian Borneo) or by Sukarno, who was in his third year of an armed "Confrontation" of Malaysia, then being fought primarily along the Sarawak/Indonesian Borneo border.

. . . .

T hanks to my new "father," the Paramount Chief of the Iban, John and I were welcomed by a number of Dayak local officials who had been born while their tribes had still been engaged in headhunting. That notorious practice had involved killing someone from a rival longhouse (the Dayaks' traditional multifamily wood and bamboo dwelling on stilts) and bringing back the head in triumph to their own longhouse. This practice, which had *never* involved cannibalism, had been more or less abandoned well before World War II. While we lived in Sarawak in the 1960s the old trophy heads (and some Japanese heads taken in Allied-led guerrilla battles during World War II) were still hanging from the rafters of many longhouses and were venerated on special occasions.

The first time I took my daughter, age four, to a longhouse, she could see that there were skeletal heads hanging from bamboo shelves suspended from the high ceiling under the communal roof. We had brought food to share with our Dayak hosts, because this was a poor longhouse that got many foreign visitors, being easily accessible from Kuching. We contributed our canned meat and fish, which our hosts saved for another day, but they had made quite a spread for us and were exceptionally cordial.

On the way home in the car I asked my four-year-old daughter if she had noticed what was hanging down from the ceiling. She asked whether these were people's heads.

I said yes, and she asked if they still did that. I said that they didn't, not anymore.

And then, after a pause, she asked me, after all, was it any worse than having a lion's head on the wall?

. . . .

I already mentioned that I had met a Swiss woman named Heidi who was married to a Dayak my second day in Kuching, at our first July Fourth party, and we became lifelong friends. Heidi had met and become engaged to her Iban husband, Sidi Munan, when they were students in New Zealand. Sidi's elder brother had been the first of his family to acquire an English-language education; sadly, he was killed in one of the few successful raids by Indonesian forces into Sarawak, in April 1963—the first year of Sukarno's armed "Confrontation" against Malaysia. Sidi had then gone to New Zealand to become the first overseas-educated man of his family.

Heidi's entire family had emigrated from Switzerland to New Zealand when she was little, and she had been raised on a farm in New Zealand before studying for a career in nursing. In addition to these skills, her Swiss facility for learning languages and her ability to play Bach on the organ and sing in the church choir made her remarkably well suited to becoming the wife of one of Sarawak's first Dayaks with a higher education.

In love though she was—she told me after we had become friends—she had been unready to marry Sidi until she saw Sarawak for herself and met her future in-laws. Her prospective mother-in-law, Sidi had explained to her, was—of all things—the shaman of an Iban longhouse (now a village). When Sidi brought Heidi to meet his widowed mother, the two women looked each other over with care, and both sides liked what they saw. They soon realized that they shared a love of Sidi and wanted to make him happy and help him succeed in life. At the same time, Heidi's comfort level in the countryside and her practical knowledge and good sense, refined by her nursing studies, gave her respect for her mother-in-law's work as a healer and adviser to her village.

After their marriage, Heidi took in stride extended visits to their house by Sidi's cousins and nephews, who needed free lodging while they attended Kuching schools. And she was charmed when these same relatives surprised her by building her an excellent chicken coop so that she could raise chickens and have fresh eggs at home, as she had in New Zealand.

When I met her at the July Fourth party, Heidi was pregnant with her first child. When little Brangka Peter was born in Kuching, Heidi told me she thought he was "probably the world's first Swiban." She and Sidi waited only a week before taking the baby to the village to be admired by her mother-in-law and what Heidi called "all the aunties."

The Iban in those days heeded a wide assortment of omens—a wild deer seen crossing the path from the wrong side, for example—that could prevent or delay travel for days until a better omen appeared. And, sure enough, when Heidi signaled to her mother-in-law that it was time for her and Sidi to take the baby back to Kuching, the aunties protested loudly that the omens were against their leaving now. After a discreet, pleading look from Heidi, Sidi's mother stood up and said words to the effect that "Don't you know who is the shaman here?" The aunties all acknowledged that she was. "Yes, indeed, I am. And this is my grandchild. And my daughter says she needs to take him back home and that is precisely what she and Sidi will do, with my blessings."

I, too, met Sidi's mother and was equally impressed by her brains and her generosity of spirit. She came to the airport with Heidi and Sidi to say good-bye when we were leaving Kuching for reassignment to Washington in 1968 and took me aside to say (in Malay), "Please keep in touch with Heidi. She needs her foreign friends like you."

. . . .

After a year of living in Kuching, I found myself envious of the hundred or more Peace Corps volunteers who were assigned to live up-country. They were doing a great job, teaching English or public health or helping lay gravity bamboo piping to get potable water to the longhouses—and having a wonderful time. It was thanks to them that the paramount chief of the

Iban could think that all Americans spoke Iban. For me, though, it was hard to travel beyond the immediate vicinity of Kuching.

Roads were few in Sarawak in those days, and almost none of them were all-weather roads. To get out of town, you usually went by boat using the island's great rivers as highways, except in the rainy season when the rivers were too wild to be safe. During the rainy season—when it rains *all* day, as opposed to showers every day the rest of the year—it was also hard to get anywhere inside Sarawak by air, since the grass landing strips that served as runways in all but the biggest towns, would be under water. Even in Kuching, trips by car to visit friends who lived in low-lying parts of town had to be put off until drier weather.

At last, in June 1967, with the rainy season behind us, it was my turn to travel. I had already joined the Kuching branch of the Women's Institute, an organization begun long ago in Britain for bettering rural women's lives and health, and I found that the Kuching branch had some interesting women whom I liked spending time with. A dozen of us—mostly Malay, a few Chinese, one New Zealander, and I—had accepted the invitation of a Women's Institute branch in an Iban longhouse on the Skrang River. We were to attend their annual festival to celebrate Dayak Day (the native Borneans' "national day") and spend the night in their longhouse.

Using roads that were barely more than dirt tracks, our chartered bus broke down six times on the way. Finally, we got as far as the bus could take us. We left the driver, after arranging that he spend the night there; we would walk back to him the next day. We scrambled up and down just one hill (thank heaven) to the Skrang River. There we took a small, motorized "Chinese launch" for about an hour to our destination, a big old longhouse on top of the riverbank.

The Skrang Iban had been notorious headhunters in the old days, but our Iban hostesses waiting for us were very friendly. The young girls were dressed in scarlet cloth with beaten silver tiaras framing their lovely faces and were wearing as many silver chains as a Christmas tree. Men were beating gongs and drums, and there was a traditional blessing ceremony involving offerings of colorful, if not very tasty, food. Next, a live cock was dangled over our heads. We were less enthusiastic participants in the ceremony than we might have been, having been on the road for nine hours by then in a cloud of dust, under a much too clear sky.

After the ceremonial greeting, we were led by the women to their bathing place, which was more like Eden: an inlet of the river with a crystalline, swift current pouring down from above us. We had all been told to wear sarongs, under which we could dress and undress without immodesty. Up until 1963 when Sarawak joined Malaysia, these Iban women would have normally been naked to the waist, but covered from waist to ankle in tight sarongs. Now they were covered on top as well.

We doused ourselves blissfully in the refreshingly chill water as we stood on a smooth sandy river bottom. I have never been anywhere more beautiful, inviting, or satisfying than that bathing place.

In the evening, during a formal banquet in our honor, the longhouse headman gave a speech in Iban that I could sort of catch the sense of, because of similarities to Malay, but which left me rather puzzled. He seemed to be saying something along the lines of: "We don't think women should interfere between husbands and wives." I noticed the men were all looking rather grim.

I looked over questioningly at Rugayah Majid, our able trip leader, a Malay woman with a university education and a lot of common sense. She subtly motioned me not to ask her about it now. The formal dinner continued on the longhouse veranda, and we were all urged to drink some rice beer that they made themselves. We were also strongly encouraged to dance the ngajat, an Iban dance that was not too hard to learn. At about midnight, having visited what seemed to be a makeshift latrine down below, but away from where the pigs wandered freely under the longhouse, we climbed back up the notched log ladder to the longhouse living quarters to sleep on beautiful woven reed mats. We had each brought along a sarong to sleep in and a pillow. Thanks to a recent antimalaria campaign, there were no mosquitoes or other bugs to bother us. And we brushed our teeth, after learning that our hostesses routinely boiled all their drinking and cooking water.

We said grateful good-byes the next morning. It was not until we were in the Chinese launch on the way to our rendezvous with the bus that Rugayah explained what the headman's speech had been about and the accompanying glumness among the men. It seems that, well ahead of our visit, the women had said to their husbands: "We have Malay guests coming in the next dry season and we cannot ask those women to fight their way among the pigs or just go over the side of the veranda the way we do. They will need to have an outhouse." The men had answered that these foreigners were the guests of the wives, and it was the wives' job to build an outhouse if such a thing was needed. So the women managed for the first time to build an outhouse except, of course, for the roof.

Everybody knew that roofing was exclusively the men's job. But once again, the wives were told: "These are your guests; you handle it."

This was during the rainy season, when there is very little for men to do in a longhouse. They can't go hunting or visiting other longhouses. Even fishing opportunities are limited, and life can get pretty dull—especially if a Lysistrata-type strike by the women against their husbands is in progress. The men held out for a while, but the women held out longer, and eventually the husbands put a roof on the outhouse. But, understandably, they transferred their resentment to us, the unwitting cause of the crisis. We all laughed uproariously as our leader told us the story.

It was good to have that lift to our spirits because, when we trudged over the hill to where the bus should have been waiting, it wasn't there. Somebody said that the driver had taken the bus to the next town for repairs. Meanwhile, we stood under the broiling sun till about 10:30—more than two hours—until an Iban woman with a betel-stained mouth came along and convinced us to go to her longhouse, a short walk away. We did, and there the ambience was not as sedate as at the place we had spent the night. The men were all in bed, sleeping off the effects of the previous evening's drinking in honor of Dayak Day, but the women seemingly had more staying power. There they were, in the late morning, wildly and riotously but cheerfully drunk.

Some of them were flapping their elbows to simulate birds' wings and their feet did not seem to touch the ground. They could not have been more cordial and begged us to stay the night. But they terrified some of the Malay women who were totally unused to being around inebriated women. Most of the Malay ladies cowered when the Ibans urged them to dance with them, and so the Chinese, the New Zealander, and I had to try to dance with them. As they swooped around the veranda with us, they did not seem to notice our clumsiness.

Finally we were told that our bus had returned. We climbed aboard and drove off, but soon it blew a gasket. Other misadventures followed. The last stage was accomplished thanks to our being rescued by a Public Works Department Land Rover that managed to cram in all of us on the way to Kuching; it dropped me at my door at about 7 p.m., just after dark. My morale was much revived by having finally got out of Kuching to see a bit of the rest of Sarawak. The bad part had been waiting for hours in the sun, but then it had rained for the last part of the trip, damping down the dust—and us, too. Like elderly Land Rovers I have since come to know elsewhere, this one leaked.

. . . .

The Malays led the federal government in Malaysia's capital, Kuala Lumpur, and Malays—or at least Muslims—were disproportionately represented in appointed offices in the East Malaysian states of Sarawak and Sabah; however, as in West Malaysia, the economic and financial power was in the hands of Chinese, most of them children or grandchildren of immigrants from southeast China.

By the time we got to Borneo in 1966, the Indonesian "Confrontation" (President Sukarno's effort to bully Malaysia into abandoning its ties to Britain and the West in order to join a left-wing "non-allied" bloc that Sukarno favored) was drawing to a close. This was thanks in part to the work of British and Australian Special Forces. And so the focus of the Western powers—especially the Americans and British—was now on whether the Chinese communist rebels based along the Sarawak border with Indonesian Borneo and supported morally, militarily, and financially by Mao's China would become more active. If the disgruntled Chinese in Sarawak joined hands with the Maoists across the unmarked border, that could, conceivably, lead to the eventual loss to the West of all of Borneo's strategic supplies of oil. Furthermore, in 1962, a rebellion against the government of Brunei, to the north of Sarawak, that involved armed takeovers of some towns on Sarawak's coast had been quashed with British help. Nobody knew whether the Brunei Rebellion would be rekindled after the British left. In short, there was a general nervousness about security in East Malaysia.

The question of which way the economically powerful Chinese community of Malaysian Borneo would tilt, West or East, focused the attention of diplomats like John on the political tendencies of Sarawak's most influential Chinese-led political party, the Sarawak United People's Party (SUPP) and its founder and leader, a brilliant, fortyish English-educated Chinese lawyer named Stephen Yong. One of John's highest priorities on arrival in Sarawak was to try to find out which way SUPP would move, given that Yong had longtime friends among the leadership of the covert Chinese communists as well as among wealthy Chinese businessmen who were inclined to favor Sarawak's remaining within Malaysia.

John found Stephen to be the most interesting man in Sarawak politics at that time—an idealist who throughout his political life handed his entire salary as an elected member of Sarawak's parliament directly to SUPP. He had founded SUPP, Sarawak's first political party, as an effort to represent all of Sarawak's ethnic groups, not just the Chinese. John and Stephen took an immediate liking to each other, and, since both loved to talk politics, they would have long chats at regular intervals, often at Stephen's house. It was clear that Yong was weighing which way to take his party—to the right and Malaysia, or to the left and closer to China.

When John found that Stephen had never been to the United States, he nominated him for a "leader grant" that would give Yong a trip to the States, all expenses paid, that John helped map out to ensure that Yong saw just about everything and everybody that Yong wanted to see. In the course of a three-week trip, Yong would spend time in cities, tourist sites, slums, farmlands, prisons, and the homes of ordinary and extraordinary people across the United States. The US Information Service's leader grants—also known as the International Visitor Program—provide selected individual leaders, whom diplomats in the field anticipate will become important to their countries over the following ten years, the chance to learn firsthand about the United States; the program is perhaps our single most effective diplomatic tool.

Stephen Yong did not begin his trip until just after we left Sarawak in the fall of 1968, but, luckily, John and I and our kids were in New York City, visiting my mother, when Stephen turned up there in late November 1968. We invited him to Thanksgiving Dinner at my mother's modest apartment in the government-subsidized Peter Stuyvesant Village in Manhattan. Stephen came and seemed to enjoy the traditional turkey dinner that my mother and Louise had prepared. Then, as he and John walked the length and breadth of Manhattan, talking politics as they so enjoyed doing together, he let John know how surprised he was that John's wife, whom he had last seen in her beautiful Chinese house in a garden of orchids and fruit trees in Kuching, came from a family of such modest means. John was amused enough to pass this on to me. We were both delighted when Stephen went back home and pushed SUPP into an alliance with the pro-Malaysian parties. I like to think that for Stephen, having seen with his own eyes that, despite what his Marxist friends were telling him, money was not the only consideration in determining one's status and one's options in the capitalist United States of America may have helped tip the scales for him against the Maoists.

. . . .

During our last year in Borneo, 1968, I was getting restless. John was sometimes able to fly on government business to Brunei and Sabah and Hong Kong and Kuala Lumpur, but, given the high cost of air travel outside Sarawak, we had to wait almost a year before I was able to get out of Kuching again. It was worth waiting for.

An invitation to attend the coronation of the new Sultan of Brunei came to John and me on thick creamy vellum stationery headed with a gold seal. I was expected to be present at all the ceremonies, and they proved to be as grand as money could buy. At the new Sultan's palace, the coronation ritual went on for many hours and involved long speeches in Court Malay that I could hardly get the gist of. Still, it was the only time in my life I ever had my own lady-in-waiting, a pretty young woman dressed in the right colors (black during the day and white at night) who stood behind me the whole time, and would have waved her fan over me if I had needed more air.

By the time we got back from Brunei we had only a month or so left of our assignment to Kuching, much of it spent in farewell parties. But one morning, a group of Iban laborers came to Kuching to do road repairs near our house.

Several of these Iban road workers came to the front door one morning and asked Ah Fong if they could speak to me. At the door, I found several men in loincloths, with long ears and tattoos, their straight black hair cut in bangs in front but hanging down their backs—Iban men in traditional dress, such as you rarely saw in town. The headman asked if I would allow him and his men to help themselves to some of the rambutans. It was the time of year when the rambutan trees in our garden were full of fruit. I knew we had tons of them and said yes. I went back indoors to continue with my book or the letter I was writing.

John came home for lunch and said, "Who are all those Dayaks sitting under our trees eating rambutans?" I explained what had happened and he said, "Okay, but with them there, this doesn't look like an official American residence. It looks like a painting by Henri Rousseau or Gauguin. Can't you ask them to take the fruit and leave?"

So after lunch I went outside and asked the headman if he and his men could take the fruit and move on. He then explained (in Malay) that that would not be proper, according to the rules of his tribe. He said it was quite okay to eat fruit from someone else's trees, if you had permission from the owner. But you must only take what you could consume right there and then. That way, nobody would think that you were taking his fruit and selling it to others. I told him that he and his men could continue eating under the trees.

That evening I told John what the headman had said. John was as touched as I was by the charming explanation the headman had given me. In a couple of days the Dayaks went back to the jungle, removing the Gauguin painting from our garden.

It would not be until years later, when I was doing research for the first of two books I wrote that involved events in Borneo during World

War II, that I learned that the Dayaks had been crucial in providing intelligence to the Allies in preparation for the retaking of Borneo—especially the vital oil fields—from the occupying Japanese. The Dayaks had also rescued, fed, hidden, clothed—and even fought the Japanese on behalf of—a dozen American airmen whose B-24 bombers had been shot down over Borneo. "Beautiful, wonderful people" is the way the surviving airmen described them.

Chapter 10

A "Tandem" Wife on Trial

• • • • • • • • • • • • • • •

FOUR YEARS AFTER LEAVING BORNEO
and after fifteen years as a diplomat's wife, I finally became—at John's urging and with his coaching—a diplomat myself; I was one of the first two Foreign Service spouses to enter via the Foreign Service exam. John already knew he had been assigned to the economic section in Brussels, and our kids, aged twelve and ten, were looking forward with mixed emotions to attending Belgian schools.

Then, the day before my orientation classes ended, I was told that my assignment—to be personal aide to our ambassador to Belgium—had fallen through. The ambassador, a political appointee, had announced his unwillingness to have in such a confidential post someone married to another of his officers.

I was crushed, and John had his work cut out trying to help me achieve something resembling professional composure. He made me (literally) dry my tears and helped me draft "nonpapers" (informal statements of policy) to take to my assignments adviser in the State Department to see what could be done. Finally, it was agreed that John would keep his assignment to Brussels, and I would be sent there on my own orders but would then be immediately put on leave without pay until or unless a job could be found for me.

It was a real downer for me, after all the excitement and delight at becoming a Foreign Service officer, to be back again overseas, jobless, and paying calls—with white gloves but without a hat—on the wives of embassy officers senior to John. But then after I had finished those calls, John said, "You are an officer now. They can't take that away from you. Take your calling cards and go call on all the officers at the embassy, starting at the top." I thought fleetingly of Hester Henderson and my first calls in Jakarta when she had explained to me that a woman never pays a call on a man. What would she think of my violating that rule? I somehow felt sure she would be rooting for me.

The ambassador who had broken my assignment to be his aide refused to see me, but his number two, the deputy chief of mission (DCM), Lou Boochever, was most gracious. After nearly an hour's chat while he gently drew out my experience and interests, he rose to signal the end of our meeting and asked: "Do I understand correctly that you are prepared to do any job in this mission?"

"Yes," I said, "I'll even do windows." He laughed and walked me out of the office to the elevator.

Four months later, in part thanks to the DCM's efforts, I was assigned to be the sole vice consul in our embassy's consular section, a job in my career specialty. I would be supervised by an able and pleasant boss, Consul Cy Richardson.

John told me that to do my new job properly in Belgium, I would need to be fluent (as he was) in not one language but two: French, which was spoken in Brussels and in Wallonia (to the south); and Dutch, which was spoken by the Flemings (or Flemish) who lived in Flanders (to the north).

I had studied French in high school, so I first strove to bring my fluency up to working level, with an hour's noontime lesson three times a week at the embassy. At the embassy and even at the foreign ministry, one could get away with speaking only English; but speaking French turned out, to my surprise, to be a great help when visiting Americans in jail, or on their way to jail.

Consular work was divided into taking care of our citizens—chiefly providing passports and birth, death, and marriage certificates, and helping indigent Americans get back home—and giving temporary or immigrant visas to foreigners. As the consular officer in charge of American Citizen Services, I was also supposed to visit any American citizens in prison in Belgium. The Belgian prisons in those days were ancient and austere, with prewar plumbing, but they were not overcrowded or too badly run. My boss, Cy Richardson, had alerted me that I would probably enjoy making jail visits because the American inmates were usually glad to have a visitor, especially one who spoke English. He was right, and I also was curious to see the inside of prisons, after years of reading about them in detective stories.

One of the first people I met in jail had been caught at the Brussels airport with a large quantity of hashish at a time when a lot of young hippies were paying their way around the world by serving as "mules" for drug dealers. He was a tall, strapping young man of twenty-two from a rural community in upstate New York. I had the impression that his parents were of modest means. He said his mother had a heart condition, so he did not want her or his father to know about his arrest. Since he had no money, we got him a pro bono lawyer, but the Belgian authorities decided to make an example of him. They sentenced him to the harshest penalty permitted for a first offender: two years in prison.

He had been caught while changing planes and knew nobody in Belgium, and continued to insist on our not contacting his parents. Although my consular duties were limited to seeing he got as good treatment as any Belgian would receive, I felt a special obligation, because he was entirely alone and in my consular district, to see him as often as I could: about once every two months, so long as he was in Brussels. When I went to see him in jail the first time after sentencing, he had that same air of fecklessness that he had shown when first arrested and which probably contributed to his sentence. He told me he had no complaints at his treatment but asked if I could get him something to read. He said the only English language book in the prison library was *The Godfather*.

The next time, I came with some good books, including Steinbeck's *Grapes of Wrath*, I remember. I went to the *greffier*, the clerk of the court at the prison who determines who may visit prisoners and under what conditions. I showed him my foreign ministry ID and my diplomatic passport and asked—in pretty good French by then—if I could bring the prisoner these books. I said I had bought them in a bookstore, and I alone could know for whom they were intended. The greffier accepted that statement but then wanted to know how well qualified I was to choose books for a prisoner.

The sacred name of Harvard and my degree in English literature clinched the deal. (I did not say anything about the presence of *The Godfather* in the prison's library.)

. . . .

One jail visit I will never forget was to see our own passport clerk, a young American army private who had grown up on army bases, the son of an officer. He had been on loan to our consular section from his unit at Supreme Headquarters Allied Powers Europe (SHAPE), near Mons in southern Belgium. He had enormous charm. I remember once when the kids were having a heated argument at home and called me at work to resolve the matter. I was not there and the passport clerk took the call. When he said I was out of the office, one of the kids said, "Well where IS she then?" Without missing a beat, the passport clerk said, "It's Tuesday. I guess she's out streaking." The thought of their mother running naked through Brussels was so deliciously outlandish that the kids stopped fighting.

By the time I went to see him in jail, our passport clerk had been found helping run a drug ring selling hash and marijuana to kids at the Brussels-American High School. With his charm, he had drawn some of the high school kids into his delivery system. A few of my motherly Belgian colleagues burst into tears when they learned what our passport clerk had been up to. They had loved him like a son; some still did.

When I saw him in jail, I could see that he was still trying to use his charm, but it was as if the mask had loosened and I could for the first time see behind it to the selfish, manipulative person underneath. All I could think was how glad I was that I had been rigorous about supervising the issuance of passports, so that there was no way he could have misused them.

One of the high school students he had drawn into his network was an undersized seventeen-year-old boy with wavy blond hair falling to his shoulders in the hip style of the day. The boy had been arrested and was about to be put in jail, to await trial. Having seen him several times hanging around our passport clerk's desk and knowing that his family lived in Hawaii and had left him in Brussels in the inadequate care of a cousin, I went with him and the arresting officer to see the *juge d'instruction* (sort of equivalent to our public prosecutor). We walked through the great bronze doors at the intimidatingly huge, hideous Palace of Justice in the center of town.

The building, said to have been Mussolini's favorite in Brussels, takes up an entire city block but—like an ancient Egyptian temple—has very little usable space inside. We wandered along various narrow corridors until we found the small office of the juge d'instruction handling this case.

In theory, my hands were tied. I had no right to ask for anything more than the best treatment a Belgian would receive under similar circumstances. I had (according to US consular regulations) no permissible alternative to his being held in jail. Nonetheless, unable to subdue my own conscience as a parent, I had decided to ask that the boy be turned over to me, and I would make sure he left the country within twenty-four hours.

I made my pitch to the juge, and he replied in French with a Gallic shrug, "Why should I do this?"

I answered in the best French I could muster, "*Monsieur*, just look at him! If he were to spend a night in jail with the other prisoners, could you guarantee that he would still be the same boy tomorrow morning?"

He grimaced, like a cat twitching its moustache, and said: "If you guarantee to get him out of here tomorrow, I guess that is good enough. But [looking at the boy] if I ever hear that he is back in this country, I shall *sortir mes griffes* [let out my claws]."

I took the boy home, where my teenage kids and the cleaning lady were—John was still at the office—and told them that this boy would be spending the night with us. I told the boy to stay there or risk going to jail. I then headed to a nearby grocery store to get more food for dinner. When I got back to our apartment, though, he was gone.

There was no way I could have asked the maid or the children to bar his way. I stood there thinking: "Oh boy, Judy—you've gone and done it now!" I hadn't the foggiest idea what to do next.

Just then, the phone rang, and it was the boy's girlfriend saying that our hero would be back to my place later that evening. He just needed to say good-bye to his friends. With only bluff on my side—since I had no idea where he was—I said, "He had better get back here immediately or I will have the cops pick him up." And then I thought to add a carrot, "But he can see his friends at my place, just so long as he stays here." After an anxious hour or so for me, he turned up with his girlfriend; a few other high school kids appeared over the next several hours. In the morning I felt a great burden fall from my shoulders as I put him on a plane with connections to Hawaii.

. . . .

Another time that speaking French was crucial was once when I was trying to help an American man marry a German-born woman in our consular district. Usually, when Americans sought to get married in our district, our role in American Citizens Services was merely to register the marriage and provide the happy couple with a piece of paper that could be used back in the States as proof of the marriage.

It was fun to get married in Belgium. Many town halls had beautifully maintained rooms dating from centuries earlier that were used for civil marriage ceremonies. The civil marriage was the only one that was binding; couples could have a church marriage, too, but it had no legal standing.

In this case, though, the betrothed couple was being prevented from marrying by the Belgian civil authorities because the German woman could not produce a birth certificate. She had a valid passport attesting to her name and date and place of birth but the Belgian official was insisting on a birth record. She had been born in some town behind the Iron Curtain and the authorities there, during a particularly chilly period in the Cold War, were unwilling to provide her with a copy of her birth record. The prospective bride and groom were both near tears when they came to me as a last resort.

I telephoned the Belgian *commune* (municipal district) where they had planned to marry and spoke in French to the official who was insisting on the birth certificate. His response was polite, if chilly: "Madam, you must understand that we have our rules and regulations. My hands are tied without a valid birth document and this young woman cannot produce one." I answered, "Sir, I do understand, but—tell me—what do you do about people coming from Dresden or somewhere else where the Town Hall archives were burned down? Can they never marry?"

He: "Madam, in such a case, if they provided proof that the birth record had been destroyed, of course we would use another document, such as a passport or court record. But that is not the case here."

I: "Then does the fact that this young woman's birth record was *not* burned by a bomb mean she cannot get married?"

He: "Oh,"—and I could almost see him shrug his shoulders over the phone—"tell them to come back here and we'll see what can be done. I make no promises, though!" They came in to register the marriage with us a week or so later, bringing me a piece of the wedding cake. At times like that, I really loved my job. It was one of those times in my life when I could be the good face of my government to our own citizens.

Before the summer holidays when Cy hoped to be away, leaving me as the only consular officer, he began to launch me into visas. By then my French was good enough to conduct visa interviews. American visas in their passports were the biggest gift American embassies or consulates abroad could give to most foreigners. Then as now, how we go about granting or denying a visa probably has a greater influence on how foreigners view the US government than anything else we do overseas.

In the days when I began, unlike now, there were no visa waivers for most European applicants. Every would-be visitor to the United States had to fill out a visa application form. Looking through these forms, our Belgian consular experts would pick out those they felt could be a problem, such as someone applying for a visa to visit the States who did not live in Belgium. Such applicants would have difficulty showing that they intended to return to Belgium at the end of their US visit. Cy or I usually interviewed such applicants and always conducted such an interview when the applicant came from one of the countries famous for having "visa shoppers." Cy explained to me that visa shoppers were people who went to our consular offices in different countries trying to find a way to get to the United States, which they would then plan to make their new home.

It was drilled into us consular officers that, once a foreigner got inside the United States, there was no reliable way that our authorities could keep track of him or her. And there was certainly no way we could prevent that person from abusing the visa rules by staying on, getting a job, or becoming a public charge. In preventing illegal immigration, the consular officer plays a crucial role.

That being said, in those days when every foreign visitor had to have a visa, 95 percent of those who applied at our consular section got them, after a routine examination of their application form raised no questions. Brussels was a small consular post, not a "visa mill," like Mexico City, for example, or Lagos or Tehran; and the habit of saying yes to visa applicants—which was almost always the correct answer—made for a pleasant work atmosphere. We consular officers spent the bulk of our visa time simply signing off on the hundred or more applications per day, but we set aside enough time to examine the doubtful cases at length, if necessary.

I found the hardest cases to decide were when a young Belgian, not yet married, had finished his or her schooling and wanted to travel. What could be more natural than that the young person would want to visit the States at this time? But we consular officers were obliged by our regulations to assume that anybody seeking to visit the States might decide—or already be planning—to find a job there or, failing that, to live there as a public charge. We were under orders to grant a visitor's visa only if it were more reasonable to suppose that this particular visa applicant would in fact *not* seek employment in the United States and would leave the US before the end of the authorized stay. The permitted stay was usually a maximum of about three months, and was a period to be determined not by us but at the border by the immigration authorities.

Our granting a visa depended on what we could determine about the applicant's plans after visiting the United States. Obviously, a ticket out of the United States—normally the return half of a round trip ticket from Belgium—was essential. But without evidence of a job or a school to come back for, it was hard to argue that this person would not be job-hunting in the United States. Throwing away one half of a round trip ticket would be a small price to pay to get past the border guards. Politically, making decisions about the veracity of young visa applicants was tricky. Some of the young people who had the money to travel had parents who were friends of important people in the country and also possibly of our own higher-ups, such as the ambassador. And yet the law and the regulations instructed us consular officers to say no unless there was a strong case for saying yes. The blame fell entirely on the visa-issuing officer (me) if I gave a nonimmigrant visa to the wrong person.

Back when I started doing visa interviews, the applicant would come into my office and sit on a chair opposite me and try to convince me that he or she was a bona fide nonimmigrant. I soon found that I didn't like how we were seated: opposite one another, me in a good chair with a big desk between me and the applicant on a little chair, no doubt feeling like a petitioner before a judge. It might be an accurate reflection of our relative standing in that circumstance, but it did not encourage the applicant to be forthcoming.

I decided to get the petitioner's chair replaced by a three-seat sofa, where the applicant and I could sit side by side. I would stand up to shake hands from behind my desk and then, having offered the visitor a seat, would sit next to him or her. At that point I would say something like this: "You may not know it, but a visa is not a permit to enter the United States. All it does is get you as far as the US border, at which point somebody in the Immigration and Naturalization Service will decide whether you can come in and if so, how long you can stay. If that official says you cannot come in, you get back on the plane, the plane gets charged a fine and you fly back here poorer and without having visited the United States.

"Now, I am sure you don't want that to happen to you. Remember, the Immigration person is there to keep out people who are likely to try to get a job in the United States or to stay there beyond the time allotted to them.

"Let's assume we are at the border and the Immigration guy is there, behind my desk [both of us looking that way]. If I were to give you a visa, what could you tell him that would convince him that you don't intend to work in the United States and that you don't intend to outstay your permitted time there?"

Sometimes the applicant didn't have an argument that could convince anybody that he was a bona fide nonimmigrant. And then he would often thank me for sparing him the misery of being turned back at the border.

But sometimes, as we sat side by side on the sofa, both of us trying to find arguments that would convince the tough guy at the border (we could imagine him sitting in front of us behind the desk) the applicant would come up with a reason that was convincing. Maybe she was going to get married in the fall—and showed me pictures of the fiancé and, better still, the wedding invitations. Or maybe he was temporarily going to take over his father's little grocery store when he got back because Papa had to have an operation; and he could return to the consular section the next day bringing evidence of this. Or he had a job offer, a good one, and had been told by his future employer to get his holiday in now because he would not get another one till next year. And the new employer could write a letter on office stationery that the applicant would be able to bring me. When I had some reasonable evidence, I would grant the visa and remind the applicant, if asked at the border, to say what he or she had told me.

Giving a visa in such cases was satisfying to both sides. Nobody likes to have to say no to a young person trying to go on an innocent trip to our country, and an unjust refusal makes such a bad impression on everybody to whom the disappointed applicant tells his story.

Since the bombings of our embassies in East Africa in the 1990s, my kind of visa interview can no longer take place. Instead, the applicant, if not eligible for the visa waiver program, stands in the waiting room, on the other side of a small, thick, bulletproof window from the consular officer, while he or she, speaking loudly enough to be heard through the thick glass, answers intimate questions about financial resources, personal plans, and other matters that nobody likes to discuss in public. Under these conditions, even if the visa is granted, the process often leaves a bad taste in the mouth of the applicant. I often ask myself: How many people on the visa lines do we make angry at the United States every day in the cause of protecting us from the possibility that someday an enemy might manage to get into a consular section and do harm?

Chapter 11

A Moment of Cold War Intrigue

• • • • • • • • • • • • • • • • • •

I ENJOYED MY CONSULAR WORK CHIEFLY for the way it parachuted me into the lives of strangers. But I had long given up hope of getting involved in anything as exciting as what I was reading those days in John le Carré's thrillers when the phone rang on my desk one afternoon in Brussels. My boss, the consul, was away, and I was asked to walk across the street to the office of the deputy chief of mission—a new one. The new DCM struck me as a bit cold, compared to his warm predecessor, but capable. He introduced me to another American I had not met before, who (the DCM said) had come from Paris to see me.

The DCM left the room, and the man from Paris explained that he had a delicate problem that I would have to handle. He asked first if I had read recent stories in the local press about a sailor on a Soviet vessel who had jumped overboard in an attempt to defect while the ship was moored in a Belgian harbor. Unfortunately, the sailor had been recaptured by the Soviets before he could make good his escape.

I said that I had read about it in the papers. The man from Paris said, "Good, then you will understand that we don't want to lose any more Russian defectors—and we have a pair of them now, with their daughter, who have turned up here in Brussels." He explained that, until given formal status as refugees by the Belgian office of the UN High Commissioner for Refugees (UNHCR), these defectors were in grave danger of being caught by the Soviets and sent back to Moscow to face who knows what retribution. Once they were formally UNHCR-vetted refugees, the Soviets were unlikely to risk the bad publicity that would come from bothering with them, unless the defectors knew very important secrets—which seemed unlikely in this case.

He said it did not really matter if the defectors knew anything that would interest our intelligence people—though that would be great. But we simply did not want the word to get back to potential defectors behind the Iron Curtain—as in the case of that poor sailor—that it was not a good idea to try to defect because the Soviets would always catch you. "So that means," he said, "that after I hand these folks over to you, I will leave you to it. Your job will be to keep them safe and hidden until the UNHCR does its job. Any questions?"

I was too stunned to have any questions for this stranger, except to ask how long I would be away from my office today, because I was the only officer there. He said a couple of hours should do it, so I phoned my office and left word that I would be back before the end of the workday.

The man from Paris drove us in a car with French plates to an apartment building in a middle-class Brussels neighborhood I did not know. He rang the doorbell and, after the peephole had been looked through from the other side, the door opened partway. There stood two adults about my age or a few years older but slim, trim, dressed as well as any of my Belgian friends, and with very alert expressions. The man had a thin face and pale skin and graying hair but was as lithe and fit as a Russian wolfhound; the woman had some red in her curly short hair, and had fierce bright blue eyes that were sizing me up without any effort to hide what she was doing. I must have passed the test, because she opened the door wider and let me and my escort come in.

Standing in the front hall, the man from Paris spoke to the two of them in Russian and then, including me, in French. From what I gathered, he had met them once before and was telling them what he had told me—about the need for them to stay hidden until the UNHCR had made them officially UN-protected refugees. He then shook hands with them, and asked me if I had enough cash to get back to the office, ideally catching a tram or bus or cab a few blocks away from where we now were. He then said, "Good luck," shook my hand, and disappeared.

The husband invited me into their living room, where their dark-haired daughter, just about my daughter's age, was waiting with lowered eyes. I asked how long they had been in that apartment and what the arrangement there was. Were they safe to stay or should I find them other housing? They said they had been there just overnight and thought it would be okay to stay there since only the man who had brought them there—the same one who had brought me—knew where they were.

We talked—their French was better than mine—and it turned out they were both mathematicians and teachers of math and had worked in Cambodia and other Third World countries as technical advisers, part of a Soviet AID program similar to ours. It had been while working in one of the least developed postcolonial countries in Africa that they had come to realize that what they had been told back in Moscow about how the world outside the Soviet bloc runs did not square with the facts as they encountered them abroad. One of the couple had been in the Party but no longer had faith in it. They said they did not want to raise their only child behind the Iron Curtain.

Excited though I was at being involved in such international intrigue, my stronger emotion was fear that somehow I would do something by mistake that would expose them to danger. I did not dare ask anyone for advice. Soon thereafter, however, I was notified that someone from the Tolstoy Foundation wanted to see them and I was told by a reliable source that I could trust the Tolstoy Foundation, which was the best-known Russian émigré group helping Soviet defectors settle abroad.

I took the Tolstoy representative to see "my" defectors, but I could tell right away that this meeting was a mistake. The woman defector's bright blue eyes shot rays of hatred at this older, overweight woman dressed in the typical Russian aristocratic émigré style of the 1930s—what John would have called "a costume made up of old bathrobes, bell-pulls, and doormats." A greater contrast to my sleek, modern Borzois would be hard to imagine. The defector woman left me in no doubt about her views: "Get that creature out of here!" she said.

I am not sure so long after the fact, but I think I arranged for them to move again, not wishing anybody but me to know where they were. In any case, I clearly recall having phone conversations with the husband, to pass on where things stood on the efforts to get them UNHCR refugee status. By prearrangement, I would be standing in a telephone booth some distance from my office and waiting for the man to phone me. Once the phone was ten minutes late in ringing. I said when I finally picked up, "I now know what it must feel like to be waiting for an extramarital lover to call." He laughed, as I hoped he would. There had not been much laughter in our exchanges thus far.

Then one day I was asked to see the DCM again, and he had another man with him whom I did not know. The other man said something along the lines of: "The Belgians are uneasy about having these defectors here, so we want you to encourage them to move on to France, where they have the language and probably know people who can help them, don't you think?"

I stood there for a minute, in shock at what I had heard. These Russians were just barely beginning to trust me. They were still as nervous as cats. Who knows what desperate thing they would do if we—if I—abandoned them at this point? After pausing another few seconds to reflect that my brief Foreign Service career might now be approaching its end, I said, "You know what I think? I think that if the Belgians want them to leave, then the Belgians can tell them so."

I walked out the door and back across the street to my office. I was thinking that, like my bosses, the Belgians probably would not be able to tell these defectors to leave, because they didn't know where they were. In my anger, I was also thinking that if my bosses wanted to discourage efforts by dissidents to escape to the West, what they had asked me to do would be a perfect way to go about it.

I had not told John anything about "my" defectors. It literally was not my secret to tell, and I knew he would understand, as I had done, when he had not told me secrets he had known in Indonesia. But that evening I did say to him that I might have just maneuvered myself out of my job. If so, we would probably know soon. He did not press for details, and we both waited to hear my fate.

But nothing happened, except that the new DCM was much warmer to me than before. As my reviewing officer, he must have had something to say about my being promoted early, within the next six months, to the next higher grade, so that I became a consul, no longer a lowly vice consul.

The Russian defectors *did* get their UN refugee status and went on to lead happy and productive lives as math professors in Western Europe.

Going to their house for dinner was something John and I came to enjoy doing, beginning in the 1970s. There, we would be served wild mushrooms our hosts had picked in the nearby woods, and we would hear how the husband had done in the local chess championship. John would sit next to a defector ballet dancer named Tatiana, and the general conversation would be about the latest famous writer defector to emerge with news of the Gulag. Their daughter was doing well in the local school, and the parents were engaged in strenuous efforts, eventually successful, to get the wife's mother to join them in the West. We are still in close touch, all these years later.

Chapter 12

Getting Out in Public

· · · · · · · · · · · ·

ONE OF THE THINGS I WOULD advise diplomats arriving in a new place to do is to get out and walk. And also, where practicable, take public transportation. It is amazing what you can learn about the new place by doing that, and it can change your whole attitude toward it.

Looking back, though, I am embarrassed to say that one of my scariest moments abroad was at our first post, Jakarta, when I first tried to walk around the corner of my street. Though it was already evening, I had assumed I would have no problem. I was a New Yorker, after all, and had been raised to be out in public on my own. I had traveled alone in the subway for an hour or more to my summer day camp from the age of nine. My parents had divorced a year earlier (1944) and we had moved back to Manhattan (my birthplace) from Albany, where my father, Warren Moscow, had been the *New York Times* bureau chief for the previous six years.

After the divorce, my mother had had little money and no car and was at work all day. She had made a virtue of necessity and taught me at age eight how to manage by myself in a busy city: avoid empty streets—even the fancy ones with awnings—and seek out instead the streets where people sat out on the front stoop or looked out the window from behind their lace curtains. "Make eye contact," she would say, "and smile, but keep on going as if you have a place to go to and somebody who expects you there." But not even she, nor my nearly equally astute nanny Louise, who had insisted on coming down from Albany to stay with us, without pay, would have known how to advise me to get around at night in a new Jakarta suburb.

On one of our first evenings in Jakarta, John was invited to some all-male event—probably a chance for some of the other embassy officers to talk frankly about their jobs and to help break in John, the newest, most junior officer in the political section. Rather than have me stay home alone—the servants did not live on the premises—he had encouraged me to accept an invitation to take part in a play reading at the house of an American businessman and his wife "just around the corner."

I accepted gladly, but it was only when I stepped outside that I realized that it was pitch dark—as it always is in the tropics by 7 p.m. if not earlier. Not having learned to drive, I had not noticed that our street had no streetlights. With no flashlight, I bent down and could just make out a darker place next to the fence. I assumed it was a tarred sidewalk and stepped onto it. Wrong guess! It was a *kali* (a drainage ditch), and I was in its mud up to my waist.

Trying not to panic, thinking always about snakes (of which I have an unreasoning terror), I scrabbled back out and walked the rest of the way around the corner, staying well to the middle of the street. I was wearing white—visible to cars except where the mud had turned me brown—and emerged at my hosts' house awash in tears of self-pity. I saw the alarm on my hostess's placid, tanned face turn to amusement and then to sympathy as I told her what had caused me to appear at her door in such a state. I suppose I could have gone back to my house after I fell, but at that moment I needed to hear English and be surrounded by my own countrymen. My gracious hostess took me in and straight to her tiled bathroom where she toweled off the mud on me the way she would have done to her own child. Then the other guests soothed and petted me, giving me the choice role of Rosalind in *As You Like It*. I ended up enjoying the evening and being glad I had come.

Looking back, despite that rocky start, I realize that some of my favorite memories overseas are of events that occurred when I was out alone in public among ordinary people in a new place.

When we lived in Kinshasa in the late '70s, we were assigned to an apartment building just a short walk from the embassy. Though I had begged for a house with a swimming pool in the hills, I came to be glad that we were in town instead. That meant that John and I did not spend several hours each day commuting during Kinshasa's infamous rush hour from and to the fashionable parts of the outskirts of Kinshasa, where many of our colleagues lived in villas with swimming pools.

Perhaps the biggest advantage of living in that apartment—that I only came to realize years later—was that I *walked* to and from work. I usually did that walk alone because my workday started earlier than John's; he had to stick around later in the day after Washington woke up, to deal with questions to and from the State Department.

One day, I was wearing a wash-and-wear blue striped chambray shirt-dress that had been advertised as up to any travel challenge; it got tested that day. I was maybe halfway to the office, on low ground, when suddenly there was a rush of water—a flash flood, or maybe a failure of the drainage system—and I was in water to my waist. I was so amazed that all I could think to do was to keep on walking in the same direction.

Then I heard a small group of Congolese women—I think they were on their way to their market stalls—higher up on the far side of the deep water from where I was. They were shouting at me and pointing. I could not understand what they said, not speaking Lingala (the one of the four national languages most commonly used in Kinshasa). But they kept on shouting and pointing and a couple of the women started to wade out into the deeper water toward me. I finally realized that they were pointing to where the higher ground was on my side, so that I would be less at risk of being swept away in the flood.

I waved my hand and shouted my thanks in French and made for the higher ground. The dress dried quickly in our air-conditioned office and that afternoon, going back home, I saw I was walking on dry sand and could hardly believe what had happened to me earlier that day. I have never forgotten that incident, though, and especially the women's efforts—at some risk to themselves—to go to the aid of a stranger. It helped change my whole attitude to the place and the people. And, I realized, it would never have occurred if I had been in a car, rather than on the public thoroughfare, on the same level as they were.

Remembering my wonderfully unconventional mother's advice on how to handle myself on the streets of New York, I avoided the "good" neighborhoods—where the well-to-do did not look out their windows. And I would try to make eye contact with the people on the street whenever I had to stay out late alone.

In Kinshasa, when seeing my Congolese dissident contacts at night, I would often end the evening by parking my car in the embassy courtyard, where it was in less danger of losing its windshield wipers and hubcaps, and walk home. As I passed in front of the closed shops, the night watchmen for those shops would be lying on the sidewalk stretched out on mats, and they got into the habit of greeting me, "*Bonsoir, Madame.*" And I would reply, "*Bonsoir, Citoyen.*" (Mobutu had ordained that Zairians should address each other by this French Revolutionary title.) These friendly exchanges formed an antiphonal chorus that accompanied me nearly to my front door and (I still believe) kept me out of harm's way.

The only time I was ever physically attacked in Kinshasa was in a fancy residential neighborhood in midafternoon when I had walked over from our apartment to go to a friend's swimming pool. I was going down a street that—I barely noticed—had a fallen tree across it, preventing the circulation of cars.

It was a Sunday and the hour of siesta, so nobody noticed my teenage Congolese attackers emerge from behind one of Kinshasa's many abandoned partly built villas, where they were hiding, waiting for a good target to come along. That I was—especially since I was wearing a wide-brimmed straw hat such as the wheelbarrow pushers liked to wear. I stood stock-still, frozen by fear, as one of the boys lifted my chin. He might have slit my throat and I could not have stopped him. But all he and the others wanted was the straw hat. While they were at it, they took my twenty-dollar watch from off my left wrist, but seeing my other arm clasped rigidly to my side, with my handbag firmly fixed between my arm and my body, they quit and ran off with their booty. This incident reinforced for me what my mother had taught me: When walking alone, avoid empty streets in fancy neighborhoods!

. . . .

A happier memory of being on the street is from 1964 when John and I and our kids were newly arrived in the capital of Malaysia, Kuala

Lumpur. With a Malay name that means "muddy estuary," Kuala Lumpur in those days was a town in appearance halfway between the steamy, sleepy administrative headquarters of the tropical British colony that it had been until well after World War II and the ultramodern urban center that it is now.

As in Jakarta, we were living in a house in the suburbs, but it was as clean, comfortable and—to my mind—boring as New Rochelle would have been to me. And, like many matrons my age in New Rochelle, I spent much of each day transporting the kids (aged five and three) to kindergarten and nursery school, to playdates, to the club with a big swimming pool (that functioned as the social center for us foreigners and some of the more well-to-do Malaysians), and, of course, taking John to the office and back home again.

The New Yorker in me looked upon all this commuting by car as a total waste of time. To keep my sanity in the rush hour traffic when I was alone heading to pick up a child or my husband, I kept a book and a manicure kit in the glove compartment; I would occupy myself with one or the other, depending on the expected length of the traffic jam.

Then one morning I was heading for the big supermarket downtown and feeling glad that the rush hour had ended, the kids were otherwise occupied, and the road was nearly empty. But I had barely gone half a mile from the house when the car coasted to a stop—luckily near the curb—because it was out of gas. (Though farseeing in many respects, John was *not* good about refilling the gas tank after he had driven the car.) As in many American suburbs, there were no sidewalks, so I stood in the empty road next to my un-air-conditioned Ford Consul, opposite a street vendor's *warung* (a portable stall where soft drinks and snacks were sold), and tried to think what to do next.

Eventually an Indian in a dhoti (a white cotton loincloth such as Gandhi used to wear) came along on a bicycle. He stopped and asked me in Malay if he could help. I explained that I was out of gas and he offered to get some for me. I said a thankful yes, but then we got into the details of how to do it. Did I have a container he could put the gas in? Well, no. (As those who know me are aware, I am clueless about cars. I can go years without even learning how to raise the hood.)

"No problem, Madam. Just wait a minute." After leaning his bike carefully against my car, he walked over to the *warung* and returned in a few minutes with an empty Blue Band Margarine metal can with a plastic lid. The can could not hold much gas, but I guessed it would hold enough to get me to the gas pump.

I gave the Indian some Malaysian dollars—a rather big bill, since that was all I had on me—and briefly wondered if I would ever see him or my money again. After he took off on his bike, of course, various Westerners I knew slightly drove by and paused to offer help. I said I thought I had things under control and thanked them.

Time passes slowly under a tropical sun as the noon hour approaches, but finally the Indian returned. He had pedaled cautiously because—quite rightly—he did not trust the seal on the lid of the Blue Band can to hold if the can tipped over,

But then a new problem occurred to him. "What do you have to pour the gas into the tank?"

Hunching my shoulders in embarrassment, I said nothing.

"No problem," he said for the second time, and walked over to the *warung* and came back with a handful of shiny dark green banana leaves. (These are often used for wrapping up the Malay equivalent of a sandwich—a portion of cooked sticky rice around a piece of meat or vegetable, to make a portable meal that many rural Malaysians carry in a small basket on their back.) Taking my car key to open up the gas tank, he then made a funnel out of a bunch of the leaves and stuck it into the opening of the tank, and carefully poured in the contents of the Blue Band can. He screwed the gas cap back on, handed the car key back to me and, with the ignition back on, I could see on the dashboard that there was now a small amount of gas in the tank.

I was about to thank him and drive off when he called out, "Madam, your money!" and poured a surprisingly large amount of bills and coins into my hands. I tried to give him some back as a tip but he would not accept it. "No problem," he said for the third time, and pedaled away.

Such kindness is extraordinary anywhere, but I am convinced that he would not have been so ready to help me if I had still been sitting in my car.

That I was standing on the street meant that I was in his world, a world where you "made do" with what you had or could easily find, a world we both could share, a world that would be, perhaps, affected by what his and my governments would do—or not do—together.

．．．．．．．．．．．．．．．．．

I hate commuting—always have—yet my longest period of commuting, three years in the mid-1970s, was then the best part of my day. During those years John was consul general in Antwerp, and I was commuting to a job at our embassy in Brussels as assistant commercial attaché.

John was put in charge of our consulate in Antwerp, the biggest city in Flanders, at a time when the Flemish (the 60 percent of Belgians who speak Dutch as their primary language at home) were starting to play political and social roles proportionate to their numbers. Just before we moved to Antwerp, Belgium acquired a Flemish prime minister, Leo Tindemans, who was the first ever in that office to use Dutch as his primary official language.

Up till then, in the Belgian corridors of power, only French could be heard; virtually all higher education had been in French, and any Fleming who wanted to be a politician at the national level or a civil servant or run a business of more than very local dimensions had to speak fluent French. But times were changing. This was therefore not the best time for our embassy to lose John, its only foreign service officer who spoke adequate Dutch.

I had started commuting by train from Antwerp to the embassy's commercial section when the DCM called me to his office and asked if I would like to learn Dutch. I was delighted at the idea, having already felt the need for more than my kitchen Dutch as hostess at John's business dinners. Were it not for me, I realized, such dinners could have been conducted entirely in Dutch.

The DCM agreed to let me have two hours of free lessons a day, I agreed to come in an hour before the workday began, and John found me the perfect teacher. A classically educated, older Flemish semiretired journalist, Guido Eeckels had a wealth of wonderful stories drawn from all of twentieth-century Belgium and its European context up to then.

Eager to hear Guido's stories, I found my passive knowledge of Dutch improved rapidly. But to speak it, I needed to perfect my pronunciation of the weird-sounding diphthongs that only Dutch has, and to remember that the verbs often do not come until the end of the sentence, where they pile up like extra railroad cars waiting to be hitched to the rest of the train.

I was given a textbook with its title in screaming big letters across the cover: SPEAK DUTCH. I carried the book outside my briefcase so that I could open it up and start studying as soon as I sat down inside the train. Like commuters everywhere, I always seemed to sit in the same car. People would comment aloud on the absence of one of our regulars. Somebody would say something like: "What happened to the dark-haired girl with the red raincoat? Her university is in session; I hope she has not got that flu that is going around." And another would say, "'No, she got a grant to study in Paris this term."

I enjoyed this chance to observe ordinary Belgians going about their everyday lives; it was something I rarely got to see in diplomatic settings. And it was not long before the other commuters, all Flemings, began to take an interest in my lessons. Finally, one of my bolder car-mates reached over and, with just a glance to ask permission, took my book into his hands and began to drill me, using the sentences at the top of the page. From then on, most days, both ways, my fellow commuters took over the task of drilling the sentence patterns for declarative, interrogative, negative interrogative, and other grammatical structures into my head. I learn best orally, so this kind of instruction was perfect for me.

One evening as I was heading home, I found that our car in the train had been officially reserved by a group of travelers and we regulars were scattered into other cars. In the car I chose, I sat down where there were two seats facing two seats. Next to me sat a fair slender woman in her forties and opposite her was a trim, dark-haired man who might have been a bit younger. (The seat opposite me was empty.) The man was talking earnestly to the woman, and it was clear that they knew each other well. At one point, the man reached above his head and pulled down from the rack a box which, when opened, proved to contain several paper cups, plates and napkins, plastic forks, a frosted oblong fruitcake, and a metal knife to cut it with. The last item was a bottle of good quality dry Spanish sherry.

He served the fruitcake to the other woman and me, and poured sherry into paper cups for the three of us. When I thanked him in English, he continued in that language so that I would be included. He had a little speech prepared—just as he had the cake and wine—to mark the last day, after fifteen years, that the woman would be commuting to their common workplace. From now on, he would not see her on the train but only at the office. It was a graceful little speech—nothing embarrassingly intimate—during which we ate and drank. The little ceremony finished in time for him to pack up the remnants of our feast and hand it to the woman before she got off the train at Mechelen.

Standing up ready to disembark, she turned to me and said softly, "When you see him in the train, take care of him, won't you?" and turned back and out the door to the platform.

He, too, had something to tell me before we got off the train at Antwerp: "Remember this," he said. "One must always celebrate life's little occasions."

That little ceremony stayed in my mind as dramatizing one of the major differences between Belgians who—like most Europeans—had opted to stay where they were, and Americans of European descent whose families had chosen to leave for a new world. And when the Belgians stayed where they were, they really STAYED where they and their parents and grandparents back through the centuries had lived. For most of them, an hour or more daily commute for their whole working life was a reasonable price to pay for sticking close to their roots. I gradually came to realize that this difference between us, the adventurers versus the stay-behinds, was a crucial one.

The next day I was back in my usual car and, though the man and I smiled at each other when we would both come onto the platform at Antwerp, we never sat near each other again.

John and I left Antwerp in 1978, when we were transferred to our next post, our embassy in Kinshasa, capital of the ex-Belgian Congo, which its dictator Mobutu had renamed Zaire. But two years later, in 1980, we were back in Belgium. John by this time was the political counselor at our Brussels embassy. One evening he was in Antwerp giving a speech (in Dutch, of course) to a business group; it may have been the Rotary.

I was up on the platform sitting behind the speaker's rostrum with the hosts and the other senior wives when I sensed someone staring at me. It was a trim, dark-haired man, and, as I watched, he poked his wife's side with his elbow and said loud enough for me to hear, "*Kijk eens, die dame van de trein.*" (Look! There's the lady from the train.) I realized then that he had followed his own advice and had remembered at least one of life's little occasions.

TO LEAD PARADE ... Mrs. ESTHER MOSCOW puts the finishing touches on the "Miss Liberty" gown her daughter, JUDITH, will wear when she heads the Children's Parade on Broadway the morning of April 23. The parade will open the national $60,000,000 fund-raising drive on behalf of American Overseas Aid-United Nations Appeal for Children. New York's share is ---- ,000. Spyros ᴾ Skouras is city chairma

Judy (age twelve) being helped into her UN Appeal for Children parade costume by her mother, Esther Moscow, April 15, 1948. *New York Journal American,* courtesy of the Harry Ransom Center, The University of Texas at Austin

John's mother, Doris Olsen Heimann, and her Chinese lover, Yao,
en route to Shanghai, 1940

John (age eleven) and his mother, back in the United States,
living with John's father, 1944

John (age twenty), a freshman in Harvard Yard, Autumn 1953

Judy (age seventeen), a freshman in the Radcliffe Quad, Autumn 1953

John and Judy and most of their Jakarta domestic staff, 1958

John walking behind Ambassador Howard P. Jones in Bandung, Java, during the Indonesian constitutional convention, 1959. Department of State

Women's International Club buffet lunch, Surabaya, 1960 (Judy in white dress)

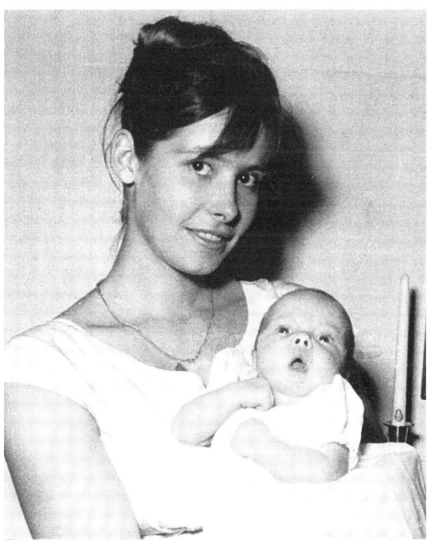

Anita Hubert Cunningham holding newborn Nathalie, Surabaya, 1960

Judy in a *becak* in Java, Indonesia, 1960

View of Kuching, Sarawak, East Malaysia, 1957

Iban women bathing in a stream, Sarawak, 1957. After 1963,
they would normally be covered on top.

John and Judy heading off to their first tandem assignments in Brussels, 1972. Department of State

Judy and a Congolese student friend on her Kinshasa terrace, 1979

Back in Brussels, John (dressed for presentation of credentials by his ambassador), Judy, and John's visiting father, Harry Heimann, 1984

To John Heimann –
on an occasion to remember.
John Shad

The Hague, senior embassy officials preparing for John's last call on the Queen of
the Netherlands, to present the new ambassador, John Shad, 1987.
Department of State

Staff members standing in front of the US Consulate General, Bordeaux, France,
1989 (Judy second from the right, wearing glasses). Department of State

Louis Longequeue, Socialist mayor of Limoges, France, gives Judy a piece of Limoges porcelain while US ambassador to France Joe M. Rodgers looks on, 1987. Department of State

Gaullist mayor of Bordeaux Jacques Chaban-Delmas (*on left*) making a point to Judy while the prefect of Aquitaine looks on, 1988

Un long flirt américain

CHRISTIANE POULIN

Le consulat des Etats-Unis de Bordeaux a 200 ans. C'est le plus ancien poste diplomatique américain au monde. Deux siècles après la nomination de Joseph Fenwick, Judith Heimann, quarante-septième consul général, perpétue la représentation américaine dans le Sud-Ouest.

Il s'appelait Joseph Fenwick. Né à Cherryhill dans le Maryland, et négociant de son état. Dès la fin de la guerre d'Indépendance, ce citoyen américain a franchi l'Atlantique pour se fixer à Bordeaux. Une ville parée de bien des charmes aux yeux du jeune Fenwick : il y fonde la firme Fenwick, Mason et Cie, et il y épouse Catherine Menoire, fille d'un négociant bordelais.

A l'angle du Pavé et du quai des Chartrons, un hôtel particulier, construit par l'architecte Dufart, deviendra la demeure du couple. Joseph Fenwick s'y éteindra à 87 ans, le 25 novembre 1849. Près d'un siècle et demi après sa mort, le 26 novembre, une plaque apposée sur la façade de l'hôtel Fenwick, à l'occasion du deux centième anniversaire de la création du consulat des Etats-Unis de Bordeaux, témoignera de l'empreinte laissée dans le port de la Lune par ce pionnier américain. D'octobre 1790

— il avait alors 28 ans — à juin 1801, Joseph Fenwick fut le premier consul des Etats-Unis dans le Sud-Ouest, nommé par le président George Washington qui créait ainsi le plus ancien poste diplomatique américain au monde. (Voir ci-dessous).

Deux cents ans plus tard, la bannière étoilée flotte toujours dans la capitale de l'Aquitaine. Quarante-septième consul général des Etats-Unis pour le Sud-Ouest, doyen du corps consulaire de Bordeaux, longs cheveux blonds et sourire inaltérable, Judith Heimann y perpétue aujourd'hui la représentation américaine. Extrêmement attachée aux « liens d'amour tissés entre Bordeaux et les Etats-Unis », en particulier, remarque-t-elle, « grâce au vin ». En trois ans, Mme le Consul a eu l'occasion de progresser dans la connaissance de ces crus dont Jefferson, voilà des siècles, avait entrepris le classement. Spontanément, cette New-Yorkaise de Greenwich-Village confie qu'à son arrivée, elle distinguait le bordeaux du bourgogne... à la forme de la bouteille !

Hien, absolument rien, ne destinait Judith Heimann à la carrière diplomatique. Elle aurait pu, par exemple, être journaliste. Comme ses deux oncles ou comme son père, spécialiste dans l'information politique au « New York Times ». Elle y songeait, d'ailleurs, à l'époque où elle étudiait la littérature anglaise à l'université. Mais elle rencontre John Heimann et, l'ayant choisi pour mari, s'empressa de le suivre lorsqu'il fit son entrée dans « la carrière ». En Indonésie d'abord, puis en Europe et un peu partout dans le Vieux Monde.

« Je suis la femme de mon mari », s'exclaffe Judith Heimann dans un éclat de malice qui plisse son regard bleu, indiquant comment la voie choisie par son époux est plus tard devenue la sienne. En tant qu'épouse de diplomate, elle avait la possibilité d'accéder, par le biais d'un examen, au service diplomatique. Ainsi procéda-t-elle en 1972, après s'être consacrée à l'éducation de ses deux enfants. Aujourd'hui, ils vivent l'un à Oxford, l'autre aux Etats-Unis, et c'est John Heimann qui a pris sa « retraite » pour rejoindre Mme le Consul en Aquitaine.

Après bien des pérégrinations — elle a notamment occupé des poste en Belgique, aux Pays-Bas, au Zaïre — Judith Heimann a pris ses fonctions à Bordeaux en 1987. Autrement dit, à l'époque où, pour des raisons budgétaires, le consulat des Etats-Unis de Bordeaux était menacé de fermeture. Grande fut l'émotion au sein de la communauté américaine de la région et de Judith Heimann si ses concitoyens n'ont pas oublié la campagne lancée par « Sud-Ouest » pour sauver le consulat. Le danger semble actuellement écarté.

Si Bordeaux conserve une petite enclave américaine sur son territoire deux diplomates américains et onze employés locaux. En bonne diplomate, Judith Heimann ne néglige aucun de son rôle commercial, ni le rôle culturel ni tenu par le consulat mais insiste aussi sur son rôle politique « Parce que, dit-elle, des malentendus peuvent surgir même entre des peuples amis et parce que, pour comprendre un pays, on est obligé, il faut le connaître en profondeur ».

Dans quelques jours, à l'instar de plusieurs millions d'Américains réunis autour de la traditionnelle dinde farcie, Judith Heimann fêtera Thanksgiving Day. La question est de savoir où. A La Rochelle ? Limoges ? Toulouse ? Ou Bordeaux ? Les ressortissants américains dépendant du consulat de Bordeaux sont non seulement nombreux (quoique leur recensement soit difficile, on parle de huit à dix mille), mais disséminés sur une zone très étendue : vingt départements. Voilà une situation géographique faite pour compliquer la tâche du représentant officiel des Etats-Unis pour le Sud-Ouest de la France. En vérité, pas du tout. Qu'il s'agisse de rencontrer ses compatriotes à Toulouse, d'inaugurer une exposition à Angoulême, d'assister à un dîner offert par le maire de Pau ou à une réception à Biarritz pour fêter l'anniversaire de l'indépendance, Judith Heimann est prête. Deux ou trois fois par mois, Madame le Consul s'évade

hors de Bordeaux dans la voiture du corps diplomatique. Pour affronter les longs déplacements et les retours tardifs, elle est munie d'un oreiller et d'une paire de pantoufles.

« A mon arrivée, j'ai été très bien préparée par l'accueil qui m'était réservé, avoue Judith Heimann. Pas question de prendre un rendez-vous avec le maire d'une petite commune sans accepter une invitation à déjeuner ! Je me suis aperçue que les gens de votre région savaient harmonieusement concilier le travail et la détente ». Toutes choses qui font que Judith Heimann dont la mission diplomatique s'achèvera l'été prochain, regrettera sincèrement Bordeaux. La preuve ? Elle en partira, à sa demande, en un plus tard que prévu ■

JUDITH HEIMANN, quarante-septième consul général des Etats-Unis pour le Sud-Ouest de la France. — « Attentive aux liens d'amour qui se sont tissés entre Bordeaux et son pays, en particulier grâce au vin ». (Ph. Jean-François Grivault)

John Bondfield en 1778

L'entrée en fonction de Joseph Fenwick fixe historiquement la naissance du consulat des Etats-Unis à Bordeaux au mois d'octobre 1790. En réalité, l'établissement de relations franco-américaines entre Bordeaux et les treize colonies constituées en Congrès continental est antérieure. A partir de mars 1778, en effet, John Bondfield, négociant comme Fenwick, sert les intérêts américains à Bordeaux en qualité d'agent commercial. Entre autres tâches, John Bondfield, nommé par un agent commercial du comite secret du Congrès, organisera des envois d'armes vers l'Amérique qui se bat pour son indépendance.

On trouve également trace, à Bordeaux, d'un « consul » pourvu d'une mission officielle en France, de 1778 à 1790, Thomas Barclay, mais c'est parce qu'il y a été emprisonné, pour dettes (en raison de sa qualité, il sera relâché par arrêt du Parlement). L'affaire défraye la chronique du « Journal de Guyenne » et le procureur du roi s'indigne en ces termes : « Nous déférons un fait inouï chez une nation policée : le représentant d'une République dans les fers; un négociant arrêté sous le prétexte d'une dette particulière ». (Bordeaux, 19 mai 1787). ■

A la santé de Jefferson !

Premier consul des Etats-Unis à Bordeaux, Joseph Fenwick ne se contente pas de certifier les demandes de passeport, d'intervenir au sujet de capitaines de navires américains emprisonnés ou de signer les déclarations d'entrée des marchandises étrangères. De temps en temps lui échoit la mission de faire acheminer vers Philadelphie les meilleurs vins de Bordeaux, à l'intention d'un compatriote, Thomas Jefferson, secrétaire d'Etat du président Georges Washington, et grand amateur de vin qui deviendra plus tard président des Etats-Unis; a eu l'occasion de visiter le vignoble bordelais en 1787 alors qu'il était ministre des Etats-Unis auprès de la France.

En 1790, il écrit au comte de Lur-Saluces : « Le vin blanc de Sauternes, de votre cru, que vous

avez eu la liberté de m'envoyer à Paris au commencement de l'année 1788, a été si bien approuvé des Américains qui y ont goûté que je ne doute pas que mes compatriotes ne le trouvent aussi conforme à leur goût.

Actuellement je me suis établi ici, j'ai persuadé notre président, le général Washington, d'en essayer un échantillon. Il vous en demande trente douzaines, et moi, je vous en demande dix douzaines pour moi-même... M. Fenwick, consul des Etats-Unis à Bordeaux, recevra les emballages et aura le bonheur de vous payer le montant, dont il est muni... » (Philadelphie, 6 septembre 1790).

Ainsi les vins de Bordeaux furent-ils introduits à la Maison-Blanche. ■

Sud Ouest, Sunday edition, November 11, 1990, page 2. This was carried in its frame to the scene of the French hostage-taking in March 1991. By kind permission of the archivist of the journal *Sud Ouest*, Bordeaux

Judy, as refugee coordinator at the US Embassy in Manila, visiting a class for children of Vietnamese boat people at the US refugee camp for them on the Bataan Peninsula in the Philippines, 1992. Department of State

Judy and John in their retirement home on the Chesapeake Bay, 1998

Chapter 13

Latin Tags

• • • • • • •

SOMETIMES IN DIPLOMACY YOU
really need to hunt to find something in common with your negotiating
counterpart that will help lead you to a fruitful partnership. That may be
why the old Foreign Service exam contained a lot of questions designed
to test your knowledge of trivia, so-called useless bits of information that
educated people—at least in the West—carried around in their heads.
One example of how useful trivia could be occurred during the mid-
1970s when, for three years, my job was that of assistant commercial
attaché in Brussels.

While John was consul in Antwerp, getting to know the people who
would run Belgium for the rest of the century, my train ride to and from
work and my early morning Dutch lesson were the best parts of my working
day. I heartily disliked my commercial officer job.

I knew nothing about private enterprise and had very few friends in the
business world. I was good at any kind of research including doing market
surveys, but the US Department of Commerce often took years before publishing the time-sensitive marketing information that we in the embassy's
commercial section had so painstakingly collected; we often wondered why
we had bothered. Perhaps fortunately, foreign service officers no longer do
commercial work; the Commerce Department has its own separate foreign
service to do it.

The one market survey I wrote that I *know* was used looked into the
opportunities in Belgium for American food franchises and what they would
need to do to succeed. I had barely finished it when my boss, the commercial
counselor, brought some McDonald's executives straight from the United

States to see me for advice on how to begin inserting their restaurants into the Belgian market.

For once, I felt I had an audience for my timely data. Belgians were discriminating eaters, and the country was full of good restaurants. But although in those days most Belgian office workers wanted a hot meal at lunchtime, there were almost no places where they could get such a meal in less than an hour or at a price they could afford. I told these executives that McDonald's could fill that niche provided they did the following: situate their franchises in walking streets and arcades in town, not drive-ins; have a license to serve beer and wine; and spend as much money as necessary on quality control. I said they should promptly shut down any franchise that ever let the oil in the *friture* go bad, but they need not waste a penny on advertising. The McDonald's name was known. If the *frites* were up to standard and the place was kept clean, the Belgians would come. If not, no advertising would get them there. I may not have been the only person to give McDonald's this advice, but it is what they did in Belgium and it worked. It still does.

I think of this time in the commercial section of our embassy in Brussels as the nadir of my career and one of the low points of my life. All bureaucracies have their weak members and I found my boss, the commercial counselor, to be an insensitive supervisor. Worse still, one of the Americans he supervised, in addition to me, was a foreign service officer who, I later learned, was notorious within the State Department for getting away with doing no work whatsoever while making his co-workers miserable. By the time both he and our boss left for onward assignments, one of our Belgian colleagues had retired on grounds of mental illness, and everybody else at the embassy had come to dread visiting our office. Fortunately, such office situations are rare in our service; I was just unlucky in having to work there then.

At the same time, John was starting to have occasional bouts of what his doctors called "fevers of unknown origin." He had enough willpower to keep doing his job well. But when the fevers struck he would have a wiped-out look. At times, he seemed barely able to keep awake for my daughter and me in the evenings. (Paul, age fifteen, had already begun boarding school in the United States, as part of our long-term plan to have the kids participate in the teenage life of Americans without being ghettoized overseas.) No-body knew what was wrong with John. Blood tests gave no clue nor did physical exams, including a sigmoidoscopy. Was he just bored? With his job? With his life? With me? Not knowing what was wrong with him, the kids felt the same worry I did, though we did not share these fears with each other at the time—undoubtedly a big mistake on my part.

My commuting didn't help. During half the year, I would leave our big, ugly, dark, furnished apartment above an old-age facility before dawn to walk to the Antwerp railroad station, and return in the dark after a dreadful day at work. In the summer, it was almost worse. I would come home when there were still hours of daylight left, only to find John too tired to want to go out—even to a café—while it was still sunny and pleasant out of doors.

My boss went on several months' home leave, leaving me in charge, but he could not have given me power to make personnel changes if he had wanted to. Those months with the boss away were miserable for me. I was doing all my malevolent colleague's work and mine while trying to protect the Belgian staff from his onslaughts. By the time our boss got back I was exhausted, infuriated, and demoralized—and I saw no way out. I could not ask for a transfer; I didn't want to quit the service; John was in no state to advise me. It was one of the rare occasions in my adult life when I felt truly helpless.

Just then, an invitation came for two of my Belgian colleagues and me to attend a two-week commercial training session in Vienna, a place where I had never been. "Two weeks out of this hell hole!" I thought. "How wonderful!"

My boss, however, though fresh from home leave, said he could not spare the three of us at one time; so I should go and the two others stay behind. That seemed wrong to me; they needed the break as much as I did. I argued for the Belgians going to the Vienna course. I pointed out that they would be staying in the commercial section whereas I, in a cou-ple of years, planned to move on and never do commercial work again. My boss then said, "OK, Judy, let them go and you stay here." I walked out of his office in despair.

After tossing and turning all night, I appeared in his office the next morning and said, "Ed, I think I understand your position, but I don't think you understand mine. I really need to get away right now. If I don't, I don't know what may happen." Then, looking at his face, which showed that he might be finally ready to pay attention to what I was saying, I added, "Think of this as the rattle of the rattlesnake." He was standing, and he leapt back as if the snake were lunging at him. I walked out the door, closing it behind me.

The next morning Ed called me in and said he had considered the problem overnight. He now had thought of a way the section could manage without two of my Belgian colleagues and me for two weeks. Looking back, I still think I did him a favor by letting him know in terms even he could not ignore that I needed a break right then. If I had not had it, I would have been so consumed by resentment that I would probably have been unable to avoid worsening what was already a bad office atmosphere.

. . . .

The Vienna trip gave me time to myself without pressure and a chance to examine what was going wrong in my life. One weekend afternoon I was sitting in the wonderful Vienna Fine Arts museum among the Breughels. There was one enormous painting, *Hunters in the Snow*, that showed men with spears and dogs hunting game in a snowy landscape. It was all in shades of brown and white, no jewel-like colors such as Pieter Brueghel the Elder and his contemporaries usually used, but it was so beautiful that one did not miss the colors. Sitting there, I quietly took stock of myself and concluded: "Judy, the only thing that makes you tolerable is your ability to take absolute delight in so many things. For the moment, life is not ideal. But stick to enjoying what you can enjoy and eventually you'll be okay."

. . . .

Soon after returning to Belgium from Vienna, and because I had previously been "control officer" for the First Lady's program during the visit to Belgium of President and Mrs. Nixon in 1974 and of President and Mrs. Ford in 1975, I was asked to perform the same role during the January

1978 visit of President and Mrs. Carter. (I was glad to see that none of these presidential visits were as imperial as the Johnson visit to Malaysia had been.)

I welcomed the job of being Mrs. Carter's control officer for the fun of seeing again how the Belgian Royals and our First Family went about their official lives. But even more, I welcomed it as a temporary escape from the commercial section. Morale in my office was still low, not least my own.

I realized I had not felt this unhappy for a prolonged period nor in such a hostile daytime environment since those five years from age eight—when my parents divorced and we all moved back to Manhattan after six years in Albany—to age thirteen, when I finally reached high school and found school friends who shared my interests.

My mother, having asked for the divorce and not wanting to ask for much alimony, had had no option but to send me at age eight to neighborhood public schools. There, I had felt very alone among classmates who had no books at home, who did not seem to trust anyone who was not mad for spectator sports and wanted to read instead, and who—the greatest sin—got good grades. My grades may have been why, out of the blue, I was chosen at age twelve by the Board of Education of New York City (not by my schoolmates) to lead a parade down Broadway to promote the United Nations Appeal for Children. That led to my becoming interested in the UN and in the prominent role that women such as Eleanor Roosevelt and Madame Pandit of India played in it, but it also increased my unpopularity at school.

Fortunately, when I was thirteen, I gained admission to Hunter College High School, a public school for "gifted" New York City girls, and within a week of my being at Hunter my life was transformed. The previous Friday, our Latin teacher Dr. Corrigan had given us a quiz, and I had that awful feeling I used to have at my other schools, that I had aced it. And worse still, this marvelous teacher—who was bent with age and frail but with the firm voice of a Roman senator—was reading the test scores out loud. She got to my name and announced: "100 percent, the class's only perfect score." In my previous schools, such a grade usually led to days of merciless teasing and bullying, so I was sitting there sick at heart, and then I noticed that the whole class was applauding. Applauding? Me? My life as a happy person began that day. I soon learned that many of the other girls had school histories similar to mine. And now that we were all together, there was no more bullying or meanness to be afraid of.

My love affair with Latin continued throughout high school. That was when I learned that Latin had long been the lingua franca of the elite throughout Europe and that it was still the basis of a "classical education" there, including among diplomats.

So, trying to apply my Vienna insight about the need to concentrate on what I enjoyed, I decided to try to remember some of my Latin. It seemed a pity that my facility at reading it had long since melted away. All that now remained were a few so-called Latin tags (famous quotations that everybody who studied Latin would know).

I recalled that Dr. Corrigan had taught us one of the best-known Latin tags: *Carthago delenda est* (Carthage must be destroyed). It is a quotation from the Roman senator Cato the Elder in the days of the Roman Republic. The senator was convinced that Carthage (in what is modern Tunisia) was the greatest threat that Rome faced, and so he would append that statement to everything he said in the Senate, regardless of the subject then under discussion. Dr. Corrigan told us that, in modern times, for someone to use that quotation is a shorthand way of saying: "I said this before and I am saying it again, and I think it is more important than anything we are now discussing." Now, having been released from the commercial section for a blissful month to prepare and run Rosalynn Carter's upcoming visit to Belgium, I found a use for that Latin tag.

I was putting together the First Lady's program and trying to get something of substance into it that would involve what I had been told was her great interest in different ways of treating the mentally ill. Because Mrs. Carter would be the guest of Belgium's Queen Fabiola, I had to coordinate her program with the Palace's master of ceremonies, a certain francophone baron. When I told the baron that the White House wanted Mrs. Carter to visit a mental health institute or organization, he said, "I know just the thing; there is a cerebral palsy institute run as a charity of the Société Générale [the financial institution that used to own much of Belgium]."

I replied, with regret in my voice, that for an American, cerebral palsy was a physical, not mental, illness and would not particularly interest Mrs. Carter. I did not tell him that I liked the idea even less when I learned that, although this institute was situated in Flanders, it was run entirely in French.

I knew that the main purpose of visits by our president and first lady was public diplomacy, to make the right gestures that would please the host government and people, and make appealing photos for the front page of newspapers back in the States. Such visits, however, also offered nearly infinite opportunities for things to go wrong and create a lot of bad publicity. I could easily imagine the field day that extreme Flemish nationalists could have, criticizing Mrs. Carter and the Queen for visiting an establishment that, ignoring the country's language policy, was French-run in the Dutch-speaking part of Belgium.

I seemed unable to get anybody with clout to focus on my problem. I was a very junior diplomat and the part of the presidential visit involving Mrs. Carter was minor. The focus of the Palace and my embassy was on President Carter's planned visits to the king, to NATO, and to European Union headquarters. Yet I knew—this being my third time planning such a program—that what was proposed would not satisfy the White House, and that the White House was perfectly capable of just saying no at the last minute. It might then go off to do its own thing, offending Belgium's king and queen in the process.

There was a big meeting at the Royal Palace in downtown Brussels at which all the eagles were gathered a week or two ahead of the arrival of President and Mrs. Carter and their White House staff. The baron, who was running the meeting, finally looked over at me and said, "Mrs. Heimann, have you anything to say?"

I had been sitting there throughout the meeting thinking: "How do I tell this guy that the thing he planned for Mrs. Carter won't work? How can I say, 'I understand where you are coming from, but the White House will not'; that 'you and I have to work together to solve this problem.' What, after all, will convince him that I *do* understand him, that to some extent I share his world, and he must trust me on this?"

There he stood, a gentleman of the old school with a classical education—and then it came to me. Standing up, I looked at him and, enunciating carefully, said: "*Carthago delenda est.*"

He laughed and repeated what I had just said, in an interrogative tone.

I said yes, and he said softly, "Stay after the meeting and we'll talk." We ended up with a panel of mental health experts from all over Belgium, but more than half of them Dutch-speakers from Flanders. The panel discussion was held at the cerebral palsy institute, but all the press photos were taken during the panel discussions in a room that could have been anywhere. It was a good solution that satisfied everyone. A Latin tag had solved my diplomatic problem.

Once again I was grateful to Dr. Corrigan, who had told us that story about Cato the Elder. I also have never forgotten what she wrote in my senior yearbook: "*Forsan et haec olim meminisse iuvabit.*" It means (my translation from Virgil): "Perhaps some day it will bring you joy to remember even such things as these." Yes, indeed, Dr. Corrigan, it does.

Chapter 14

Heroics in the Hinterland

· · · · · · · · · · · · · · · ·

AFTER SIX YEARS IN BELGIUM, WE
were sent in mid-1978 to Kinshasa, where, as I already noted, I was assigned
to a low-ranking job not in my specialty and did not expect to enjoy my time
there. In fact, it became one of my favorite assignments.

In early 1979, I had become the officer at Embassy Kinshasa responsible for dealing with members of the nonviolent opposition to Mobutu's
dictatorship and was also responsible for reporting on human rights matters
and trying to improve Zaire's human rights record. And then I acquired yet
another specialty, that of acting consul in Bukavu, in the Kivu region, in the
mountainous northeast of the country.

Our Bukavu consul was going to be temporarily away—with my boss,
Bob Remole. The two of them were going to collect the consulate's new
four-wheel-drive vehicle at the Congo River port of Kisangani (formerly
Stanleyville) and drive it back to Bukavu. But the main reason why my
boss wanted to go along to collect the consulate's car was that it would be
a trip both ways through the great Ituri rain forest, a jungle full of different
kinds of wild animals and birds, and home to the legendary pygmy people.
Given the road conditions, my boss and the consul would be gone at least
two weeks, and I was asked to fill in for the consul, staying at his house in
Bukavu with his wife and children.

Remole and I flew on January 30, 1979, by way of Bujumbura, Burundi—the nearest place to Bukavu that we could get to by a reliable (i.e.,
non-Congolese) airline. From there, we were driven in a Land Rover by
an Embassy Bujumbura driver, on a road that crossed and recrossed the
borders of Burundi, Rwanda, and the Congo before reaching the lovely lake-
and-volcano landscape around Bukavu.

Once there, after bidding bon voyage to my boss and the consul, I thought this was a good occasion for me, as human rights officer, to visit the leader of an evangelical American missionary church in Goma. Goma, due north of Bukavu, was on the other side of the big, beautiful blue Lake Kivu that I could see from the consulate office. I had met the missionary, an African American married to an American-educated Congolese woman, when he and his wife had come to Kinshasa to try to get support against some new antiforeigners rules that threatened to interfere with their mission's work. I had pleaded with the then minister of justice on their behalf, and I don't know if it helped, but it certainly made them feel that someone at the embassy cared about them.

As for traveling from Bukavu to Goma, as the saying goes, "Getting there is half the fun." I waited at the Bukavu airstrip for a day and a half to catch the scheduled daily flight to Goma across Lake Kivu. Goma was less than twenty minutes away by air, but it was a seven-hour drive along the west side of the lake. Despite the printed schedules, no planes going that way appeared. Eventually a Congolese man who had waited as long as I had said (in French), "Come with me. We'll go by ferry." At the docks was a ferryboat ready to launch. The man helped me aboard with his bags and mine and paid for our tickets.

From chatting with the crew, I gathered that my companion regularly smuggled alluvial diamonds from the Kasais (in central Congo) and gold from surface mines in the Kivu region to markets abroad, but was otherwise an upstanding fellow. I was also told that the ferry had lost one of its two engines and therefore would take a full seven hours to cross Lake Kivu from south to north.

I was exhausted and slept on my luggage. I woke only once during the trip, when I detected a delicious scent in the air. I opened my eyes to find my travel companion offering me a slice of fresh pineapple cut from a bunch he had bought from a fruit stand on an island in the middle of the lake. He was gallantly serving slices to all the women on deck. In my conversation with him I learned, first, that the island was famous for the quality of its pineapples and, second, that Lake Kivu was one of the deepest lakes in the world and thus we should all hope that the second engine on our boat would not fail.

When I turned up outside Goma at the missionary's door, guided by a flashlight held by my travel companion—who then slipped away before I could thank him—the couple was astonished to see me, but very ready to take me in for the night. It was Evensong time, and would I mind just sitting there with the group while they sang some hymns and offered some prayers?

I must explain at this point that my delightful late stepmother, Jean, Jewish though she was, had learned a number of swinging Baptist hymns from her cleaning lady in New York. Jean had taught them to me years before (after having taught me camp songs, folk songs, ragtime songs, and naughty ditties from the 1890s that her father had taught her).

As I sat on a kitchen stool in the missionary's living room-cum-prayer hall, I heard their miniature electric organ play the opening chords to one of my favorite Baptist hymns, "Leaning on the Everlasting Arms," and earned much merit by being able to sing along without a hymnal. (In its own way, knowing this hymn proved to be as useful knowledge as sharing a Latin tag with a Belgian baron had been.) I have to admit, I was beginning to enjoy my new assignment.

From then on, my hosts treated me like an honored family friend. I liked them too, and soon realized that they were the undeclared leaders of all the American missionaries of the Kivu region north of the lake. They kept track of who in the missionary community was where and in what state of health, the call numbers on their radios, and if they had access to a private airplane. This sort of information would prove useful to me sooner than I had expected. Meanwhile, I got back to Bukavu the next day in about fifteen minutes, when a plane belonging to a friend of one of the missionaries was available to cross the lake.

I soon got to know the number two in our Bukavu consulate, an able vice consul and his vivacious German wife. There was at least one other German consular wife in Bukavu, the remarkably pretty wife of the Belgian consul. The Belgian consul was a brilliant senior diplomat who had been exiled to this minor post for having caused a scandal by stealing his wife from her German husband at another post. I had been urged to meet the Belgian by a Flemish friend of mine back in Belgium who said he was her favorite cousin. The Belgian consul—whom I shall call Hans—and I liked each other immediately. His office was just down the dusty arcaded street from mine.

Bukavu's tiny consular corps also included, among others, a Swiss man from the International Committee of the Red Cross, an Italian with the World Health Organization, and a rather glum German or Danish honorary consul involved in agricultural investments, as best as I can recall. There was a surprising number of Americans in town, not only various rival American evangelicals but also at the Peace Corps language-training school set up there because of its mild climate. Nearly a hundred Peace Corps volunteers were at the Bukavu school, studying one or another of the Congo's four main languages (other than French, which few but educated people spoke fluently): Kikongo, Kiswahili, Lingala, and Tshiluba.

I had been at the consulate just a few days and was beginning to find my feet in consular work again when I had an unexpected morning visit from my Belgian colleague, Hans. He looked slightly uncomfortable to be asking me: "Judy, have you heard any odd rumors lately—anything at all, but that might have a security dimension to it?"

"No," I said. "What's up?"

"Probably nothing. But let me know if you hear anything odd."

I did not have long to stew over Hans's question. My vice consul, who was well integrated into the local foreign community, came to me within the hour to relay a rumor that a bunch of white mercenaries had gathered on the eastern shore of Lake Kivu, in the Rwandan town of Gisenyi, and were waiting for a signal to attack Bukavu. The mercenaries allegedly included a handful of the fifty notorious Belgian, French, and South African soldiers of fortune, rumored to be led by French Colonel Bob Denard, who in 1967 had helped lead a thousand anti-Zairian gendarmes from Katanga (the cobalt- and copper-mining area of southeast Congo) in pitched battles on the streets of Bukavu and elsewhere against some 30,000 soldiers of the Mobutu-led Zaire central government.

I thanked my colleague and told him to keep tracking this story while I went to see Hans. Hans, relieved that I now had heard the rumors and so he could talk freely, said that there were only a dozen or so mercenaries sitting around a hotel bar in Gisenyi, but they expected to pick up a sizable crowd of ex-gendarmes and others in Kivu who were ready and willing to try to topple the Mobutu regime. The awkward thing for Hans was that most of these guys sitting around in Gisenyi had obtained their passports or their visas in Liège, the Belgian home of one of the world's biggest producers of small arms, the famous Fabrique Nationale.

We agreed to stay in close contact and to share any further information. I hurried back to the consulate and quickly typed up my notes on a typewriter with a much-used ribbon. I wanted to get into the vault to see how to send this message to the embassy in Kinshasa, which would no doubt have heard something of what was going on and would be waiting anxiously for word from me. I went upstairs to the vault door and punched in the code. But as I turned the big shiny wheel (such as bank vault doors have), the wheel came off in my hands, though the door remained locked.

The vice consul and I looked at each other blankly until I remembered John having once said to me when he was running our little consulate in Borneo: "You know those vault doors are bulletproof steel and inches thick. But I bet the walls are only one brick thick." I passed on this thought to the vice consul, and he ran off to find the hulking teenage son of one of the Bukavu-based missionaries, who came back with an impressive-looking hammer that, sure enough, broke through the single row of bricks into the vault in less than half an hour.

After we made our way into the vault, I was trying to think what my next step should be. It was then I suddenly was brought up short by the fact that I knew of no way to send confidential messages from my office to Embassy Kinshasa—or to anywhere else, for that matter. My vice consul showed me a moldering pile of "one-time pads"—the standard way to send a secure message by radio over an open line—but it required a familiarity with the process that both the vice consul and I lacked. I fumbled around for a few minutes with a pencil, destroying several pages of one of the pads before putting my typed draft message in my handbag and announcing: "I think I'll just walk over and see Hans for a minute."

"Hans," I said, "do you have a way to send a classified wireless to Kinshasa?

"Of course," he said. "Be my guest!"

Within a few hours, a wireless message came back via Hans from our Kinshasa DCM Alan Davis (who was our chargé d'affaires at the time) thanking me for the prompt message and telling me that this was the safest way for us to communicate. He added that I had the Belgian Embassy's permission to continue to do so. The chargé also kindly provided a bit of background to the mercenary story and why—though it was not yet confirmed as fact—the possibility of such a threat was likely to greatly upset the people of Kivu, who had lived through such an incident less than a dozen years earlier. I was glad Alan was in charge. He was a bit given to nitpicking when things were going smoothly. But, at the first sign of a crisis, his great good humor and sense of proportion would rise to the top like cream in a milk bottle, and working for him became a joy.

Thinking like a consular officer again, I realized the most important thing to do right away was to get word out to the American citizens in my district of what we knew regarding a possible mercenary attack and to figure out a way to get our people out of the district—and perhaps out of the country—if that should become necessary.

Every American diplomatic and consular post is required to have a list of American citizens and their "fireside aliens" (a term John and I loved) and a plausible plan for getting them to safety should the need arise. The vice consul and I read Bukavu's plan carefully and found it was good for the names and locations of Americans on the south side of Lake Kivu. Thanks to my Goma missionary friends, I had an up-to-date list of the more numerous group of American missionaries and other strays north of Lake Kivu. My vice consul went off to the Peace Corps training center where he had friends and came back with a list of all the Americans there.

When he returned, I asked if he knew Adrien De Schrijver, a Belgian "white hunter" who had been recommended to me by adventurous Belgian friends back in Brussels. The man was allegedly involved in protecting the elephants and gorillas that lived in the region. He also flew photographic safaris and possibly other kinds of safaris in his own Piper Apache, a little twin-propeller bush plane. The vice consul knew where the man garaged his plane and drove me there. Luckily for me, the hunter happened to be standing next to his Apache. I invoked his friendship with my Belgian adventurers, and he agreed to fly me to Goma the next morning.

Meanwhile, I got my Goma missionary friend on an open radio line and said I needed to see him urgently—he could perhaps guess why—and would arrive by private plane tomorrow morning around 10 a.m.

The vice consul and I then spent the evening with the Bukavu missionaries, who had heard the rumors of the mercenary threat. We discussed possible ways out if the balloon went up. By the end of the evening we had tentatively decided that—aside from using the missionary planes, which were the best way out, if we could not get to the airport—the best alternate choice was to use everybody's motorboats, sailing yachts, canoes, or other craft to go east across the lake to Rwanda and seek safety there. Romantic as this Dunkirk-style exit would be, I had little faith it would work. To my mind, the safest way out, bar none, was if the region's commissioner (the Mobutu-appointed governor for all Kivu) could assure that we foreigners got to the airport safely and onto whatever planes could take us.

The next morning when I got to the Apache's hangar, the man I was counting on to fly me to Goma asked: "How long do you plan to stay on the ground there?" When told him that I thought I could do my business in an hour or two, he said, "Make it an hour. I feel a malarial attack coming on and really shouldn't be flying." With that, he opened the door and helped me into the seat next to the pilot's.

I hardly dared breathe while he flew us across that incredibly deep blue lake, but he got us safely to the other side, and there was my dear missionary friend, along with a few of his colleagues, waiting for me. They too had heard about the Gisenyi gathering of mercenaries and were preparing to leave if they had to. Ironically, it seemed more likely that they would rescue the Peace Corps volunteers and us at the consulate than the other way round. We set up a code of simple words that I would pronounce over our radio, each word indicating a different stage in our evacuation plan. A quick hug of my friend and his colleagues and I was able to get back to my fading pilot within the hour.

I sent a quick wireless message via Hans back to the chargé who was at that moment (he later told me) apologizing to John for having unknowingly sent me into such a potentially dangerous situation. The chargé later told me that John had said, "Don't you worry about Judy! I'm sure she is having the time of her life." John always knew me better than I knew myself.

The next days brought confirmation that the mercenaries were indeed in Gisenyi and were waiting for a signal from whoever was paying them to begin their attack. The emerging consensus had the attack on Bukavu beginning on a certain day in February during what, for Americans, would be the George Washington's Birthday weekend, more than a week away.

With time to reflect, I began to worry about our Peace Corps volunteers. The hirsute young men in their Banana Republic slacks, tabbed shirts, and military-style caps in camouflage colors looked just like everybody's image of a white mercenary. How to keep them safely off the streets as local tension mounted? Discussing the matter with the vice consul and his party-loving wife, we decided the best way to keep the Peace Corps kids safe would be to invite them all to spend Washington's Birthday weekend at an extended house party divided between our two houses. (The consul's wife and children had gone on a visit elsewhere by then.)

I asked the vice consul to issue the invitations and to say that the crazy temporary consul didn't care what they drank, smoked, or whatever, or who slept where, but we wanted them all to stay on either my premises or the vice consul's for the weekend. They should bring their own booze to the extent possible. Amused and bemused, they all accepted the invitation.

I also began to think about what to do if the balloon really went up. We started to burn unnecessary classified files. This proved a distressingly long and tedious process involving throwing files into a big perforated metal cylinder and then setting the cylinder on a rack like a barbecue over an open fire. It took many hours to turn one file drawer's contents into ashes. We took turns at it.

Then I thought about the arsenal inside the vault room. We had a couple of rifles, several pistols, and a number of cans of Mace pepper spray. My belief was that any effort to use any of those items in case of attack would be nearly certain to escalate the situation and lead to us and others being hurt, even killed. Given the odds, our only chance was to throw ourselves on the mercy of the Congolese loyalists—or, if that failed, of the mutineers. My vice consul, a red-blooded he-man, didn't much care for that idea, but he reluctantly agreed to bury the guns and the Mace in his garden.

By this time some of the other foreigners in our sort-of-consular corps were beginning to get anxious and came to see me. They wanted primarily to learn what I planned to do about an invitation we had all just received from Kivu's regional commissioner to attend a mass rally to be held at Bukavu's football stadium on the day when everybody expected the mercenary attack to be launched. Some felt strongly that this was a trap, and that we would be made into hostages or worse. I said I didn't think so, but I was prepared to go see the commissioner and find out more about his intentions. They agreed, seemingly relieved to be able to put off making a decision for now. Hans favored my approach, I think, but was prepared to let me do the running; he would still have to live here in Kivu afterward.

I was too ignorant and preoccupied at the time to question why these old-timers were turning to me, a very junior and inexperienced diplomat, to lead them. Years later an American Foreign Service colleague who had served in Zambia helped me see why. He told me of a time when his Belgian colleague in Lusaka had been trying to get the Zambians to allow a plane filled with Belgians escaping from a rebellion in Eastern Congo to land in Zambia en route home to Belgium. After a long and fruitless day, he had said over a beer with my colleague: "Just once, for a day or so, what I would not give to be an American diplomat, not a mere Belgian!" The moral to my colleague's story seemed to be that the mere fact that we represented the United States gave us clout that we would never have had otherwise.

. . . .

I made an appointment to call on the commissioner and was received— possibly accompanied by some of the other consular officers, I forget— by a roly-poly man in a well-cut high-collared short-sleeved jacket and matching suit trousers (the Mobutu-instituted national dress). His French was excellent, and his wit sparkled, lending credence to the rumor that one of his numerous wives was francophone Swiss. I remember saying that my concern for all American citizens in the region—a concern shared by the other consuls with respect to their communities—was that his government, his police, and the national government forces in Kivu all be in agreement that, whatever happened next week, this was not our affair. We needed to be protected from danger and, if necessary, extricated from Kivu in the quickest, safest manner possible before any violence began. Specifically, when the time came, we would count on him to see that we and our fellow citizens were protected by armed escort to the airport and given priority passage onto planes out of Kivu.

He said that this was precisely why he had invited us all to the stadium next week. He was going to carry that message not only to his subordinates but also to the people at large. He urged me to convince all the other foreign community leaders, especially from the West, to come to the stadium. I shook his hand and said I would try my best and that in any case I would be there.

A day before the rally at the stadium, I left the rowdy, cheerful crowd of Peace Corps volunteers at the consul's home under the supervision of the vice consul, who was a perfect host for this sort of occasion, and drove our beat-up Land Rover off to see somebody across town. I no longer remember whom I went to see, but I do recall the rush of adrenaline that came to me steering between the potholes of this eerily empty city, everybody waiting for what might happen tomorrow. It gave me such a high that I suddenly thought this must be what soldiers feel when they set off to do battle. No wonder there have always been—and will always be—wars.

. . . .

The next day the whole consular crowd, led by Hans and me, got to the stadium on time. We were given seats on the platform directly behind the rostrum. Looking out at the sea of faces in the stands, I never felt so white in my life. The commissioner stood up. Over the next hour in a graceful mixture of fluent French and Swahili, he caressed the crowd with his voice. I don't speak Swahili and can't remember all of the French, but I can recall bits:

> We are, as you may know, going to be imposing a curfew tonight, for the next several nights. So try and find a girl nearer home! [Pause for laughter and applause.] And if a gendarme or a soldier asks to see your ID, just show him that—no money, no food, no cigarettes, nothing else; just the ID. [More applause.] . . . .

Now, all of you remember or heard about white soldiers who did harm here before—and threaten to do so again. Look behind me! Look at those white faces [motioning us to stand up]. These people are NOT mercenaries. They are decent people who mean no harm. Some of them are useful to us, are here to help us have better health care and a more healthy economy. Some are here just to care for their own fellow citizens. In any case, they are our FRIENDS and our GUESTS. Do not let anybody harm them. You understand? [Applause]. . . .

In the end, the signal to the mercenaries to attack never came. A few days after the stadium rally, the curfew was ended. Word had reached the commissioner that the members of the Gisenyi round table had flown back to Europe. Our Peace Corps guests tottered home, and life went back to normal.

Bob Remole and the consul drove back into town in the new car and seemed puzzled by the vestiges they could see of a big party in the consul's residence. I figured I could wait until later to explain things; all I wanted was a good night's sleep and to get back to John in Kinshasa. And then I remembered a line from one of my favorite mystery writers, Dorothy Sayers: "Heroics that don't come off are the very essence of farce."

. . . .

It had already been an adventure to get to Bukavu in the first place. Starting out from Bujumbura (the capital of Burundi), our driver and my boss and I had been held up by Congolese border guards who wanted money. Having very little cash, we had offered the sandwiches we were carrying instead, and they accepted them but said, "Don't you have anything else to give us?"

I said, "What kind of thing?" and they answered they could use some books or newspapers, explaining that they were forgetting how to read for lack of practice. Remole and I handed over what French-language reading material we had with us and were allowed to continue our trip.

The next time I was asked to go to Bukavu, to replace the consul again, was a few months later. Remole came with me this time, too. I was glad to have the chance to go back to Kivu, and this time Remole wanted to add on a visit to the Congo's biggest game park at Virunga, accessible by road from Bukavu. The night before our planned departure on Air Zaire, we learned through a contact who worked at the airport that the flight was going to take off at 5 a.m. the next morning rather than at 9 a.m. Congratulating ourselves on our good intelligence network, we were there at 4 a.m. prepared to board.

At this point we ran into a new obstacle. My luggage was overweight, they claimed—and it may even have been true—and I would be charged excess baggage fees that, given the exchange rate we were using, were rather steep. Remole said, "It can't be helped. I will see that you are reimbursed for this." At 6 a.m. or thereabouts, we were allowed on board. There were few other passengers, presumably because others had not learned of the change in departure time.

After takeoff, the pilot made an announcement about "this flight to Mombasa," and my boss and I looked at one another. My boss said, "They don't even know the difference between Mombasa and Bujumbura. What a country!"

In a little while I went forward to use the toilet and, peeking into the first class section, found there were no passengers. This was puzzling. Usually flights from Kinshasa to Bujumbura were fully booked.

Back in my seat, I heard the next—and most memorable—announcement: "Passengers for Bujumbura, we aren't going to Bujumbura."

Remole, his face flushed with anger and disbelief, summoned the stewardess. She calmed him down, explaining that the plane was running late and would now not stop before Kenya. But not to worry, she said, it would stop in Bujumbura on the way back and we and our luggage would be disembarked then.

Our next stop turned out to be Nairobi, where only one passenger got off and nobody got on, though someone in an Air Zaire uniform—possibly our pilot?—got off and came back stuffing an envelope into his pocket. The next stop was, indeed, Mombasa, Kenya's historic East Coast port, where we all got out while the plane was refueled and many cartons of British cigarettes were loaded from floor to ceiling into the empty first-class cabin.

No passengers got on, though I seem to recall that there were fewer aboard when we took off again.

At some point as we were heading back westward across Africa, my boss asked the stewardess when we would be getting to Bujumbura. Perhaps that is why, some minutes later, an announcement came over the loudspeaker: "We are sorry to say we shall not be able to land at Bujumbura." The hostess then told my stupefied boss that, the flight having been delayed, it was now too dark, and Bujumbura's airfield had no night-lights.

The upshot was that, nearly twenty-four hours after check-in at the airport in Kinshasa, we were back there again, not having ever got off the plane except during the refueling. Oh, and we were charged a second time for my excess baggage. My airgram about this trip, widely circulated in Washington, began with a sentence from *Alice through the Looking-Glass:* "It takes all the running you can do, to keep in the same place."

Airgrams are yet another thing that no longer exist. Airgrams were sometimes described as "thumbsuckers" because they allowed the writer to give a rounder, fuller statement of a person or place or situation than one would normally do by cable. We were allowed to use upper- and lowercase in an airgram, instead of all caps, and could type it on a regular typewriter, making it much more readable. Airgrams were intended not to present urgent news but to provide the background that would give our intelligence people and the policy paper writers in Washington a fuller sense of the subject than they could otherwise easily obtain. Airgrams were also a great exercise for the drafter, in that they forced the reporting officer to think outside the box, to get to know more about a subject than would fit on a postage stamp. I loved writing them, and my bosses urged me to do them, partly because new officers at post could learn a lot from them. Nothing that long, slow, or discursive is produced in the field anymore by Foreign Service officers.

Back in Kinshasa, I was assigned a new officer to help me—a junior officer on her first tour as a diplomat. Black, beautiful, very bright, and fun to be with, she proved a delightful colleague and became a lifelong friend. But while in Kinshasa we both found to our surprise that she had problems as a woman that I had not encountered in the Congo.

Unlike most African Americans whose skin color betrayed them to the rather racist Congolese of those days as being of mixed blood and therefore not attractive to them, my young colleague was very black and could easily have been mistaken for an African. With her dark skin, good looks, charm, and single status, she attracted a lot of unwelcome attention from Congolese men. I would take her along to calls on my dissident friends and human rights contacts, and they would talk to me about the subject I had come to discuss. But they would often later phone her at home to ask her out on a date. By then, she was involved with an Englishman whom she later married. She had no interest in dating these men and was distressed not to be taken seriously as a diplomat by them. We never figured out a way to deal with the matter while we were together in Kinshasa, but she must have done so eventually, because years later she turned up in Brussels in John's old job of political counselor. She even arranged for me, after my retirement and John's death, to come back to Brussels and take over her job for some months when she had to leave Brussels early for an important onward assignment in West Africa.

On a later trip to Kivu, when I was alone, trying again to go by plane to Bujumbura and by embassy Land Rover from there to Bukavu, the obstacles to travel were more serious. Mobutu, in an effort to deal with mounting inflation, had decided to remove all five- and ten-zaire notes from circulation, replacing a small portion of them with new bills of the same denomination. In order to keep people from smuggling money and goods into and out of the country during the predictably chaotic period that followed, he had suddenly sealed the country's borders. Having flown into Bujumbura on Air Cameroun without any problem the day before, I was caught with my diplomatic passport and some diplomatic mail collected at Embassy Bujumbura to deliver to Bukavu, but with no way to convince the Burundi or Congolese border guards to let me through.

Not expecting this border closure, the Embassy Bujumbura dispatcher had assigned me a new Burundian driver, hired just that week. As usual, I had been assigned a Land Rover that looked like it was about to fall to bits. Waiting for the border to reopen, I stayed on in my rather nice Bujumbura hotel for a couple more days, watching from the terrace as the sunsets turned the hippos wading in Lake Tanganyika an improbable pink. But then I decided that nothing ventured, nothing gained. Nobody knew when the borders would reopen, and I was anxious to get to Kivu and do my job. I had already become fond of Kivu's lovely landscape and a number of the people I had come to know during the mercenary scare and was looking forward to getting to Bukavu again.

The next morning I told the driver we would go now. He shrugged his shoulders and got into the driver's seat, and I climbed in next to him.

Within twenty minutes we were at the first border barrier and the Burundian guards politely explained about the sealed border. I said, "Is this being done by the Burundian government?"

"Oh no, it's Mobutu!"

"Then let us through, and I will talk to Mobutu's guards."

Reluctantly, after warning that we would be back to them shortly, they opened the gate. A few minutes down the road we came to the barrier being manned by Zairian border guards. "Sorry, the border is sealed. You cannot come in."

I got out my diplomatic passport and my diplomatic mail: two rather unprepossessing canvas sacks but with fancy embassy seals on them. "Such rules," I said airily, "do not apply to diplomatic couriers. There are international treaties about this that your government has signed."

Both parts of this dialogue got repeated several times, but, when it became clear that short of force majeure we were not going to turn around, I saw some hesitation on the face of the senior guard and asked him, "Isn't there someone I could speak to about this matter? It could really blow up into a major issue between your country and mine."

"The only person you could speak to is the chief of police at Uvira [the subregional seat for that part of the Congo]."

"OK, let me see him!"

"I guess you could go, if two of us rode with you."

We invited them into the backseat, and under their guidance our driver found the way to the office of the chief of police. This man, who was very gracious and embarrassed, said in effect that such a decision was way above his pay grade.

"Well, who CAN decide?" I said, trying to keep the fractious note out of my voice.

"Only the subregional commissioner" (a Mobutu-appointed official).

"Then let's go see him!" Turning around to face the border guards sitting behind us, I asked, "How do we get to the subcommissioner?"

They asked the police chief, who gave our driver instructions to the subcommissioner's office. But when we got there, the men at the door said, "You've missed him. He has left to go home." It was afternoon by then.

With the bit between my teeth, I asked our passengers to ask where the subcommissioner's home was. They did, and we were on our way there when a big black car ahead of us disgorged a big black man who signaled us to stop.

"I am the subcommissioner for this subregion, and I gather you want to see me. What seems to be the problem?"

Greatly relieved to meet somebody who spoke fluent French, I said, "Sir, there really isn't any problem—or at least there shouldn't be. I am a diplomat carrying privileged diplomatic mail [pointing to the mail bags] to Bukavu. I am accredited to Zaire; I am IN Zaire . . ."

At this point he interrupted me with a smile, "So you are! So you are! And I strongly suggest that you stay in Zaire rather than try to use the road that goes in and out of Rwanda. The mountain road will mean you avoid border troubles, but do drive carefully," he said, looking at the driver. "It is a tricky road, especially at night, and we don't want any more problems, do we?"

It was in a triumphant mood that we returned to deposit the border guards—who by now had become backers of our cause—at their guard post. They gave us sticky sweet bottled soft drinks and detailed instructions to the driver how to negotiate the steep mountain passes en route to Bukavu.

The scenery was glorious, but the drive proved as hair-raising as we had been warned. There was a long stretch where, stopping first to take a stick and bang a metal gong that was positioned along the roadside, the driver proceeded to drive us along a road barely one car wide next to a steep drop of billiard-table green to a darkening valley below. Craning my neck to look down, I could just make out a black ribbon of river interspersed with dazzling white cataracts. The nearer view, while the light held, revealed all sorts of brightly colored wildflowers and flowering trees.

It also revealed that ours was the only car on the road. This was fortunate because if, despite our having sounded the warning gong, there had been a car coming the other way, one of us would have had to back up all the way along a dizzying collection of switchbacks to let the other car through. We finally got to the Bukavu Consulate late at night and I put the diplomatic mail in the vault—patting myself on the back for having remembered the combination to the metal cipher lock and grateful that the opening wheel had been restored to the vault door. I didn't want to bother my hostess, the wife of the absent consul, at that hour, and suggested the driver sleep in one office and I in another. We were beyond hunger by then and slept till morning.

. . . .

M y last visit to Bukavu occurred in 1980, after the State Department's Africa Bureau decided to close our consulate there. The US Congress did not agree, though it provided no funds to keep it open. So it was with some discretion that I was flown by our embassy's air attaché in his small US Air Force executive jet to Bukavu, where my instructions were to go to the consulate (which no longer had a staff) and collect the consular seals and any other items that must not fall into the wrong hands before the place was abandoned de facto. The air attaché, who was a tall, slim man who strongly resembled Steve Canyon of the comic strip, with a shock of white hair in a brush cut, was to wait for me and fly me back to Kinshasa.

I felt a little blue that the post was closing. I had lost my heart to this beautiful part of a mostly ugly country, and to its people who hailed me like a returning hero every time I came back after the mercenary scare.

Mainly to comfort myself as I sat in the copilot's seat, I had recited a sonnet I knew by heart by Edna St. Vincent Millay, about permitting her memory to recall the features, smiles, and words of a loved one "only until this cigarette is ended." We were flying at sunset, which I thought fit well with the last lines of the poem, addressed to the loved one: "But in your day, this moment is the sun / Upon a hill, after the sun has set."

To my surprise, the pilot then recited Robert Frost's entire poem "Stopping by Woods on a Snowy Evening," ending with the memorable lines: "But I have promises to keep / And miles to go before I sleep / And miles to go before I sleep." Many people are familiar with that poem, but I was not sure that I could recite it from start to finish as perfectly as he did. I said as much, and asked the attaché how he happened to know it so well.

He said, "I spent seven years in solitary in a North Vietnamese POW camp. And the chief prisoner of us Yanks taught me that poem by spelling it out, tapping on the wall I shared with him. I could never forget it. It kept my mind alive." It certainly put my little sorrows in a new perspective.

. . . .

Our assignment to the Congo led to my being advanced to the next higher rank. And the promotion board had, unusually, added a recommendation to the personnel bureau to the effect "Either give this woman a decent consular job or move her to the political cone [career specialty]." I replied by return mail to request transfer to the political cone; the request was granted and I remained a political officer ever after. John had also— more predictably—been promoted, making him eligible for the job he most wanted, political counselor in Brussels.

But quite aside from professional advancement, I had lived some moments that I would remember for a very long time. One was when John and I had been flown in the air attaché plane to a lunch hosted by Mobutu in Kisangani. I was included as one of the bag carriers for visiting State Department VIPs and for our ambassador. It was a memorable meal, though I must confess that, were it not for the honor of the thing, I might have been happy to skip the food. Mobutu liked to make his Western guests eat what he knew they would find repulsive, foods that were delicacies to some Congolese. Our ambassador was very brave on these occasions, and when he tasted things before his wife and children were served, they would wait to hear his comment. Putting a locust in his mouth and crunching it, he was heard to say in an upbeat voice, "That was not so bad . . . as the caterpillars."

Soon after that presidential lunch in 1979 came Thanksgiving, which John and I celebrated in typical Foreign Service tradition, by inviting any stray Americans who might be around and had no family to eat turkey with. Our choice was David and Sharon Shapiro, a Penn State demographer and his Canadian wife. We did not know them yet but had been told that, between the two of them, they had made friends all over the Congo, especially at the universities. At the same time we had been asked to provide a bed for a couple of nights—which we did gladly—to one of our best career diplomats, Bill Swing, an Africanist who spoke beautiful French and German. He was already on his way to being a legend in Africa and the Caribbean. He could take stenographic dictation and could do without sleep for days at a time, dancing and socializing when he was not working. Also staying with us at the embassy's request was Sophie Porson, a fabled State Department simultaneous interpreter from Portuguese or French into English.

Our houseguests had just been to Angola, on a hush-hush trip, and Bill Swing was writing up with great care what had been said on both sides to send to the anxiously waiting State Department and National Security Council. We had no diplomatic relations with Angola at the time, and so he had had to come to Kinshasa before he could write up his message and send it out. Sophie Porson (Swing told us) was such a good simultaneous interpreter that, during the discussions in Luanda, the Angolans had asked if she would interpret for their side, too. On Thanksgiving Day our houseguests were so busy writing up their notes that we served them some of their dinner in their bedrooms so that they could quickly get back to their work. We used the evening after the meal to get to know the Penn State couple, with whom we subsequently got into the habit of having Thanksgiving dinner whenever our paths crossed to make it possible.

The next night, Bill Swing was looking over his almost finished draft cable at about 2 a.m., while a bunch of us, including Robby and his wife, Linda, were lying down, practically asleep, on our well-padded carpet after an exhausting day. I was awake enough to hear Swing say to Sophie, the interpreter: "I have gone over my steno notes of what the Angolan side said, and I seem to be missing part of a sentence. Can you help?" She got out her steno pad, and I was amazed to see she had just a few big squiggles penciled on each page as she intoned, like a Delphic Sibyl, the exact Portuguese words that were echoing in her ears and then translated them into English. It was impressive to watch. Swing followed along from his steno notes and said, "Ah yes, thanks. These are the missing words!" At that point, John put on the CD player our favorite new disk, the then little-known Pachelbel Canon, performed by the St.-Martin's-in-the-Field orchestra under Sir Neville Marriner's baton. We all lay there, stretched out on the carpet, taking in the ravishing music. Being there and being accepted as part of this group of able and adventurous colleagues is one of the happiest memories of my life. I finally felt that I had started to be the kind of diplomat I wanted to be.

Chapter 15

Farewell to Africa

• • • • • • • • • • •

OUR TIME IN AFRICA ENDED SOONER than we had expected. Starting in the first half of 1980, John grew very thin and had more frequent attacks of what had been occasional "fevers of unknown origin" that had begun in Antwerp. He was still able to work, but would often get that wiped-out look again. Eventually our excellent Embassy Kinshasa doctor told John, "I don't know what you have, but it may be serious, and I don't believe it can be dealt with here. I want you out of here and am formally recommending that you curtail your assignment." (Our assignment had another year to run.)

Our new ambassador, Robert Oakley, on hearing the news, bowed to the inevitable, and, being himself married to a Foreign Service officer, graciously agreed to my curtailing too, to go wherever John went. His only price for my curtailing was that I write up four long analytical airgrams that I had promised to do in 1980 and which he now wanted me to do before I left, less than six months into the year.

John had already left weeks earlier, to go back to Washington to be seen by a round of doctors and to look for jobs for us both in a more salubrious place. The ambassador in Brussels, Anne Cox Chambers, whom he'd worked for two years earlier, soon tracked him down in Washington to offer him the job of political counselor, which had suddenly come open on her staff. John was delighted, but, again, he insisted there be a job for me; we were still waiting to learn about that.

Alone in Kinshasa, with nobody to tell me to stop writing and go home to bed, I managed to get the four reports written, while also saying good-bye to as many of my contacts as I could. There were numerous parties given for me, and I was feeling sad about leaving.

On my last day, I was still at the apartment before leaving for the airport, and my new political counselor, Tony Dalsimer, and I tried to trap my frightened but cunning Siamese cat, Pounce. Pounce wanted at all costs to avoid being put in the carrying case—which he no doubt associated with visits to the vet. My new boss (a spry, slender man) and I had most of the sofa cushions down on the floor, as well as a couple of the bed mattresses, trying to create barriers to this streamlined, speeding animal, with its ears back, determined to escape us. The doorbell rang, and it was my giant Congolese friend, the man who had taught me the first rules of being a political officer nearly two years earlier sitting in a café in Kinshasa's least Europeanized quarter. He looked on, holding his shaking belly, as Pounce continued to outmaneuver us until, finally, we caught him and put him in the carrying case.

My Congolese politician friend then explained that he was here now to protest my departure and to ask where on earth I was going and why. I told him John had left for health reasons, and so I of course wanted to be with him. "All right," he said, "but where are you going?" I told him it was almost certainly going to be back to Brussels.

His face cleared. "Brussels, eh! Then you're not really leaving us." (And indeed, I learned that no Congolese traveled to Europe without spending some time in Belgium. This meant that, though I never returned to the Congo, I was able to keep up with a number of my best Congolese contacts for years afterward and occasionally report to Washington on how they see political developments there. All these years later, this is still true.)

I remember even more clearly the night before—my last evening in the Congo. I had invited to dinner at my apartment David Shapiro, the Penn State academic (whose wife was away), and a college-age intern whom I had been mentoring in the political section.

Why dinner at home? I was well known to the secret police (as "Madame Judith") because my job was by then primarily that of cultivating the theoretically lawful opposition to the Mobutu regime. I could reasonably assume that the secret police would always be looking for an excuse to expel me. That meant I was obliged to cash in my dollars for zaires at the legal exchange rate, which imposed five or more times the going rate for zaires on the world market. The irony is that I would have been better off if I had still been just a wife and not an officer. The wives of my embassy colleagues could earn lots of zaires teaching English at a school set up by the US government. Paid at the going free market rate, the wives earned enough zaires to live on, enabling their husbands to bank much of their dollar salaries. Other resident foreigners avoided the official rate by exchanging their foreign currency on the black market. (The nearest currency black market was at the Catholic Church's national administrative headquarters, next to our embassy.)

So, for John and me, though not for most others, a loaf of French bread in a Kinshasa bakery cost five dollars, a pineapple from a fruit stand cost even more, and dinner at a restaurant was out of the question. I was cooking out of my Julia Child *French Chef* paperback, using groceries from our embassy commissary, which got most of its supplies in South Africa.

Thanks to the commissary, I was able to serve for that last meal sea scallops (frozen ones from Sydney, Australia) and American frozen broccoli, with a dessert of baked South African Granny Smith apples, all accompanied by good French Sancerre. The table was set with what was left in the apartment after the packers had left: dented metal measuring cups and measuring spoons, paper plates, plastic knives and forks, empty peanut butter jars, bathroom glasses, and paper towels.

Since the scallops would only take a few minutes to pan fry in South African butter, dried herbs, and garlic, I had not put them on the stove yet when the doorbell rang. My best Congolese friend, Makanda, one of a small but well-known group of parliamentarians who dared to press publicly for genuinely democratic governmental institutions for their country, had come to say good-bye. There were enough scallops, so I invited him to stay for dinner.

Makanda could see I was on easy terms with the other guests and did not freeze up, as he might have done with other people he did not know. In any case, this was my last evening in Kinshasa, and he wanted to be there. The intimacy and ease of our friendship—like brother and sister or school friends since first grade—was well established by then. (His wife had met me and had clearly decided I was not a threat and so he could come see me alone.) We were close in age and had found that we could use the same eyeglasses, so if one of us forgot to bring them and there was something to be read, we would pass the glasses back and forth. He was a professor of sociology, and we had a common interest in how ethnic politics and urban and rural allegiances affect how people think and behave. (That was one of the subjects I had been writing about before my ambassador would let me leave.) Over the previous eighteen months or so, Makanda and I had spent many hours together, alone or at dinner parties with John and with other opposition figures.

He had explained to me once why Mobutu's regime was so corrupt. He said that if somehow Mobutu were out of the way—run over accidentally by a truck, say—and (more unlikely) Makanda were given the job of president, "By a week from Tuesday, I would be as big a crook as he is. Why? Because, without adequate political structures, checks and balances such as Montesquieu envisioned, you have to choose whether to kill all the competition—à la Sékou Touré—or behave like Mobutu, who would much rather buy off his potential rivals or opponents. In the latter case, however, you need to have infinite amounts of cash."

Makanda did not see himself as a potential president of his country, but he was a man of influence within the opposition. The Carter administration was approaching its end, and the Congolese pro-democracy dissidents came to believe that now might be their best chance to force concessions from Mobutu. Makanda had therefore encouraged—from within his own small band of open opponents of Mobutu's dictatorship—the two who had the best chance of becoming the next president if there were fair elections (one of them being my giant friend) to put aside their personal rivalry and keep their group united. To that end, he persuaded them to always go to see Mobutu together, never alone. That way, Mobutu could not seduce one of them to join him, or claim that he had done so.

I nominated Makanda for an International Visitor grant before I left post. I was in the United States in the fall, on home leave and preparing for my new assignment in Brussels (where John had finally wangled a job for me) when Makanda's grant program brought him to New York and Washington. I took the train to New York to meet him and we walked across the

Brooklyn Bridge together one mild Sunday morning, starting at Brooklyn Heights, and enjoyed the iconic view, ending up eating Chinese dim sum when we reached the Manhattan Chinatown end.

In Washington, we walked down Dupont Circle streets together, a white woman and a very black man, with nobody paying the slightest attention to us, so unlike what would have been the case there a mere dozen years earlier.

When we got together that evening in Washington, Makanda was looking really happy and was eager to tell me about his call that morning on a senior official in the Africa Bureau of the Department of State. In answer to Makanda's question as to whether the new (expected to be Reagan) administration would be as pro-human rights as the outgoing Carter regime was, this official had gone on at length about how human rights was an enduring American value and, of course, it would be the same in the Reagan administration.

I was so angry I could barely speak. While in the Congo, I had spent a lot of time telling these opposition figures, who had so bravely raised their heads above the parapet, that they must not count on us to protect them. I would habitually tell them, "If you want to take the risk, by all means do so, but you must not expect us to be there for you. This is YOUR country and YOUR risk." In everything I said to these brave men, I was always thinking back to 1956 when our Radio Free Europe broadcasts had encouraged the Hungarians to rise up against their Soviet-led oppressors, only to be mowed down when we would not—or, more likely, could not—come to their aid.

Walking alongside Makanda on a Washington street in mid-1980 with Ronald Reagan the favorite to succeed Carter as president, and given the Cold War games being played in Africa, I was convinced that our government would not be willing to turn against Mobutu, a noncommunist, however crooked or dictatorial he might be. I knew that many people, especially those likely to be setting policy in the future administration, were fed to the teeth with the heavy focus on human rights of the Carter years; they thought it impractical at best and irrelevant at worst. I was sure the State Department official Makanda had called on was equally aware of this.

When I had control of my voice again, I told Makanda that, however convinced his State Department informant might be that the United States would always come out strongly for human rights, he, Makanda, must assess the risks for himself. I said he should do what he felt comfortable doing, keeping always in mind that Washington might not be able to intervene on his behalf or that of his fellow members of the opposition.

I had pushed for the International Visitor grant for Makanda and for other political dissidents as a way of saying to Mobutu: "Watch out! Uncle Sam will notice if anything happens to these people." It was all I could think to do to protect them. But, ultimately, sometime after John and I had left Africa, Mobutu found Makanda too articulate an opponent and had him jailed.

At least Makanda's jail was in Kinshasa, where friends and family could provide food, so he did not starve, unlike some convicts sent to prisons too far from their families, where the guards stole the prisoners' food money after the guards' pay had been stolen by others up the line.

Once Makanda returned to Kinshasa after his US visit, I had not dared to complicate his life by writing to him. Thus I did not learn that he had been sent to jail until 1986 when John and I were living in The Hague, where John was chargé d'affaires.

Then one day I received word in The Hague that Makanda was in Brussels and had called our consular section there, trying to reach me. I was given a phone number to call, but the person at the other end was highly suspicious. She had not heard of a Madame Heimann and did not know where Makanda was. Feeling frustrated, I finally said I had been asked to call this number, and if she was in touch with Makanda, would she please tell him that Judith had tried to contact him.

"Judith? Madame Judith? Sa soeur Judith?"

"Yes," I said, "Yes, yes."

"Oh," she said, "Makanda is in hospital and he wants to see you. You can reach him in his room there. Here's the number.'"

I called. He sounded bad. "I am very ill," he said, "so come soon." I drove down from The Hague the next day, and his doctor waylaid me in the corridor. He wanted to know who I was, and if I could explain to the patient that he had this dreadful new illness, AIDS.

I arrived in Makanda's room, steeling myself for what he would look like. Having always been slightly plump, he was now emaciated, but the mild expression on his face was the one I was so fond of. We talked about what each of us had been doing in the intervening six years. He said he had spent most of the time in jail and had caught some sort of bug there and (as a routine part of being medically treated in the Congo) he had been given a shot of something.

Since the 1940s when the previously prevalent disease yaws was shown to be curable by a single inoculation of penicillin, much of the Third World continues to believe it has not received adequate medical treatment unless a shot is administered. The irony is that, because there was hardly a clean, sterilized needle to be found anywhere in Kinshasa, it was almost certainly the needle that infected Makanda with the HIV virus.

I bent over my friend's hand and kissed it, my tears falling on his knuckles. Initially worried that my tears could carry germs that would make him sicker, given his degraded immune system, I gradually accepted the evidence of my eyes. He was going to die—probably soon. I told him what the doctor had told me, and he did not seem surprised. He looked up at me and said evenly, "It is just an illness, like any other." This common-sense approach to his malady—at a time when in my own country people who might carry the HIV virus were being treated like lepers—took my breath away.

Faced with the new fact I had relayed to him, Makanda was as usual thinking of others rather than of himself. He asked me to tell his wife, because she needed to know. He said I should also speak to his son, who was a pediatric heart surgeon in Belgium, but he said he wished his daughter Françoise was there. He wanted her to be the head of the family after he was gone. I nodded agreement. I knew her, and agreed that she had the brains and guts needed if, after Makanda's death, his family still faced persecution by the Mobutu regime.

I went to see Makanda half a dozen times over the next six weeks, driving down in my VW Jetta from Holland. We talked about everything and nothing, and it was as easy as it had always been. Through the influence of a Belgian friend, Marc Van Montagu, who is one of his country's greatest scientists, I got the offer of a new and very scarce drug, AZT, for Makanda. But when I got the news that he could have it, his doctor said it would be a waste to use it on him. The disease was too far along.

The last time I went to see Makanda was the day before he died. There was nothing much to say; we had said it all. I stumbled out blindly to the elevator and back to the parking lot and drove home somehow. The next day, a phone call told me he was gone. But in my heart and in the hearts of many of his countrymen, he will always have a special place.

Chapter 16

Back in the Heart of Europe

• • • • • • • • • • • • • • •

THE AMERICAN AMBASSADOR TO Belgium, newspaper magnate Anne Cox Chambers, had liked John's work as consul general in Antwerp. There, he had become friends with the Flemings who would lead Belgian governments for decades to come. When she learned that John was leaving Kinshasa early, she tracked him down in Washington, where he was looking for a job in a healthy place, and offered him the job of political counselor, which had unexpectedly come open at her embassy. Despite John's fevers, Ambassador Chambers was sure that he was the person most likely to accomplish what her embassy had been assigned as its highest priority: to get Belgium to agree to the stationing of intermediate-range ground-launched cruise missiles on its soil.

The government of Belgium's position on the basing of these nuclear missiles was ambivalent. The cruise missile question brought to the surface the intrinsic contradictions between different strands of opinion simultaneously held by many of the same people in the government coalition and the opposition. Regardless of party and linguistic affiliation, Belgians favored any policy that reduced the chance of war breaking out in Western Europe. Belgium had been the battlefield for two such wars in the twentieth century, and its people were anxious to avoid that happening again. After World War II, Belgians exhibited a strong pacifist strain, especially apparent in Flemish politics, a visceral dislike of nuclear weapons, and an uneasy recollection that America had been the only country ever to use them—and on a civilian population. And many Belgians (like many other Western Europeans, especially those on the Left) had opposed the Vietnam War and our Bay of Pigs attempt to overthrow the

Castro regime in Cuba. They were not ready to support the United States unconditionally on defense matters.

The cruise missile deployment issue increased the tension between Belgian antinuclear, pacifist instincts and the Belgians' equally strong desire to behave like a good NATO ally. NATO, by then headquartered in Belgium after de Gaulle had kicked it out of France, was as popular with the Belgians as was the European Union, also headquartered in Brussels. This pro-NATO feeling arose in part because, under NATO, the United States picked up the bulk of the tab for the armed forces and the weapons required to deter a Soviet attack on Western Europe, thus allowing the European Union's political and economic union to advance and its member states to devote much of their national budgets to building up enviable social safety nets.

In the early 1970s, when we first arrived in Belgium, it had been a revelation to John and me—and is a fact still little known to Americans at large—that Belgium under a government then headed by Christian Democrats—not Socialists—had a social safety net Americans could envy. Belgians—like their French, German, Dutch, and Scandinavian neighbors—had almost free, good public education through university; reasonably priced infant-care facilities; low-cost, excellent health care; ample old-age pensions; generous paid vacation time; and long-term unemployment compensation. Belgian salaries and wages were low, but people did not need to save for anything big, except to buy their own home if they wanted to and maybe a car—though most people used the excellent network of buses, trams, and trains to get to work.

With this widespread popular support of NATO and the EU, Belgium in the late 1970s was ready to show solidarity with other NATO allies in allaying anxiety in West Germany about the recent deployment of the Soviet SS-20 missile by agreeing to deploy Pershing II and cruise intermediate-range nuclear missiles on their own soil. In 1979, the Belgian government, under a Christian Democrat/Socialist coalition, formally agreed to accept some of these missiles, as did four other European countries, namely, the UK, West Germany, Italy, and the Netherlands.

But soon thereafter, for various reasons too complicated for this memoir, deploying intermediate-range nuclear missiles in Western Europe became deeply unpopular with Europeans, including the citizens of Belgium and the four other countries that had agreed to deploy them.

In the summer of 1980, while still in Washington after leaving Kinshasa, John had been briefed about the mid-range missile deployment issue and told, basically, "You won't be able to get the Belgians to accept these missiles, given the feeling there these days, but you have to try." John had long hoped to become the political counselor in Brussels. And now, heading off to that job, he was determined to do his best at it.

Thanks to his fluent Dutch and his previous assignment as consul general in Antwerp, he was already on excellent terms with the successive Belgian prime ministers and foreign ministers from the Flemish Christian Democratic party that had headed virtually every Belgian government coalition since 1974. Also, from our earlier time in Brussels in the early 1970s, thanks in part to introductions by Kenneth Brown, a Foreign Service colleague and friend ever since, John and I had many close friends in the Flemish Socialist Party, a party that had been in almost every Christian Democratic–led coalition. Even when the Socialists left the government in 1981 to join the opposition for the next six years, John continued to have easy access to the Socialist party leaders, who, in opposition, had become the most vocal opponents of basing nuclear missiles on Belgian soil.

By 1981 (John's first year back in Brussels), the NATO-Soviet arms race was speeding ahead. There was popular alarm among our European allies, and even among some prestigious Americans, that NATO deployment of intermediate-range missiles in Western Europe might make conceivable a nuclear war fought in Europe using these missiles.

In mid-1981, a movement composed of tens of thousands of women protesters established semipermanent "peace camps" along the perimeter fences of more than a dozen suspected nuclear weapons bases and ordnance factories in Britain and on the continent, making headlines worldwide. Within months, newly elected President Reagan offered a "zero-zero option" by which the United States would eliminate its new intermediate-range missiles if the Soviets would dismantle all their newly deployed SS-20s and their earlier intermediate weapons: the SS-4s and SS-5s. During the next two years of US-Soviet talks, the United States continued to favor its zero option but also suggested an interim agreement under which both sides would have equally low numbers of intermediate nuclear weapons deployed.

In the fall of 1982, hundreds of thousands of marchers turned out in New York's Central Park to support the demand of such esteemed US foreign policy experts as George Kennan, Madeleine Albright, and former CIA head William Colby for a total freeze on the production of nuclear weapons by everybody.

There was no likelihood that the Reagan administration or Britain would be deterred from cruise missile deployment in Europe by such protests, but what countries like Belgium and the Netherlands might do was more of a question. During roughly the same years as the original US-Soviet talks on the subject, Helmut Schmidt's Social Democrats in Germany and Belgium's Socialists moved from government to the opposition, where they led strong popular movements opposing the basing of these nuclear missiles in their lands.

I recall many complicating factors that would temporarily influence how the Belgian government and the public viewed the missile deployment issue. For once, Washington and much of the world were following closely what little Belgium might decide to do. Conceivably, if Belgium refused to accept deployment of the missiles on its soil, so might the Netherlands and even—if it fell into Social Democratic hands again—West Germany.

John and I left Belgium for the States in 1984, a couple of years before the last act in this drama. In the end, Belgium followed through on its 1979 commitment to deploy the missiles on its soil. John's role was undoubtedly only one of many in bringing that result about; but as recently as January 2015 I was told again—this time by a former political-military adviser to Louis Tobback, who had been the leading Flemish Socialist opponent of the cruise missiles' deployment in Belgium—that Tobback was one of many Belgians who saw John's role as crucial in getting those missiles deployed.

. . . .

In order to get John to Brussels, the State Department's European Bureau had done its best to find a job there for me, on virtually no notice. They came up with a job that existed for only a year, the product of a late Carter administration idea to base a handful of Foreign Service officers around Western Europe. These officers, of which I was one, were to report back to state and local governments in the United States about European solutions to problems at subnational levels. These included such matters as district heating, care of the elderly, restoration of historic monuments, waste disposal, and coordination of firefighting. Some of the European ideas that I reported on were new to Americans, such as a Dutch program for refitting ordinary housing to suit the needs of elderly tenants or owners, coordinated with visits from medical and social service providers to allow people to "age in place."

The motive behind this new State and Local Government Office in the State Department was to try to build a state and local political constituency at home that would appreciate the work done by the Foreign Service abroad, given that the bulk of our diplomatic achievements could not be made public and did not seem to directly affect the welfare of ordinary Americans.

Although we all assumed from the beginning that my job would disappear as soon as President Carter left office, I had fun traveling all over Italy, BENELUX, and France, finding interesting solutions to various subnational problems that might also work in America. I would then write them up for publication in state and local government newsletters back home.

When it became clear that my job would soon evaporate, our ambassador to the European Union, George Vest, conspired with our new ambassador to Belgium, Charles Price, to find me another job for at least the next six months (January–July 1981). My new job would be to become the first "European Community rover" to provide an extra pair of hands in Embassy Brussels's political section during the Belgian "presidency" (Eurospeak for the six-month-long chairmanship of the European Council, the political decision-making body of the European Community).

During Belgium's six months at Europe's helm, I worked alongside an able, seasoned political officer, Ed Fugit. Ed had a number of good foreign ministry contacts who spoke French; I cultivated the ones who spoke Dutch; he knew West and South Africa; I knew Central Africa and Southeast Asia. At one point, to express his pleasure that I spoke Dutch, the Fleming who chaired the EU Africa working group walked me to the elevator of the

Foreign Ministry in order to quietly slip a copy of the Dutch-language confidential minutes of the last meeting into my hands.

It was through this assignment that I learned the single most important fact an American diplomat could learn about the EU in the early 1980s: that the EU was the biggest, richest, most powerful international organization that the United States would never be able to join. Not only could we not join it, but we outsiders were not supposed to be told what was discussed in their meetings in any detail, nor which country espoused which policy, who said what to whom, or what were going to be the next topics for serious discussion and decision.

Given that all ten EU member states at the time (Greece, Britain, Ireland, Denmark, France, West Germany, Italy, Netherlands, Belgium, and Luxembourg) were also in NATO, the barring of American diplomats from knowing what some of our closest allies were saying and doing together regarding foreign policy matters that we cared about was a problem for Washington.

I was surprised to learn that many foreign policy matters in EU countries were being handled almost entirely by junior and midlevel diplomats. These young people would send draft policy statements to their counterparts in the other member states via their classified EU wireless circuit without even informing *their own* superiors. Then, unless the matter was a sensitive one to a member state, the policy would be rubber-stamped at a ministerial meeting held in whatever country currently had the EU chair.

The US mission to the UN would meet in New York with its NATO allies in the autumn, ahead of the UN General Assembly session, to discuss foreign policy matters that were coming up at the UN General Assembly that were not specifically within NATO's purview. And to our UN ambassador's dismay, he and his staff would raise topic after topic with these allies, only to be told repeatedly that the subject we wanted their support on was no longer open for discussion. The EU ten, despite their NATO membership, had already committed themselves to a common EU position on the matter.

I go into this level of detail because to some extent the problem remains. The European Union has twenty-eight member states as I write, and there is even less willingness on the part of the EU presidency (which now does most of its work in Brussels and has a permanent president and its own foreign service) to reopen subjects on which the EU member states have already reached consensus. Though the State Department deals better with the EU bureaucracy now than in the past, the White House often prefers to deal with the big NATO members—Germany, Britain, and France—as if these countries were entirely free to determine their own foreign policies (with the exception of trade matters) without regard to commitments they may have made to their EU partners.

This problem does not seem to go away, no matter who is in the White House. The Europeans noticed, for example, that President Obama spent several days in India during one of his trips abroad in his first term in office but did not pay an official call on EU headquarters in Brussels until he was in his second term.

Awkward as the EU is for us to deal with, given that we are not a member, I am not alone among people following European affairs in believing the EU's existence is the most positive political development since the end of World War II—and that it is generally in America's interest to strengthen the EU's ability to act as one in political and security matters. By providing a common market that stimulates economic growth in countries that believe in individual rights and respect the rule of law, the EU was crucial after World War II in attracting former dictatorships such as Italy, Spain, Portugal, and Greece toward a stronger commitment to democratic principles and practices. Similarly, I am convinced that the EU's economic success in those days, as witnessed on East German television sets, had as much to do with the fall of the Wall in 1989 as did the United States' making the arms race too expensive for the Soviet competition.

After doing this EU "rover" job in Brussels, I was asked to do the same job in Copenhagen, which was the next place to hold the EU presidency. My first call there was on a very young-looking man who headed the United Nations office in his Foreign Ministry and who, ex officio, chaired the EU working group on UN matters. I had brought along to share with him a "non-paper" on US policy about imprisoned Ethiopian princesses, which I asked him to share with the EU United Nations working group. He was frank in admitting that this was the first he had heard of the matter, but when the EU Council came out a few weeks later with a position on the subject very close to ours, I felt this was proof that I had reached the right person at the right time.

Bonn (then the capital of West Germany) had the EU presidency after Copenhagen. When I was assigned as the rover there, I would work from 8:30 a.m. until 10:00 p.m. Monday through Thursday without stopping for dinner and often without lunch. I had the loan of a wonderfully competent—if hilariously foul-mouthed—secretary who liked to work late, typing my cables into the tricky format then used for sending them. She caught all my grammatical errors as she went along. I would be back in Brussels in the early hours of Friday morning, having driven four hours straight from work, returning to Bonn on Sunday night.

I had not expected to like Germany or the Germans. I had imagined that they would all look like the beefy Bavarian politician Franz Josef Strauss. I was therefore unprepared to meet the German political director, Franz Pfeffer, who looked like a dark-haired version of the willowy British actor Leslie Howard and had at least as much charm.

At one point early in my stay in Bonn, I was dismayed to find I had to call on this very senior Foreign Ministry official three times in one day. Wilting with embarrassment the third time, I started to shake the political director's hand while making excuses. He kept my hand in his while gently saying, "I think we are beginning to get the right rhythm."

Although not all his colleagues were as handsome as he, they outdid each other in making me feel welcome, letting me know what I needed to know, and taking account of my government's views. If I only had time to phone an EU working group chairman at his German Foreign Ministry office, I learned to allot at least a half hour to the call and to have my notebook and pencil handy to write down all the useful things he would tell me.

Our Bonn embassy was then headed by Ambassador Arthur Burns, who had been chairman of the Board of Governors of the Federal Reserve System from 1970 to 1978. An Austrian by birth, Burns was enormously respected by the Germans. He had the personal style of a brilliant, cranky, and intimidating elderly professor who liked to skewer his students with awkward questions.

As one of America's leading economists, Burns got annoyed one day at an embassy staff meeting and asked if anybody knew what "M1" meant. The question went round the table until a new assistant military attaché said, "It's a gun." It is, a .30 caliber rifle. But what Burns meant was the term, familiar to anyone who has taken an introductory economics course, denoting all cash and other assets in a money supply that are easily convertible to cash.

Another time at a staff meeting, a young Foreign Service officer reported on a visit by a congressional delegation for which he had been the "control officer." The officer ended his report by saying a bit fatuously that the visit had been "a great success."

Most ambassadors would have let the remark go; it was the sort of comment often made in such circumstances. But Burns, after a few puffs on his pipe, said to the poor guy: "Tell me, [puff, puff] by what criteria do you judge the visit [puff, puff] as having been a great success?"

Standing up, with his eyes popping out, the young man named a couple of policy issues that the visit had moved forward and ended by saying: "And furthermore, none of the principal visitor's luggage was lost." He sat back down amid a hail of applause.

I had one moment of interaction with Ambassador Burns that I won't ever forget. This was my third EU presidency, and I was struck anew in Bonn at how clueless Washington seemed about how to engage with the EU on foreign policy matters. In those days, the State Department and the White House tended to ignore the fact that, in an EU context, our NATO allies were making policy behind our backs and without consulting us. Our policy makers at home seemed to feel that if the United States was not a member of an organization, its activities could hardly be important. They continued to try to deal with each member state bilaterally and were surprised each time at how ineffective this approach was.

I finally got riled up enough to draft a cable that I wanted Ambassador Burns to send out as his own personal message.[1] I wanted this one to indicate that Burns had sent it himself, because I wanted him to be seen as alerting Washington to what I saw as a serious problem in our diplomatic relations

_____

1. As became clear at the time of the WikiLeaks scandal, few outsiders know that all cables from the State Department go out as if signed by the secretary of state (unless the secretary is out of the country), and all cables sent from one of our embassies go out as if signed by the ambassador (unless he or she is away); but few outgoing cables are actually seen by the secretary or by the ambassador.

with some of our most important partners. At one point in the cable, I contrasted the speed and frequency of our dealings with the EU member states with the way they dealt with one another, and used the image of our Pony Express trying to catch up with their superfast Trans European Express trains.

The political counselor and deputy political counselor in Bonn were intrigued by my draft message but cautious. They suggested we all go up to see the DCM, an immensely able officer, who made an appointment for all of us to see Ambassador Burns. The next day, sitting at a long table in Burns's office with my bosses seated some distance from me, I sat opposite the old professor, puffing on his pipe between half-sentences.

The ambassador said something along the lines of: "I have read [puff, puff] your cable with interest. And [puff, puff] if I were writing it [puff, puff] I would have eliminated all the adjectives and [puff, puff] most of the adverbs." He paused and nobody said a word. " But I am not sure [puff, puff] that it isn't better the way you wrote it. [Puff puff.]" Then, looking over to my bosses, he said, "Add a sentence [puff, puff] that says 'I read this cable and approve it' and send it!" I walked on air for days.

. . . .

A month before the German presidency ended, Embassy Brussels called me back to be a policy aide to Ambassador Charles Price. (John and I worked for many political ambassadors, those chosen from outside the career service because they were alleged to be friends of the president. The rationale was that their ignorance of foreign affairs was offset by their ability to "get the president on the phone." In my experience, Charlie Price was the only noncareer ambassador actually able to do so on a regular basis.) Ambassador Price got me reassigned to Brussels, he *said*, so that I could write speeches for him and do research on political-military subjects. Thinking back, I now suspect he wanted me to be there with John, who was still handling his office duties brilliantly but was looking very thin and wiped out.

Soon after I got back to Brussels to stay, we learned what had been making John ill for seven years: a previously undetected cancerous tumor in the colon. Stunned by the news, John phoned Betsy Schell, a good friend in Brussels who was a Harvard-trained medical doctor, and asked her if he shouldn't get a second opinion. She said, "This is your second opinion. I know your doctor. Get the thing taken out tomorrow."

Although it was good to know what John had, it was not exactly cheery news. The surgery went well but was followed by a long series of radiation treatments meant to kill off any cancer cells that might have metastasized into nearby organs. The treatments had the side effect of exhausting John further and giving him nausea and stomach cramps. In those days there were no chemotherapies for colon cancer.

On the plus side, we were ideally placed to handle an invalid, with a wonderful cook/housekeeper and great friends and colleagues. Not least of these were Ambassador Charles Price and his wife, Carol, who always seemed to know just what to bring or send to make John more comfortable.

John's bosses in Brussels and Washington were still anxious to keep him on the job because of his knowledge of how things worked in Belgium and his unrivaled access to the key players. We did not talk much to others about John's illness. In those days the word *cancer* was seen as a warning that death would come soon. If it were widely known that John had this disease, it might make it impossible for him to get good jobs if he did recover. Meanwhile, for a month after John's surgery, I had been moved back to the political section to help his deputy mind the store.

Then, in November 1983, about the time a new ambassador arrived, John recovered his strength and went back to heading the political section, and I went upstairs to work as speech writer and aide to the new noncareer ambassador, Geoffrey Swaebe.

At the time, I found it a hardship to be moved around on almost no notice and never to be sure whether I would have a job a few months hence. Looking back from this distance, I realize how lucky John and I were to have been given such special treatment by the Department of State and two embassies in Belgium.

. . . .

In January 1984, John and I learned we were being reassigned to the State Department in July. Thanks in part to that Pony Express cable sent from Bonn, I would be working in the Regional Political-Economic

Office of the State Department's European Bureau—the office that I had been reporting to from Europe. There, I would be on the other end of the phone while the new "rover" reported to me over the next two years what was happening during the successive six-month "presidencies" of another four EU member states.

Returning to the States that summer, after so long away, required great adjustments for John and me. (The kids were then grown-ups who had been in American schools from the age of fifteen.) I did not know how to be a diplomat at home. For example, when we were invited to the Nixon White House because John had arranged the program for the state visit of Malaysian premier Tun Abdul Razak, I went off to buy a dress for the occasion and turned up at the White House as the only female of the State Department contingent in a dress suitable for office wear; the other American women all knew to wear long dinner dresses. I looked around the room and noticed the only other woman who looked to be as ill at ease as I was: Pat Nixon. I took little comfort from that.

In my office in the State Department, everybody seemed to be isolated in his or her cubicle, nobody telling the others what he or she was doing. Most of the officers were pleasant people and capable at their work, but many of the secretaries were not as ready to help the officers as were those I had known abroad. They were all in the Civil Service, not the Foreign Service, and were recruited, trained, promoted, disciplined, and rewarded by an entirely different system. For me, the last straw was that all the windows were sealed closed, and the air-conditioning in the office was so icy that I had to buy silk ski underwear to wear under my summer suits.

This was the first and only time while a career officer that I worked at the State Department, and I now understood why John used to say, "I would rather sweep up in a Chinese store than any job in Washington." John was now serving as a Foreign Service Inspector, swanning around interesting capitals in Europe and Africa, checking out how well our embassies and consulates functioned, and how they could do their job better. It was work he loved and did well—seeing and solving management problems. Meanwhile, I needed to find a way to make my workplace tolerable.

Some five months into my time there, I was asked to organize the Christmas party. Given the atmosphere in the office, it would require herculean efforts to make the event other than dismal. I discovered that one of the Civil Service secretaries had a really good singing voice, and so I built from that. In high school and summer day camp, I used to write parody songs to known melodies and would get the other kids to sing them with me. So I sat down at one of the office's three new computers. These were the first computers in the office for officers to use and were lined up side by side in the middle of the room.

At the computer keyboard, I quickly composed a number of comic lyrics about the European Union and set them to Christmas season melodies. My favorite was to the tune of "Angels We Have Heard on High":

> Sources close to Jacques Delors
> Say he finds Brussels a bore.
> Nothing that he tries to do
> Will make one market by '92.
> Oh, oh oh oh oh oh, oh oh oh oh oh, All they say is no to me
> When I ask for unity.
> Oh oh oh oh oh oh Why don't I just go
> Find a job in gay Pa-ree.
> Brussels is too slow-ow for me.

Writing these songs out and humming them with my new secretary friend, we began to attract the attention of some of our colleagues, who got in the habit of doing work on the computers and sharing jokes, comments, and information with others sitting alongside. John had once said to me that every well-functioning office has a village well where people gather informally. The three computers had become the village well.

The singing secretary had a good memory as well as a great voice, and I was able to get us both word perfect on several songs covering every aspect of our office's work. We then invited the staff of the European Mission to the United States to our Christmas party. We had printed out copies and rehearsed the more willing of our colleagues to sing with us. After that party, colleagues would ask me to write parody songs for a birthday, promotion, or onward assignment of one of our number, and the office ceased being a place I dreaded coming to every morning.

. . . .

Soon, though, something occurred that I had dreaded more. In the spring of 1985 John felt ill again, enough to get another physical exam. It showed he had cancer in one of his lungs. The surgeon spoke to me while John was being prepped for the operation. He said that nobody knew yet whether this was a new cancer or a spread from the colon. I knew so little; I asked him which would be better for John's prospects. He said a new cancer would be better, because if it was a spread from the colon, that meant it was able to move to all parts of his body. I remember waiting in what would be John's room at George Washington University Hospital to learn how the operation had gone. After a few hours, the surgeon came in before John returned. Looking grim, he said the biopsy was not back yet but he knew for sure, by the ugliness of the cells, that this was a metastasis of colon cancer.

"What happens next?" I asked. The doctor said we should ask the oncologist, but, as best he could guess, nothing more would be done now except to let John's body adjust to having not as much lung as before. There still was no chemotherapy for colon cancer.

That was the last that we heard of John's cancer until twelve years later, in 1997. We had no way of knowing that John would go on so long without any more symptoms—or why. Meanwhile, however, we were determined not to wreck our lives waiting for a recurrence. Looking back on it, I think that was the smartest decision we ever took.

. . . .

At work, I began enjoying different aspects of my job. In those days, the mid-1980s, the State Department cared so little about exclusively European multilateral political organizations that one middle-grade officer (me) in the department's European Regional Political and Economic Affairs office had the entire job of dealing with the EU's political cooperation and with the Council of Europe, the European Parliament, and other European non-EU political organizations. The rest of the office was concerned with following our economic and commercial relations with the European Union and the Organization for Economic Cooperation and Development (OECD). The staffing of that office has vastly improved since then, I am glad to say.

I liked working with the Council of Europe (COE), the first multinational European organization to develop after World War II. In my day, it was of interest to the United States chiefly for its Court of Human Rights (in Strasbourg, France) and because the COE provided a waiting room for possible future EU member states. The state that has spent the longest time waiting there to be welcomed into the EU—and that is still waiting—is Turkey. Turkey is a NATO ally, and US policy has long been to encourage European organizations, including the EU, to accept Turkey as a member.

In the fall of 1985 Turkey was about to be nominated by the British to become, as of November 1986, vice president of the Council of Europe's Committee of [Foreign] Ministers, a position that normally leads to the incumbent becoming the next president of the COE's leading political body. But then I got word from my colleague at our consulate in Strasbourg (where the COE is headquartered) that the French and the Scandinavians were going to block Turkey's chance to be vice president—and subsequently president—because of Turkey's spotty human rights record.

France, Sweden, Norway, and Denmark were among a group of five countries that had in 1982 introduced a request that the COE's European Commission of Human Rights look into civil rights abuse allegations against the Turkish government, and these countries were still unsatisfied with Turkey's responses thus far. If those four countries persisted in opposing Turkey, there would not be enough votes to give Turkey the vice presidency.

Thinking about how my European counterparts in Belgium, Denmark, and Germany had no trouble coordinating with colleagues at their level without bothering their bosses, I thought, "Why not try something like it to win Turkey its turn at bat?" By then I knew that France was looking for some friendly gesture to make to Germany, and Germany was looking for a friendly gesture to make to Turkey (short of support for Turkey's entry into the EU). I also knew that France was close to the Scandinavian countries and that the Scandinavians, at that moment, were not ready to listen to another lecture from a US ambassador (especially the one then in Ankara) on how Europeans should stop being mean to the Turks.

I checked the timing for the COE vice presidency decision with my Strasbourg consulate colleague and phoned a midlevel colleague at our embassy in Ankara, to suggest she avoid mentioning to her bosses the potential stumbling block my Strasbourg colleague had disclosed to me. I next phoned a midlevel contact in the political section at our embassy in Paris and asked him to go quietly to his best contact for dealing with the Scandinavians in the French Foreign Ministry and ask that person to try to change France's position opposing Turkey's becoming vice president of the COE and also to ask France to encourage the Scandinavians to remove their own objections.

My overseas colleagues worked wonders; in April 1986 Turkey was voted the next vice president of the COE's Committee of Ministers. There was some displeasure expressed afterward within the State Department's European Bureau at the way I had bypassed our higher-ups at home and abroad. But given the result, I was given a meritorious honor award instead of being scolded for lèse majesté.

Within a few months after his lung surgery, John was looking and feeling so well that we stopped thinking about his illness. A year later, when I ran into our former ambassador to Zaire Robert Oakley waiting for an elevator in the State Department, I could truthfully answer his question about John's health by saying that John was in better shape than in years.

Oakley's question turned out not to be an idle one. He was slated to become ambassador to the Netherlands. Remembering that John spoke fluent Dutch, and having admired his work as economic counselor in Kinshasa, he wanted John as his deputy chief of mission. (In the event, John got the assignment to the Netherlands, but Oakley did not become his ambassador.)

The European Bureau offered me a job in nearby Brussels, in the political section of our mission to the EU, this time to report on the ministerial meetings of the EU. It looked at first like a perfect fit, but when I found that John's only free time was likely to be on weekends, which was when I could expect to be standing around outside the EU ministers' meeting room hoping to learn something about what had gone on inside, I went to see my old ambassador to the EU, George Vest, who was now director general of the Foreign Service. He greeted me cordially and asked what he could do for me. I said, "You can give me my manumission. I need leave without pay to be with John in The Hague." A humane man, Ambassador Vest agreed at once.

Chapter 17

Being in Charge

• • • • • • • • • •

W<small>E HAD LIVED ONCE BEFORE IN</small>
The Hague, in the early 1960s, coming out of Indonesia, and we had
been relatively poor and very poorly housed. Now we were living in the
deputy chief of mission's residence, a house built for grand occasions. A
nineteenth-century mansion, it had great long windows, high ceilings, neoclassical pillars, and a splendid garden with a more than two-hundred-year-
old ash tree at its center.

The house still had the same English butler, Desmond, who had been
there in the days of our former DCM, and he remembered me, newly arrived
and pregnant, attending a dance at this residence. "I thought you might have
the baby there and then, Ma'am," he told me, "but you wouldn't sit down."
We both laughed, and I thanked my good luck that he was still there. The
house was in flawless condition despite its age. Some thoughtful predecessor
had arranged for under-floor heating in the glass-enclosed covered terrace
that ran the length of the house, front to back, with a view of the garden. The
terrace was wide enough that we could also have small lunch parties there,
which John began to do soon after arriving, in May 1986.

As John knew well, the position of DCM was always a delicate one. The
DCM was supposed to be the loyal alter ego of the ambassador, never outshining his boss but keeping him out of trouble. In Western Europe where,
then as now, almost all the ambassadors were noncareer, keeping the boss
from doing things that he or she did not realize were either illegal or very
unwise was sometimes a job and a half, and only the DCM could do it.

For a DCM to spend a long time in charge of the embassy, that is, as
chargé d'affaires, while awaiting the arrival of the new ambassador, added to

the delicacy of his or her situation. The DCM would want to do a good job as chargé. At the same time it would be impolitic to overshadow his future boss. For example, he would not seek to initiate bold new policies or practices in case these would not be agreeable to the new ambassador when he took over.

The trickiness of John's situation was compounded by the fact that he had been chosen by one man, a career officer, who had expected to be the new ambassador, only to find shortly before leaving Washington to take up his DCM duties that the man who had chosen him was not coming and somebody else, a noncareer ambassador with no overseas experience, was coming instead—eventually. The new ambassador-designate, whom John and I went up to New York to meet before we left for The Hague, wanted to keep John as his DCM and informed us that he and his wife would be unable to get to The Hague until nearly a year after John did.

The classic solution for what to do when a new ambassador arrives after the DCM has been in charge a long time was for the DCM to stick around for *at most* two weeks to introduce the new man to his embassy and to his key host country contacts, then go out of the country on leave for *at least* two weeks, inaccessible by phone, and then return—usually to a heartfelt welcome by the new boss. Meanwhile, there was a year for John to get through, walking on eggs.

As it happened, John did not need to worry about outshining anyone. The previous ambassador, still there for a couple more months after John arrived, was the career officer L. Paul "Jerry" Bremer, who seemed to have a halo of light that surrounded his Kennedy-like head wherever he went in Holland.[1]

At forty-two, with movie-star good looks, Bremer became famous soon after arriving in Holland for outrunning his security guards during his morning exercise laps. A Kissinger protégé who had shot up to become executive secretary to Secretary of State Alexander Haig, Bremer had received an enviable education at New England boarding schools, followed

---

1. Ambassador Bremer later became the diplomat in charge of the immediate postwar civil administration in Iraq, shortly after our Shock-and-Awe rapid military triumph there. Many critics contend that Bremer did everything wrong in Iraq, but my guess is that he had been chosen for the Iraq job in part because he had done everything right in The Hague.

by Yale, Harvard, and Sciences Po in Paris, before entering the US Foreign Service in 1966.

A Reagan appointee as ambassador to the Netherlands, Bremer had arrived in August 1983 in a country that—for reasons dating back to the Vietnam War—was strongly anti-American. The newest cause uniting much of the Dutch population against the United States was the cruise missile deployment issue. Yet somehow, by November 1985, Bremer had obtained the agreement of the Dutch Center-Right coalition to uphold its 1979 commitment to the deployment of forty-eight cruise missiles by 1988. At the same time Bremer had become the most popular diplomat in the Netherlands.

I was in The Hague at our residence, watching the evening news in August 1986 alongside our butler, Desmond, when Ambassador Bremer left Holland after his three years there. For fully five minutes there was no comment while the Dutch TV cameras followed this handsome man tossing his youthful mane as he reached out to shake hands with various key Dutch politicians and public figures while climbing the planeside stairs and into the plane. There was still no comment as the cameras stayed fixed for a few lingering seconds on the plane's closed door. Desmond and I shook our heads in amazement.

John, who had seen Ambassador Bremer in action from late May onward, felt that what he needed to do was avoid anything that would lessen the strong pro-US sentiment among the Dutch that Bremer had engendered almost single-handedly. Self-confident enough not to need to seek the limelight, John found it easy to walk this narrow path. I did not find it as easy to return to the "wife of" status.

We had official functions most lunch and dinner times. Many of these meals were a great bore for me, or at least the people were. This was a problem I had found at ambassadorial dinners elsewhere in the past. The flower arrangements would be magnificent; the lighted candles, the glittering crystal chandeliers, the gleaming silver and china, the women's silk and satin gowns and, above all, their sparkling jewels would be almost worth the show; but the conversation would often make me glance discreetly at my wristwatch.

That first summer in The Hague I had a respite from boredom when the State Department asked if I would be willing to be the acting vice consul in Amsterdam, thus permitting the incumbent vice consul to have his home leave. The job came to an end in the fall, and I went back to being a full-time "wife of" with regret. Mrs. Bremer had been very involved with the wives of the American business community, but that was not my scene; I did what I felt had to be done to be courteous, but did not enjoy it.

I debated going back to research I had begun when in Holland last time, on Java's Hindu and Buddhist temples, but then a new idea occurred to me. Why not write a biography of our most interesting neighbor in Borneo, Tom Harrisson. Harrisson, an astonishingly prolific English polymath, had died ten years earlier (in 1976) in a road accident in Thailand. I had contributed chapters to several nonfiction books on Southeast Asia before I became a diplomat, and I had always vaguely thought of writing a book after I retired from the Foreign Service. Thus began my biography of Tom Harrisson, a labor of love that took twelve years, trips to four continents, and more than two hundred taped and transcribed interviews, to become my first solo book. It was the perfect project for me to begin while on leave without pay in Holland. Many of the people I needed to meet lived in nearby Britain or Belgium, and his last living ex-wife lived in the Netherlands.

Once I started on my book, I no longer had irksome extra time on my hands. Thinking back on my time as a spouse and not an officer, it occurs to me that having a freelance job or a hobby that is fulfilling but allows time to carry out one's diplomatic duties is perhaps the best way for spouses to enjoy the diplomatic life abroad.

. . . .

Our family and friends from all over the world came to see us in our new splendor, but they were struck most—as were we—by the invasive presence of our security detachment, installed at the request of one of Ambassador Bremer's predecessors. A clutch of young Dutch policemen were assigned to go everywhere with John once he left the residence, except when he was safely inside the embassy or outside the Netherlands.

The physical protection of diplomats within a host country's borders is, under international law, the duty of the host government—one reason why diplomats are normally useless in a war zone. But how it is done is worked out with the foreign embassy. The Dutch police were courteous and professional, but they were very much underfoot. John couldn't walk around the block without being escorted by at least four heavily armed young men. I felt sorry for the security detail that accompanied us to Amsterdam's Concertgebouw to hear a five-evening series of Schubert piano sonatas (John's choice) and sorrier still for the detail that suffered visibly sitting in pews in various ancient Dutch churches through early music concerts (my favorite music).

John and I were going to a little Italian restaurant in Amsterdam in late December 1986 with John's father, friends from earlier postings in Indonesia and elsewhere, and our twenty-six-year-old son Paul and his pretty American girlfriend. As was standard operating procedure for protecting the American chief of mission in the Netherlands at that time, there were armed Dutch security people positioned in the little restaurant, and a driver and a heavily armed guard in the front seats of John's limousine. The limo had armor-plated doors and bulletproof windows that could not be opened. More armed guards followed in a second car.

As our party arrived in several cars, ahead of us was John's father—a smallish slender man in a dark gray cashmere Chesterfield overcoat with a white silk scarf at his throat and a Persian lamb astrakhan on his head. By then he had retired from a public health career crowned by his having helped convincingly prove the link between asbestos and lung disease. He was wearing dark glasses because his pale eyes were sensitive to the northern light. And as he led our column toward the restaurant with our beautiful French friend Anita in a fur coat on his arm, I suddenly realized that people were staring at us. Trying to strangle my hoot of laughter, I realized that we looked just like a mafia family—with John's father the *capo dei capi*, his glamorous girlfriend in tow.

John would have gladly dispensed with the security detail, despite the fact that a British ambassador had a few years earlier been shot dead through the window of his residence—near ours—by an IRA gunman. But if John were to turn off the guards now, it might be hard to convince the Dutch government to put them back on duty again when and if John's new ambassador wanted them. Until the ambassador arrived, the security detachment was the heaviest burden of John's job, making impossible any spontaneous, unplanned activity for him outside the house. This kind of security detail was an exception in those days. Since 9/11, however, most American ambassadors while assigned abroad have security details at least that burdensome, making it more difficult for the ambassador to meet people who have not been formally vetted.

When not with John, I was not under the guards' protection, so I could go about freely. I could duck into Holland's wonderful art museums frequently. For some six weeks in early 1987 I also drove myself weekly in our VW Jetta to Brussels to see my dying Congolese friend Makanda. More cheerful trips were to England and Scotland to begin interviewing Tom Harrisson's relatives, friends, and enemies. At one point I was going to the House of Lords so often that the man at the door said, "And which peer will you be calling on today, Ma'am?"

. . . .

The time came for eligible Foreign Service officers to bid on jobs for the following year. I was about to write back that I would like to extend my leave without pay for another year when John said, "No. Put in a bid. If it is good enough, I'll quit and join you."

Taken aback, I protested that he had just been promoted again and had an excellent chance of getting another DCM-ship someplace nice or maybe even an ambassadorship somewhere. But John was obdurate; he said he was anxious that I earn five more years of service to reach twenty years, the minimum required for a full pension. "And," he added, "I have been doing this work thirty years now, and I'm ready to stop. I would never get a European ambassadorship; I'm not a superstar like Jerry Bremer, and these days almost all ambassadorships in places with indoor plumbing go to political appointees. And if I got such a job, even a DCM job, you almost certainly could not work without us being apart. Anyhow, it really is your turn. You find a nice place to work, and I'll resign the next day." Then, looking at my doubtful expression: "At least put in your bids now and see what they offer you."

I could not argue with that, but I felt uneasy. I wrote my mother that, if I accepted a job, "it would mean either a long separation from John or his quitting the Foreign Service, neither of which is ideal from my point of view." In the early spring of 1987 the word came, unbelievably, that I had been assigned to be the new consul general in Bordeaux, responsible for America's relations with the southwest quadrant of France. John did not appear surprised, but I had not bid on that job nor expected anything nearly so glamorous. Luckily, John's father—whom I loved and trusted—was visiting us, and so I was able to take him out to lunch alone and lay my problem before him.

After we had toasted one another with our wine, I said: "Dad, here is your only child, your son, who has just been promoted to yet a higher step within the Senior Foreign Service. He is serving in an enviable job in an enviable place and would no doubt get even better options the next time he bids, in less than two years from now. But he wants to throw all that away to accompany me to Bordeaux where I have just been assigned. I am more than willing to stay on leave without pay. It is still early in the assignment cycle, and there are many qualified candidates who would be glad to go to Bordeaux, so the State Department would not be angry with me. Tell me, what do you think we should do?"

He slowly shook his head while smiling to himself and said, more to himself than to me, "How could he know? What made him so smart? Why didn't I do something like that for his poor mother?"

I shall never forget that moment. It explained so much about the way my husband had treated me all these years.

. . . .

In late July 1987 I drove myself to Bordeaux in the Jetta. I had never driven in France before. Getting lost several times en route, I took four extra hours to reach my destination,

Within a day or two I had our consulate driver take me to the prefect of Aquitaine's annual summer reception on a well-kept lawn attached to his handsome official residence. I was taken in hand immediately by an elderly

French couple of which the husband was the honorary consul from some Latin American country. The couple knew everybody else at the party. They introduced me to the leading regional and local officials, such as the mayors, police chiefs, locally based generals and admirals, senior politicians, doctors, lawyers, newspaper editors. They took care to have me meet the other consuls—both career and honorary (of whom the latter were often proprietors of Bordeaux's more famous wine chateaux). By the end of the evening I had been introduced to everybody I ought to meet in Bordeaux. That still left me with the capitals of my other three regions, Toulouse, Poitiers, and Limoges, where I would need to introduce myself.

I soon learned that the French people of the southwest, although few of them spoke English, retained a special affection for the English—and for English speakers—dating back centuries to before the Hundred Years' War when southwest France had belonged to England and the French wine trade had first flourished. At the suggestion of someone I met at the prefect's reception, I went that weekend to the village of Castillon, not far from Bordeaux, where the villagers did an annual restaging of the last battle of the Hundred Years' War. I wondered if I was following the plot correctly when I saw that the audience was near tears for the death of the senior British officer, Lieutenant Talbot, and I was stunned when the audience hissed at Charles VII's victorious soldiers. I said to the villager sitting next to me, "Isn't Charles VII Joan of Arc's dauphin? Why are French people hissing at his soldiers?" My neighbor said, "When the British lost that battle, there began for us hundreds of years of economic depression. For us of the southwest, St. Joan was on the wrong side." I was so struck by this discovery that I wrote a cable about it to Washington as my first message from Bordeaux.

My new house was almost as big as the one in Holland and better furnished. It was on a short street that led to a lovely public park, and, in the other direction, it was walking distance to the office. The guest rooms were immediately put to use. My daughter came first, having just graduated from university and trying to figure out what to do next. While she was with me, my giant friend from the Congo arrived to spend a couple of nights. (He had already stayed with John in The Hague.) Within a few weeks, the downstairs was in good enough shape for us to give a cocktail buffet for twenty-five—chiefly my staff and their spouses. John came down from The Hague for that and was soon back to stay, as my "consort," as the French called him.

My office car was like John's in The Hague, so heavy and clunky with armor that it was miserable to ride in. Not being able to open the windows seemed especially frustrating in the beautiful climate of southwest France. Fortunately, I was not burdened with a security detail like John's in Holland. All I had was a contract guard at our house and a couple of extra French police during working hours outside the office. The office was a four-story eighteenth-century mansion within sight of the magnificent bronze sea-horse fountain at the Place des Quinquonces in downtown Bordeaux.

Naturally, there were security risks. I would occasionally receive un-signed letters threatening my life, and there were known to be extremist organizations and individual crackpots in France who would be happy to do harm to an official American, but I felt that this was par for the course for any public servant. At John's suggestion, my office driver plotted out and numbered six different routes between my residence and the office, and kept one of a pair of dice in the glove compartment. When I got into the car en route either to the office or my house, the driver would hand me the die and I would toss it; whichever number came up, that would be our route.

At the office, I was now almost back to the situation I had been in when I had asked our Indonesian cook Chi-chi how to organize my staff of seven. My staff was now just under a dozen, a bit too big for me to handle alone and yet too small for me to not be involved in their management. While I did the political and economic reporting and much of the representation, supported by my Anglo-French secretary, two American Foreign Service officers reported to me and led a clutch of French colleagues doing the consular work—passports; visas; marriage, birth, and death documents; indigent Americans—and budget and administrative matters. There were also a French commercial specialist and a French public diplomacy special-ist. I wrote the basic annual evaluations of only some of the staff, but wrote reviewing statements for all the others. The staff was excellent for the most part. And the local staff was more pro-American than we Americans were, and full of initiative and good sense—not at all exhibiting a clerk mentality.

There were, however, two serious drawbacks to the place. First was the total absence of twentieth-century communications for any confidential material. If the matter wasn't sensitive, I could talk about it over the phone with my bosses in Paris. I could also write them a letter if there was no confidential material in it and send it via the French post office. But if it were sensitive, the only way to get it to Paris or Washington was via a once-in-three-weeks diplomatic pouch, brought by an American diplomatic courier unless a cleared American from the consulate happened to be going up to Paris. The other drawback was that, within weeks of my arrival, it was announced in the French press that the State Department planned to close Bordeaux by September 1988—a year from then. Bordeaux would be one of thirteen European consulates to be axed at that time to save money.

The consulate in Bordeaux was the oldest extant American post abroad, dating from 1790, and the French were up in arms at the thought of its closing. A year or so earlier, French protests had saved our consulate in Strasbourg by getting the US Congress to attach a rider to some crucial legislation, forbidding the closing of Strasbourg and some other European consulates—though Congress did not provide the funds to keep them open.

One of my first weeks, I paid a call on the widely read regional daily newspaper *Sud Ouest* and met its editor in chief. An experienced newspaperman, he quickly made me feel at ease. To my surprise, he said to me (in French), "We plan to run a campaign to keep the consulate open. I know you cannot get involved in this, but could we call on you and your staff to help us when we have a factual question about the consulate to verify before publishing?" I tried not to smile too broadly when I said that this would be possible.

True to his word, and despite the fact that the paper's editorials were more often opposed to US policies than in favor of them, *Sud Ouest* devoted prime columns (on the first and the back page of the front section) daily to a series headlined "Let's Save the US Consulate in Bordeaux."

All the main newspapers in Paris, including *Le Monde, Figaro,* and the *International Herald Tribune,* covered the story of the post's threatened closure, and all argued for keeping the consulate at Bordeaux. I could hardly believe this was the France about which Americans tended to sneer and where, just a few years earlier, French sneers about America had been so common. I didn't go anywhere in my consular district—Limoges, Poitiers, Bayonne, La Rochelle, Toulouse, for example—that people didn't come anxiously up to me to ask what they could do to keep us here. I had to find ways not to seem to be on their side against my government's priorities, without making the consulate's fans feel that their appreciation of the consulate was unwelcome.

The Gaullist mayor of Biarritz told me he had written *Sud Ouest* to say if they had been as nice about the United States years ago, maybe we would not be leaving now. I told him it was not for policy reasons that we were closing down, just the budget deficit and the falling dollar.

I had arrived in France at a lucky time for an American diplomat. France's Socialist president François Mitterrand had as his prime minister Jacques Chirac, from the Gaullist party. To have the president and the prime minister be from rival parties was a novelty in French politics, for which the French coined the term *cohabitation*. It was brought about by the workings of De Gaulle's brilliantly devised constitution for the Fifth Republic. There was an overlap in areas of authority that obliged the (Socialist) president and the (Gaullist) premier to agree on a few basic foreign policy goals. One of the goals they found they could agree on was to try to get along better with the United States.

I saw my job as taking advantage of this friendly period to build wider and deeper cooperation with the French government in as many fields as possible, especially in political/military matters, where southwest France had a significant stake because of its civil and military aeronautics industry. Also, some of the most senior political figures in France were elected from the southwest, and I could often see them during their long weekends, when they were relaxed among their friends and voters and unencumbered by protocol.

I loved my work, even though it took me between ten and sixteen hours a day; and Paris and Washington liked the reporting. John told me that good reporting was essential to saving the post. He advised me to let Paris know that I considered myself to be working for the various sections of the embassy, that I did not see myself as Eleanor of Aquitaine with my own little kingdom by the sea. My deputy agreed with this approach. He passed me a note one day when Bordeaux's future was looking especially cloudy to say,

"Judy, you keep on writing your reports and I'll take care of the consular stuff and we should be able to save Bordeaux."

Eventually, about halfway through my four-year stay there, the post was saved. Lyon was closed instead, along with the twelve other European posts already on the list, including Antwerp—where John had made the contacts that served our country so well during the cruise missile crisis.

Immediately upon his arrival in the fall of 1987, John had relieved me of many of the more onerous of my duties. He kept track of official residence expenses, including the costs of food and drink for official entertaining and the salaries of the domestic staff. This staff consisted of an elegant Frenchwoman as cook, who with her ex-husband had run a Michelin one-star restaurant not far from Bordeaux. Our staff also included an enchanting cleaning woman from the French-owned island of Réunion for whom our two French cats, Eleanor and Esther, waited every morning on the inside front step, just for the pleasure of hearing her say in her raucous voice, "Et bonjour, mes belles!"

The good fortune of having important people in my consular district was brought home to me when John and I went to the opening of a new wing of a museum of paleontology in the Dordogne, the district from which then French Foreign Minister Roland Dumas was elected. I had forgotten that fact and was feeling resentful at having to give up another Saturday to a long drive, just to be present when a famous American paleontologist's work was being honored, when I saw Dumas and realized that, being the senior woman present, I would be seated next to him.

This was in 1989, only days after the Berlin Wall separating East from West Germany had fallen, and Dumas mentioned he had just come back from Moscow. With no classified phone or wireless link, I was not "in the loop" enough to know that Washington and Paris were dying to know why Dumas had gone to Moscow just then and what he had learned there. But I was interested, myself, in what would happen to Germany, now that the non-NATO half would presumably be joined to the NATO half. What would the Russians say or do about it?

As luck would have it, that was the question that had taken Dumas to Moscow. And here among his old friends, on his weekend before the Paris world caught up with him, he was relaxed enough to tell me. Without naming names of the Russians he had spoken with in Moscow, he let me know that his conclusion was that the Russians would grumble a lot but do nothing to prevent all of Germany from taking part in NATO. This was news, and I could hardly wait for lunch to end so that I could go back to Bordeaux and write it up. I did so, but then was struck again with the dreadful inconvenience of having no electronic classified link to Paris or the outside world. (I dared not phone in the news to Paris. It would have embarrassed Dumas dreadfully to have it leak out then that he had given me this information before most of his own government had been told.)

Although it was a Saturday, after conferring with John, I called the very able administrative officer in Paris, Rusty Hughes. I told him I had something urgent that had to go out very quickly and asked would the embassy pay for a courier trip to Paris and back for John. (John, as an American with a current security clearance, was eligible to serve as a courier of diplomatic pouches when needed.)

Rusty said he would love to help me, but they were flat out of spare cash and feared they were going to have to put some of the local staff on unpaid furloughs for days at a time just to make ends meet. I thanked him and hung up dispiritedly, not knowing what to do next. John said, "This can't wait. Call him back and tell him I'll go up for free." I called Rusty back and told him of John's offer and he asked, "Is this urgent because of who said it or what was said?" "Both," I answered. Rusty thought for a minute and then said, "The best I can do is tell John to come ahead, and if upon reading your message the DCM says it is worth paying for, then we'll pay for it." "That's a handsome offer," I replied.

John went up that night with a sealed pouch containing my draft message. On Monday, the cable having gone out during the weekend, the DCM and the political counselor both phoned me to say they would be happy to pay for John's trip.

. . . .

The work never slowed down, but it kept being enjoyable. One of my continuing tasks was to follow developments in the French Basque country, down near the Spanish border, of Spanish Basque nationalist terrorists. It was not a high-risk activity since the terrorists were for the most part careful not to kill people or blow up places *in France*, for fear that the French would pursue them with more enthusiasm than they were currently showing. But I could sometimes learn a bit about where in France such terrorists were hiding themselves and their weapons by asking around in the French Basque community. A plus for me was the chance to enjoy the beauty of the Basque hills with their grazing sheep and semiwild Basque ponies. Then there were the spectacular ocean waves (attracting crowds of surfers in season) crashing against rocks, visible through a huge picture window in a turn-of-the-century tearoom John had found in Biarritz.

The mayors, mostly wiry older men who looked like the former rugby players they had been, made me very welcome and were happy to talk to me about politics, Basque nationalism, the economic situation, and anything else I cared to hear about. Through them, I met a number of the rising young stars of the national political scene, such as Michèle Alliot-Marie, who later was the first woman in France to become, successively, minister of defense, interior, and foreign affairs. A handsome woman with a crisp, no-nonsense air, her father, the mayor of Biarritz, to my private amusement, persisted in calling her "Fifi."

While I would be sitting at the massive oak dining table of a Basque nationalist politician, thinking "This is really fun," John would be a half hour away in another town checking out a Basque nationalist bookstore and looking for places to take our ambassador and his wife when they came down to the Basque country on a semiofficial, semiprivate trip in the spring.

The hard part was getting back to the office where piles of paper and telephone messages awaited me. If these messages were not dealt with promptly, my colleagues would be delayed in *their* work. And my head would be so full of what I had learned that had to be written down before it evaporated, that I sometimes felt my brain was stuffed with uncomfortable and spiky hay—rather like Dorothy's scarecrow.

John, though retired, had managed to keep his security clearance, and so he could speed-read through the great pile of classified cables that arrived in heavy diplomatic pouches brought by embassy courier once every three weeks. John had been allowed to keep his clearance for precisely that purpose. After making penciled notes on the relatively slim set of cables and other papers that he felt were worth my reading, he would put them aside in the vault's safe for me. Then he spent many hours standing, feeding superfluous classified messages into the shredder. If he had not done the shredding, I would have had to do it, or I would have had to call on my busy American consular officers to do it.

He also went through the old memoranda of conversations (known as "memcons") that some of my predecessors had written, and filed them so that I could retrieve them easily. Since many of the important political actors of southwest France had been there for decades, it was an enormous help to me to be able to quickly find and read what they had said to my predecessors. That way, we did not have to repeat the same old conversations. I am sure that was in large measure why my contacts were willing to see me repeatedly.

From reading these old memcons (which Foreign Service officers no longer write) I came to know whose predictions were most often correct. There was one senior retired Gaullist politician who was marvelously articulate and would make firm predictions about elections and forthcoming government decisions, supporting his predictions by carefully thought-out reasoning. Knowing what actually had happened afterward, I found that he had almost always guessed wrong. By contrast, an elderly Gaullist senator, whose memcons I had also read, was unusually terse in his comments but somehow always got it right. I learned to catch his eye across the room at a reception and approach and ask him in under ten words what I wanted his input on. He would answer in five words, and I could take what he told me to the bank.

The French politicians and other officials I dealt with generally assumed that American diplomats favored the politics of the Right, but I worked hard to get on good terms with the Left as well. For half my time in Bordeaux, the three most important national offices—president, prime minister, and foreign minister—were in the hands of Socialists elected from my consular district. It took time to overcome the suspicions of some on the Left, but eventually I had what I thought was a balanced set of political contacts.

One of the subjects I was supposed to follow closely was the aeronautics industry in southwest France—the home of both Dassault and Airbus. To do my work, I had to read widely in a field I knew nothing about (except what my pilot son Paul told me): the complicated and fascinating subject of the commercial workings of the civil airplane industry.

Washington was especially eager for anything I could learn about Airbus: its production plans; its marketing strategies; what engines it was thinking of buying and what it planned to do to counter its main competitors, specifically Boeing and McDonnell Douglas. This was when Airbus was seeking to obtain a third of the world market, which in those days seemed to many to be an impossibly ambitious goal on the part of a newcomer like Airbus. How little we all knew!

I used to go every other week to Toulouse to talk to people who worked for or with Airbus Industrie. I would usually start with a call on Airbus Industrie's chief executive, Jean Pierson. Pierson had a great sense of theater and would greet me with a barrage in French, complaining of alleged commercial practices by Boeing and the US government that he felt were unfair to legitimate competition. I would take notes of all his points and then he would say, "Ah, now that's over, what can I give you to drink?" From then on, over a glass of good wine, we would have a polite and even cordial conversation in which I would suggest that there were some valid points of disagreement with his view, and he would give me more details about why I was wrong and what Airbus's backers (four EU countries at the time) planned to do about it. I spent hours writing cables to Washington about this after I got back to Bordeaux. I think it is fair to say that having a consular post nearby made it easier for Uncle Sam to keep close tabs on a crucial foreign industrial competitor while trying to find areas where we could cooperate—airplane engines, for example.

It also proved useful to Uncle Sam that one of the people I saw frequently in Bordeaux was Jacques Chaban-Delmas. We would often be at events where we were both called upon to speak, he as Bordeaux's mayor and I as the dean of the Bordeaux consular corps—a title given to the career principal officer of a consulate who has been in that city the longest, which I became soon after arriving.

Chaban had once been French prime minister, and during part of my time in Bordeaux, in addition to being mayor, he was also, for the third time, speaker of the lower house of the French parliament. A glamorous man, Chaban had been famous in his youth for his success with the ladies. He is played in the film *Is Paris Burning?* by the devastatingly attractive Alain Delon. In the film, Delon wears a trench coat just like the one Chaban wore when he flew from Bordeaux to England to help De Gaulle set up his Free French government-in-exile early in World War II.

Chaban still wore that trench coat on special occasions, one of which was to unveil a plaque—honoring two hundred years of US-French relations—that the City of Bordeaux wanted placed on the outside wall of the eighteenth-century mansion that had been the home of the first American consul. I was standing next to that mansion on a drizzly winter day in January 1991, as part of a small crowd waiting to welcome Chaban to the plaque unveiling. The news of the day was all about the anticipated Gulf War, about to be launched by President George H. W. Bush against Saddam Hussein's Iraq, in response to Saddam's August 1990 invasion and takeover of Kuwait. In November 1990 the UN Security Council had given Iraq a deadline for withdrawal from Kuwait of January 15, 1991, after which those states opposing Saddam's invasion would be entitled to use "all necessary means" to force Iraq out of Kuwait.

Saddam had not pulled back his forces, but France, the day before the withdrawal deadline, had proposed a new Security Council resolution that appeared to give some support to Iraqi negotiating demands, causing the United States to reject it. In the days that followed, the French government had not yet publicly announced whether or not it would join the anti-Saddam coalition we headed. As the world waited to hear, I was one of many standing on the damp Bordeaux sidewalk, remembering how France in 1986 had refused overflight permission for the Reagan-launched bombing raid on Libyan dictator Qaddafi's Tripoli. Since then, general elections had brought a change of prime ministers from Gaullist Chirac to Socialist Michel Rocard, but, in any case, foreign policy was more in President Mitterrand's bailiwick, and Mitterrand's intentions were often hard to read.

What would Mitterrand decide to do now? I knew the State Department must be anxious to know. I had talked to a number of French politicians in and out of government in the preceding days and they had all said that the question was still up in the air. And now here in Bordeaux, among us during that suspenseful period of less than a week (if I recall correctly), was the veteran Gaullist and World War II hero, Chaban-Delmas, three-time speaker of parliament, a consummate politician who had always kept on good personal terms with Mitterrand and the Socialists. What, if anything, would he say about the approaching Gulf War?

Chaban almost never wrote down his speeches; he spoke so well off the cuff that he didn't need to. Standing there in his Resistance raincoat he made a few remarks about the plaque and the centuries-long ties of friendship between France and America before saying something along the lines of "I have lived through wars and they are terrible, but I also know from experience that there are times when there are worse things than war." I may not remember his exact words (in French), but the sense was clear to all of us. Before his party or his country's government came out and said so, Chaban was saying that this war to resist Iraq's invasion of Kuwait was a just war and France should be part of it.

In reporting his remarks to Paris, I commented that Chaban was shrewd and was unlikely to have said that in public if he had not had a good idea which way Mitterrand was going to go. Soon thereafter the French government announced it would join the coalition. And next thing I knew, my favorite French Air Force general—who used to stand next to me at various parades and formal ceremonies where I represented the consular corps—called me up to say he had a present for me: A base commander in southwest France wanted to host the coalition's aerial refueling planes that allowed the American strategic bombers to stay in the air and head straight for the Gulf. And, in order to win for his base the honor of doing this, the base commander was in the process of flattening large parts of his base's airfield so that it could accommodate our biggest aerial refueling tankers.

He won that honor, and I remember being flown in a French Air Force plane with my ambassador from Paris, a general from USAFE headquarters in Ramstein, and my French Air Force general friend from Bordeaux to the

French airbase where USAFE awarded a special medal to thank the base commander. Before returning to Paris, my ambassador said to me something like, "You may remember that I asked if you could send me a Valentine from your part of France, and here it is."

Some years after I left Bordeaux, the consulate was closed down. At the suggestion of a well-meaning noncareer ambassador, the State Department began instead to create so-called American Presence Posts (APP) in a few cities in France, each post with one American officer and one French assistant. These APP posts were too small to do virtually any consular work—not even add extra pages to a passport. They could not do any political or economic reporting worthy of the name. The American might occasionally attend an event, but had no time or facilities to report what happened there. It seems that APP posts devoted most of their efforts to helping American businesses seeking to invest in France—a job for which the French government should pay, not the American taxpayer. Such little posts weren't cheap, since almost all the US government legal requirements for physical security and control of expenses and materials applied to them. To my mind, it was the stupidest move possible, maximizing cost per output—rather like having a powerful train engine pull one railroad car.

Chapter 18

Encores

• • • • •

By the time we were due to leave Bordeaux in the summer of 1991, my mother had died at home two years earlier, and John's father, a widower again, was suffering from the Parkinson's disease that would kill him a few years later. John's father did not have someone like my nanny Louise to look after him, so we were anxious not to be too far from him. My assignments officer in the State Department, however, was determined to send me as far away as possible, to a job for which I had no preparation: to our embassy in Manila, Philippines, to be refugee coordinator. My chief responsibility would be the welfare of tens of thousands of Vietnamese boat people, most of them housed in an American-funded refugee camp some hours from Manila by SUV.

I found the reasoning behind that assignment unfathomable and I told my new bosses in the Refugee Bureau that, if assigned there, I would retire at the first possible opportunity, in less than a year, on the twentieth anniversary of my entry into the Foreign Service. The assignments officer prevailed and—although soon after arriving in Manila I learned I had been promoted into the Senior Foreign Service with almost double the pay—I kept my word, retiring in May 1992. John by then had made the trip back to see his father in Washington six times in eight months, enduring twenty-three hours of economy-class travel each way. He was getting that wiped-out look again, and I worried that the stress of all this travel might bring his cancer back.

Meanwhile, however, I did find the job of refugee coordinator interesting. The Refugee Bureau gave me, its coordinator at post, my own pot of money, separate from the embassy's general funds, and that turned out to place me among the grown-ups at country team meetings (the meetings of the ambassador and DCM with all the heads of sections at the embassy).

This was the first and only time that I had hundreds of people working for me, most of them engaged in running a camp—more like a small town—with its own schools, jail, health clinic, and restaurants—for some 20,000 Vietnamese boat people on the Bataan Peninsula, further south on the island of Luzon than Manila. Getting to the camp took me along steep, scenic mountain roads where communist rebels liked to take hostages to fund their rebellion. I was told, though, that the rebels preferred not to bother women and was advised to always wear a skirt so I could be seen from a distance to be female.

My happiest moment in that job was when I succeeded in relocating to more adequate quarters a hundred or so Vietnamese boat people who had arrived in Manila too late to be regarded as refugees and were being kept in a warehouse-like space near the docks that had been meant only to hold them for a few days until the Philippine government and the Red Cross figured out what to do with them. My recollection is that that had been several years earlier, and I had accidentally come across these boat people still there.

. . . .

I retired in May 1992. By the fall of 1993, John and I were living in our new home in the pretty little town of Oxford, Maryland, on the Chesapeake Bay, when the phone rang. It was my old Refugee Bureau office asking if I didn't want in retirement to earn some extra money and have some fun being the acting refugee coordinator in Zagreb, Croatia. The bureau was sure it would appeal to my adventurous spirit; the job was to be responsible for our program for Bosnian refugees in Croatia, who had fled the interethnic war then raging in ex-Yugoslavia.

The idea was tempting, but getting on with my Tom Harrisson book was more so. I said, "I am writing a book that is going to take a while longer, but my husband is also a retired Senior Foreign Service officer. Would you like to speak to him?"

That was the first of a number of assignments abroad for John or me or both of us as re-hired annuitants. When temporary gaps must be filled—anywhere in the world, including in Washington—the appropriate State Department bureau can draw on retirees like us without much fuss, provided the assignment is for less than six months of full-time work in a given year. The six-month limit is to ensure that we do not earn more annually (including the pension) than a person still in the career would earn for that job.

John worked two years in a row for months at a time as refugee coordinator in Zagreb while I sat in our Zagreb hotel room writing my book. Next, after I had finished the book, both of us were asked to work for several months each in 1997 and 1998 for a noncareer ambassador in Luxembourg.

While John provided guidance to the ambassador and the senior staff on everything from administration to the legality of some of the ambassador's initiatives, I got the embassy ready to facilitate the US dialogue with the European presidency, which was poised to move its six-month headquarters to Luxembourg.

In mid-August 1997, while on a second pair of assignments for John and me in Luxembourg, the long-expected recurrence of the metastasis of the John's colon cancer appeared—in the bone. We went home and sold our house by the bay to move nearer his DC doctors. By June 1999, John—with the help of home hospice care—was spending all his time in a rented hospital bed in our Washington apartment's master bedroom, with me at night on a folding cot next to him. My book about Tom Harrisson came out at the end of 1999, in time for John to share the triumph of it.

All during John's last year, family and friends came by in such numbers that our bedroom sometimes took on more the air of a cocktail party than a sickroom. John's best friend, retired ambassador Edward Marks, a colleague from our earliest Brussels days, came almost every day. He and his wife, Aida, always brought an air of unforced gaiety with them. Some of our friends may have started coming to see John out of sympathy, but they came back because John was such a wise and sympathetic person with whom to discuss their problems.

John died at home in June 2000, on our forty-fourth wedding anniversary, surrounded by our children, daughter-in-law, our closest friend

Edward Marks, the two French cats, and me. John's passing was so gentle that it was only after Eleanor, the alpha cat, jumped up on John's bed and puffed out her fur till it all stood on end, that we knew he was gone.

A week later, even before the various memorial services for John in Washington and Brussels, I had already returned to part-time work at the State Department. And the next year, 2001, I was called back to work in Brussels as "senior adviser to the political section." The idea of using me for this assignment came from Robyn Hinson-Jones, an old friend from Kinshasa days, who was leaving her job as political counselor in Brussels to take up her new assignment in West Africa.

This was the first of what would become parts of nine of the next ten years spent working in Brussels. There, they usually made use of me for an EU presidency, internal political reporting, political-military affairs, and Belgium's ties with its former central African colonies.

Going back repeatedly as a rehired annuitant to our embassy to Belgium, I was able to revive and expand John's and my circle of friends throughout Belgium's political, diplomatic, and academic world. This was great fun for me and perhaps also for my colleagues to whom I introduced the most useful of my contacts. Knowing that I was there for just a few months, my colleagues soon stopped worrying about my becoming a rival and accepted me for what I was, an extra pair of hands and a source of background information that they could access easily.

It was a little trickier to establish my status as an extra resource, not a competitor, when dealing with the political counselor, my boss, who was, of course, a lot younger than I. My first such boss, Mike Fitzpatrick, was small, blond, and very young looking and so, taking my courage in both hands, I walked into his office his first day (after I had been running the section for months until his arrival) and closed the door. We looked each other over for a minute or so until I broke the silence by saying, "I'm older than God and you're about fourteen."

He said, "I'm forty-one."

"Yes," I said, "precisely what I meant. Well, the good news is that there isn't any job you can give me that I won't be happy to do. And the other good news is that I will be going away in a few months' time."

A week later, together we watched on live CNN as the second plane crashed into the second of the Twin Towers. My new boss, whom I had already come to respect as a very able diplomat, turned to me and said, "Judy, you aren't going anywhere. I need you here."

Still, there was a slight hesitancy on Mike's part in dealing with me, almost as if he were walking on eggs, until about a month later, when we were both in the office at 11 at night (5 p.m. in Washington). This was during a period when the two of us were working closely together trying to do our part in carrying on a productive dialogue between our government and the Belgian government as our chase after Al Qaeda in Afghanistan began.

A wave of fatigue hit me as I tried to write a cable to Washington about recent political-military developments in Belgium that could affect Belgian support of our efforts in Afghanistan. I could sense that the cable wasn't turning out right. I tried fiddling with my draft and got nowhere, so eventually I gave up and ended it somehow, printed it out and handed it to Mike to approve. As usual, he took it into his office and closed the door. But some minutes later he came out with the draft still in his hand and said, in a puzzled voice, "Judy, what's with this shitty cable?"

I laughed and said, "It is, isn't it. Give it back and I'll start over." From then on we got on famously. He even managed to convince the State Department to keep me there a month or two beyond the usual limit of six months in one year.

. . . .

*P*erhaps the most fun for me in my postcareer assignments to Brussels was working with the Belgians to help find a way to reduce the trafficking of "blood diamonds," the alluvial diamonds mined in war zones and sold illegally to fund civil wars and rebellions throughout Africa and terrorism in the Middle East. In the course of finding out what was going on regarding this trafficking in Belgium, I got to know NGO sleuths and illicit Lebanese and Congolese couriers, as well as Belgian gemologists connected to Antwerp's world-famous diamond market.

The Antwerp Diamond Council was—maybe still is—the chief world market for alluvial diamonds, and it was anxious to have some way to vet its diamonds as having come from nonconflict mines, in order to compete with diamonds from the deep mines owned chiefly by London-based De Beers in Botswana and South Africa and Canada. It is easy for diamonds coming from deep mines to be watched over every step of the way from mine to market by their owners, whereas alluvial mining is usually done by amateurs or small entrepreneurs working along the shores of rivers in many places, including in war zones. Antwerp worried that the "blood diamond" label would mean that the diamonds sold in their market would be treated like animal fur—which had become anathema to many people who cared about the ethics attached to purchasing nonessential luxury goods. In contrast, De Beers's diamonds could continue to be the gems of choice for fiancée rings worldwide. In a small way, in constant liaison with other agencies at post and in Washington, I participated in tracking down some of the worst blood diamond offenders operating in Belgium, and helped in the setting up of the Kimberley Process, an international mechanism established in 2002 to reduce such trafficking and to provide a certificate of legitimacy for alluvial as well as deep-mined diamonds. The Kimberley Process made for a significant reduction in blood diamond trafficking until the discovery in recent years of huge quantities of alluvial diamonds in noncomplying countries, such as Zimbabwe.

When in Washington, I worked in the immediate post-9/11 period on an interagency committee that was supposed to assemble and vet a list of terrorism-financing individuals and organizations to submit to the UN, so that the financial assets of supporters of terrorism could be frozen in all UN member countries. This was my first experience in Washington of dealing with other federal departments. It gave me more sympathy than I had previously had with the State Department for its slowness in sending its embassies clear policy instructions for use overseas. I could now see that herding cats was *much* easier than getting our federal departments and agencies to agree on anything with practical consequences. I took ironic comfort in watching the four representatives of the Department of the Treasury at our weekly meetings unable to agree among themselves, much less with the rest of us, on what to do each time a new name was proposed for the assets freeze list.

Less frustrating was my job a few days each week during the winters of 2003 to 2010, writing situation reports on "hot" political-military subjects as part of the Political-Military Action Team, or PMAT. PMAT was and, at the time of writing, is a marvelous group of retirees, half of them retired military and the other half retired diplomats. For some years the only woman on the team, I was quietly amused at how careful my ex-military colleagues were to watch their language when I was around. I laughed out loud when I realized—on a day when all our computers crashed—that I was the only person in the office to use a four-letter word! All in all, my postretirement work turned out to be as satisfying as any I had done before.

Chapter 19

Honesty, the Best Policy

• • • • • • • • • • • • •

THE MOST FAMOUS DEFINITION OF
a diplomat was made in the early seventeenth century by Sir Henry Wooten:
a diplomat "is an honest gentleman sent to lie abroad for the good of his
country." It is a witty double entendre but is patently untrue in implying
that diplomats can succeed by telling lies. Their whole profession is built on
trust; and if they were caught out in a lie or betraying a confidence, not only
they, but their successors for years to come, would be unable to obtain the
trust of the people they have to deal with.

After the ability to speak the language, a diplomat's credibility is his or
her most essential tool. It was our best diplomat, Benjamin Franklin, who
coined the phrase, "Honesty is the best *policy*."

One rule I tried always to follow was never to lay claim to expertise I
didn't have. The typical host government foreign ministry has a smaller staff
than we do, and so there are subjects it does not cover at all. But, at least in
Western Europe, what it does cover is often in the hands of specialists who
spend years developing their expertise.

One day postretirement while I was our political section's acting Africa
watcher in Brussels, I was handed a demarche about Sudan to take to the
Africa desk at the Belgian Foreign Ministry. I suddenly realized I knew virtually nothing about the subject. I could claim some knowledge of the Congo,
Rwanda, and Burundi, and I knew a bit about several other diamond-
producing African countries, but Sudan was a blank to me. What to do?
The demarche was urgent.

I could have quickly looked up Sudan on Wikipedia and on the State
Department's websites, but I chose instead to try another approach. With

what diplomats call a "nonpaper" (an informal statement of some policy we want to share with the host government) containing the Sudan demarche in my briefcase, I was conducted by a secretary through the labyrinth of the Foreign Ministry into the office of the Sudan desk officer. The maps on his walls, the books on his shelves, and the man's demeanor told me that here was someone who knew his subject. I took a deep breath and confessed to my ignorance and my embarrassment to be bothering him with a demarche that I did not understand myself.

This got me a big, compassionate smile and the offer to put me in the picture. In less than fifteen minutes, he efficiently led me through the crucial facts about Sudan, beginning with the surprising fact that it was then the biggest country in all of Africa—this was well before the split-off of South Sudan—and shared borders with seven other countries. By the time he was done, I could thank him and say that I now understood what my demarche was about. I then got out the nonpaper and explained my country's views and hopes that Belgium would make similar approaches to its friends in the African Union and other relevant organizations.

We both came away from the meeting grateful, I for the excellent briefing, and he for being allowed, this once, to display his expertise to a representative of the US government. He remained a useful colleague during the years that followed when Sudan was a country whose problems we cared about.

. . . .

The biggest challenge to one's credibility is when a diplomat has to present or defend a policy that he or she thinks is wrong. On such occasions one is caught between a duty to present one's government's point of view—which is our assigned duty and the reason why the foreigners want to hear us out—and the felt need not to burn our bridges with the host government by saying things we know or believe to be untrue, ill-timed, or inappropriate. Such a challenge was forced on me during the buildup to our launching the second Iraq War, a policy with which I personally disagreed.

I am cursed with a face that is easy to read, and thus telling an outright lie would not work for me, even if I were to try. I also knew there was no way I could do then what I had done once when a minor issue came along where I could not present the arguments in my government's demarche with a straight face. The instance was when I was given a demarche defending our refusal to join the International Criminal Court in The Hague, the tribunal that prosecutes war criminals. Our argument was that the United States would never commit such crimes and so any charge against us would have to be politically motivated. In that case, I brought along a State Department nonpaper and said that I hoped my interlocutor would read it carefully and get back to me with his views. He didn't, and I didn't press. (US views toward that court have since evolved into cooperation with it, if not membership.)

On one occasion, I asked—and received—permission to eliminate an item from a demarche on the grounds that it wouldn't help obtain what we wanted and risked hurting our overall relations with the host country and damaging my personal credibility in the process. This was when I was back working in Brussels for the third time after retirement, in late 2003. News had just broken of maltreatment of prisoners at Abu Ghraib in Baghdad, and I was assigned to go to the United Nations director at the Belgian Foreign Ministry to take her a demarche that included a talking point about "prisoners of conscience." I received prompt agreement from my bosses at the embassy that that week was not the time to approach the Foreign Ministry with the word "prisoners" on my lips.

If I had ever been ordered to deliver a demarche defending the practice of so-called enhanced interrogation, I would have been unable to do so; and, if obliged to try, I might have had to resign my position at the embassy. It was lucky for me that I was never put in that position.

Still, I knew there was no way I could as an American diplomat avoid making my strongest efforts to encourage Belgium to give full support to our logistical efforts to get our men and materiel out of Germany via the port of Antwerp to the Persian Gulf in the lead-up to the second Iraq war, a war opposed by virtually all Belgians—including Belgium's then foreign minister and minister of defense. During a lengthy and delicately handled diplomatic effort by Washington and my embassy colleagues, I searched our office files for old treaties and nonpapers on the subject for a good reason—one I could defend with a straight face—for asking Belgium's support. I came up with the need to ensure that NATO would not be the unintended casualty of Belgium's refusal to support us logistically, now that another NATO member, Turkey, had already turned us down. Recognizing the validity of that argument, my contacts helped ensure that Belgium kept its word to NATO.

The fact that I had worked many years in Belgium and knew precisely which were the right people to deal with may be the single bit of diplomacy in my whole career where what I contributed may have mattered. Early in this process, while I was once again "senior adviser to the political section" at Embassy Brussels, I had run into a Belgian diplomat I had known slightly in another country where he and John and I had been assigned. John and I had entertained him at dinner at our house when we all ended up in Belgium. John was good at dealing with fellow diplomats, having learned a tradecraft tip from John Henderson, his first political counselor in Jakarta: "Never see a diplomat from an allied country without having a little nugget of fresh information to give him." A "little nugget" could be advance notice that an American VIP was coming from the United States to visit the host country soon, or saying who the United States was planning to propose for an important international position, or some gossip about the inner circle of the host country that we could share without betraying confidences.

Now, in late 2002, two years after John's death, as the George W. Bush administration prepared for its Iraq War, this senior Belgian diplomat held a very important position in his Foreign Ministry. He would normally have been above my level to contact, so I got permission from my bosses to call on him at his office, and told him roughly what subjects I was covering in the political section. He decided that, for my work, I would need to know a colleague of his at the next-lower level: the head of one of the Foreign Ministry's functional bureaus. He walked me to the other man's office and said to him, "I have known this woman twenty-five years. You can trust her."

From that moment on, the new man treated me as if he, too, had known me twenty-five years. Indeed, he became my best contact at the Foreign Ministry, giving me good advice, suggesting other people I should get to know, answering my questions as frankly as he could, and telling me even the things he knew I would not enjoy hearing—given my country's policies at the time—but that I needed to know.

During the lead-up to the Iraq War, as I have mentioned, my job was to convince him to get his government to help us with logistics, and I had to pick my words carefully to tell the truth as far as I knew it, and yet make my government's case convincingly. Years later he told me, "I understood what you were saying and they were good points to make, but your body language was saying something else." I now suspect that my visible discomfort with our policy then did me no harm in convincing him that, reluctant as we both felt about the upcoming war, our two countries needed to help make sure that NATO did not fall apart during this crucial time.

Given the unpopularity in Belgium of the approaching war in Iraq, we at the embassy had to be continually alert to events that might be used against us in the court of public opinion. While at the office late one night during this period, I learned of a group of anti–Iraq War demonstrators who were painting slogans on the hull of one of our military ships in Antwerp Harbor that was loaded with materiel from one of our bases in Germany, now bound for the Gulf. This antiwar demonstration was just the kind of event that could turn septic, I felt. My new friend at the Foreign Ministry had already introduced me to a useful person to call at the Ministry of Defense. Luck was with me and I reached her at 11 p.m., while she was still at the office, and asked her whom I should contact to call off these demonstrators. She told me and—despite the late hour—I phoned the man at his home in Flanders. Speaking Dutch, I made my case.

"But we cannot interfere with the right of free speech," he protested, "so long as the demonstration is nonviolent."

"Yes, I agree," I said. "But surely neither you nor I would want one of these young people dangling from ropes along the hull of this ship to fall and get hurt [I paused] and cause a media frenzy!" He quickly took my point, and the demonstrators were ordered to leave.

My political section colleagues were all very busy and productive during this time. For example, in this period when for various reasons US relations with Belgium were already under strain, Hans Wechsel, our most junior political officer, convinced the Belgian government to revoke a 1993 law that, if it had continued in force, could have caused enormous damage to bilateral relations between our two countries.

Wechsel, a young man on his second tour abroad, had become familiar with various parts of the Belgian judicial system during his efforts to get the Belgians on the same page as us with regard to counterterrorism. He drew our embassy's and Washington's attention to the dangers to us and to some of our allies, especially Israel, of a new use of a law that the Belgian parliament had passed nearly ten years earlier. This law asserted that Belgium was competent to bring to trial anyone suspected of crimes against humanity, wherever committed, provided the alleged criminal was in Belgium or a Belgian citizen entered a legal complaint of such a crime.

The law, referred to in Belgium as the Law of Universal Competence, had received the strong endorsement of a rising star in the Flemish Liberal party, Guy Verhofstadt. Verhofstadt was one of many Belgian politicians who felt terrible about the genocide that had taken place in 1994, when ten Belgian soldiers and other Belgians were slaughtered along with tens of thousands of Africans in the former Belgian colony of Rwanda. There had been European troops in Rwanda at the time, participating in a UN peacekeeping mission that felt it lacked a mandate to intervene. Verhofstadt, who had subsequently become Belgian's prime minister, saw the Universal Competence law as a way of maybe bringing some of the murderous Rwandans to justice.

To the surprise of most of its advocates, however, in the decade that followed its passage, the Belgian Law of Universal Competence had begun to be used against alleged criminals the law's framers had never had in mind. Complaints under this law against the government of Israel on behalf of victims of the Sabra and Shatila massacres had led Israel to temporarily withdraw its ambassador to Belgium. And then, in 2003, shortly before the Iraq War started, victims of a bombing raid of a civilian shelter in Baghdad during the 1991 Gulf War filed a complaint under this law against former President George H. W. Bush, Vice President Richard Cheney in his role as former secretary of defense, and Secretary of State Colin Powell in his former role as chairman of the Joint Chiefs of Staff.

Arrests on the basis of such complaints were not automatic under that law, and were never likely to be made of Bush, Cheney, or Powell, but the threat hung like a sword of Damocles over US-Belgian relations in what was already a tense time. Wechsel, who was kept on the case and gradually became so knowledgeable about that law that Belgian officials in various ministries relied on his expertise, helped convince the Belgian government under a Verhofstadt prime ministership to ask its parliament to repeal the law—though not before some awkward moments, such as when Washington threatened to remove NATO headquarters from Belgium.

Wechsel had a three-week training course to attend in Washington just at the time when the Belgian parliament was bringing up a bill to repeal the troublesome law. So instead of him, I was sent by the embassy to sit in the tribune above the main floor of the Chamber, the lower house of Parliament, to watch and report on the last act in this drama.

I was leaning forward over the balcony, following the debate, when I caught the eye of the Speaker of the Chamber, the tremendously able and experienced Herman De Croo, also a Flemish Liberal. He looked up and recognized me, and a few minutes later a messenger arrived by my chair with a cart holding a four-foot-high pile of documents relating to the passage of the original law that had passed unanimously a decade earlier but was now about to be repealed. It was late on a chilly early spring night, and it was cold in the Chamber as I looked over at the Speaker again and smiled. He turned his warmest smile on me and raised an invisible hat. I imitated his gesture as best I could, and within a few minutes the bill to revoke the law of Universal Competence was passed. We then knew that, after a pro forma session in the Senate, the law would no longer be on the books.

Sitting in the balcony above the Chamber that evening was both a humbling and satisfying moment for me. In much of my work in Belgium since retirement, I had felt rather proud about being able to draw on more than a decade of experience there and on my extensive network of long-time Belgian friends. Yet here was Hans Wechsel, half my age, and in Belgium less than two years, who had done something even more impressive by simply using his very good brain and a whole lot of perseverance and attention to detail. The only extra help he had was that, for once, our political section was fully staffed, so he was allowed to concentrate on this project.

Epilogue

• • • • • •

WHY HAVE A CAREER FOREIGN SERVICE? That is a question that has been asked from time to time not only by outsiders but also by some people inside it. In the days when John and I came in, the Foreign Service attracted and recruited people drawn to a life of adventure who were willing, even eager, to serve abroad and who did not expect to earn the kind of money their college classmates could make in business or the professions. I think that is, by and large, still the case.

We Foreign Service officers were expected to already know—or be ready to quickly learn—at least another world language besides English; to have some familiarity with the great art, literature, and music of the West, if not of the world; and to be reasonably familiar with America's diplomatic history of the past hundred years or so. Our written entrance exam tested our general knowledge; I remember being asked to identify a Donatello David. And the oral exam tested whether we could present ourselves to a panel of alert, intelligent strangers with sensitivity, tact, and an ability to defend a point of view convincingly. The written exam now has fewer questions of the kind of "general knowledge" that betray having had an elite education, and the "oral" has ballooned from two hours with a panel of three people to a long and elaborate "whole candidate review" process with more than a dozen dimensions to be measured, and involving extensive role-playing among candidates.

We were mostly young, many of us without advanced degrees, but were ready to serve wherever "the needs of the service" required us to go. "Needs of the service" demanded that we spend most of our time abroad and that we learn to deal effectively with foreigners, whereas even today, most Americans do not have—or plan to get—a passport.

Because of historical and social developments in the United States, relatively few women, African Americans, or members of other minorities used to join the Foreign Service. For a long time, spouses were barred from taking the exam, since it greatly complicated the assignments process if the couple, understandably, wanted to avoid being split up. Eventually, after a court case that successfully claimed that women were being discriminated against in recruitment numbers, among other disparities, the bar was lifted, and in 1971 I was one of the first spouses to take and pass the exam.

Today the number of women Foreign Service officers is rising; the aim these days is to recruit an equal number of men and women, although currently only about 11 percent of our ambassadors are women. One problem that existed in my day was that there were relatively few qualified women who were eager to join a service that had few places abroad where a spouse could legally work. The State Department has done a spectacular job in getting more host countries to improve work opportunities abroad for spouses, but that cannot solve the problem for spouses trying to build a career when they cannot know where their Foreign Service spouse will be assigned one, two, or three years hence.

Despite strenuous Foreign Service recruitment efforts, the numbers of African Americans, Hispanics, and Asians are still low as compared to their respective proportion of the US population. This is largely due to factors over which the current Foreign Service has no control, such as better pay, hours, and working conditions in other professions for those candidates who have the other credentials that would make them good diplomats. Also, the fact that they were even less well represented in the past means that many minority potential candidates today don't think of diplomacy as an option, having few friends or colleagues who have taken that path. One way the State Department has tried to attract a wider group of candidates is by offering a very generous loan repayment program to help college graduates get rid of their college tuition debt.

At the same time, the State Department has greatly increased the number of political appointees and civil service employees in jobs that had previously been held by the career Foreign Service. The proportion of the senior-most jobs in the State Department given to noncareer Foreign Service appointees has risen from one-third in 1975 to two-thirds now. Political appointees now hold more ambassadorial jobs than since before the 1924 Rogers Act, which initiated our career Foreign Service.

The competition in the up-or-out Foreign Service process to earn promotion into the Senior Service is fierce, now that there are so few jobs available to career officers seeking to enter the higher ranks. This is a problem that is likely to get worse in the next decade, because the recruitment of entry-rank Foreign Service officers has risen in recent years, and these new officers will, over the next six to eight years, have to be promoted or forced out. The problem for career diplomats has been aggravated by the fact that the percentage of permanent employees in the State Department who are in the Civil Service (with no requirement to serve abroad or to move up or out, or to meet the other special criteria demanded of career diplomats) has risen from a low of 27 percent in 1980 to upward of 45 percent now, at the same time that the percentage of career Foreign Service personnel in the State Department has fallen from 73 percent to 55 percent.

As the expertise formerly provided by Foreign Service officers has diminished within the higher reaches of the State Department, so have that department's power and access to the president. Much of that power and access has now migrated to a gigantic Department of Defense, which is heavily involved in civil affairs abroad, a hyperactively operational CIA, and a greatly enlarged staff at the National Security Council (NSC). For those who wish to know more about these worrisome trends within our diplomatic establishment, I recommend retired ambassador Larry Pope's book, *The Demilitarization of American Diplomacy: Two Cheers for Striped Pants* (Basingstoke: Palgrave Macmillan, 2014). In his book, Pope examines in detail problems currently afflicting the Foreign Service and US foreign policy much more clearly and authoritatively than I could. To give you a sense of his drift, I quote here what he said in reference to the greatly expanded NSC staff to a University of Maine audience in a 2013 speech:

> Career diplomats are no wiser than anybody else, and a White House staff of lawyers and policy wonks can do a lot of things, but a world of sovereign

nations requires *sustained and serious attention* [my italics] and that is what a foreign ministry and a diplomatic service are for.

When John and I started our diplomatic life abroad in the late 1950s, we were able to draw not only on far more generous diplomatic staffing abroad but also on what was widely referred to as "the great reservoir of goodwill" toward America that had come into existence not only by our having won World War II, but also by our having won the peace that followed it.

Over the past fifty-plus years since our unsuccessful wars in Indochina, however, we have been continuing to use up that reservoir of goodwill until it is nearly dry. We won the Cold War, in the sense that we avoided a World War III and saw the breakup of the Soviet bloc in 1989 when the Wall came down. But during the decades that the Cold War lasted, a period foretold by George Orwell as "a peace that is no peace," more and more resources were provided to our Defense Department and our CIA while, at the same time, the State Department was progressively starved of funding, staffing, and political clout at home. This tendency has worsened since 9/11. Even when we get more money for staffing, it is generally not spent on putting classic diplomats (political/economic officers) in nonwar zones.

From the 1970s to the 1990s, the State Department, in order to save money, eliminated dozens of consulates that could observe and help our government better understand and influence opinion leaders of countries we needed to work closely with, especially our NATO allies, such as France and Germany, or in areas where there was trouble brewing, such as the Middle East.

And then, beginning after Osama bin Laden organized deadly bombing attacks in 1998 on our embassies in Kenya and Tanzania, the expense of installing every metal detector and hideous barbed-wire fence festooning a US embassy (often relocated from downtown to outside of town, beyond public transportation) and overstaffing it with "regional security officers" has been paid for by eliminating essential diplomatic personnel inside the political and economic sections. According to figures from September 2013, the security bureau of the Department of State currently has some 2,000 security officers, more permanent employees (at home and abroad combined) than does any other State Department bureau. It is as if, after a bank robbery, the bank's owners spent most of their resources making the bank inaccessible to customers, and eliminated bankers and bank tellers to replace them by armed guards.

. . . .

Though mostly useless in war zones, diplomats are often needed in other places where there is danger—and sometimes they get killed there. God knows it is never easy to assess the risks that being in the new place can pose for you, a foreigner and a representative (official or not) of your country.

Regional security officers often seem to be more concerned with protecting us diplomats from foreigners than with finding a relatively safe way for us to do our job. I recall an instance when a noncareer American ambassador in Europe—after accepting an invitation to an event from an important host country political contact who sometimes opposed US policies—simply did not show up. At the last minute, the RSO had told the ambassador not to attend; he had heard of a possible threat that in his view made it too risky. Years later, that ambassador's successors were still paying for that slight, while the person slighted had become more important than ever to that country and to our relations with it.

Admittedly not in the 2012 Chris Stevens case—where our knowledgeable, experienced ambassador to Libya was killed along with three members of his staff—but often, a career officer is better able to judge security risks than can a noncareer ambassador or an RSO. Once, while working as a rehired diplomat a few years ago, I was told by the RSO that I must not go to observe what was happening at a European Union summit outside the capital because there was going to be a Leftist demonstration protesting against the summiteers. I was able to get that order rescinded by pointing out that I would be staying the night before the summit with friends in that city who would be among the demonstrators. Many career diplomats can tell similar stories of the inherent contradiction between 100 percent physical security and being allowed to do our job. It is a continual struggle that calls for common sense on both sides.

. . . .

Since World War II, more American ambassadors than generals have been killed on the job, but one should not exaggerate the dangers American diplomats face. Most days, most American diplomats don't risk the dangers faced daily in the United States by the cop on the beat, the fireman, or even the teacher in an inner-city classroom. Like many other diplomats, I received the odd letter containing a death threat and traveled roads where murderous rebels sometimes killed or took hostages. But in fifty-odd years I had only one occasion when I was faced with what seemed to me to be a credible risk to my life related to my work as a diplomat. It is a much more typical Foreign Service story than that of the murder of an ambassador.

It was late on a Sunday afternoon in Bordeaux in 1991 when I got a phone call at home from the duty officer at our embassy in Paris. An aide to a US senator from Iowa had called the Paris duty officer to alert him that the father of an American teenage girl who was in Bordeaux on a student exchange had been telephoned by his daughter; she had told him she was being held at gunpoint in Bordeaux by a demented Frenchwoman. The girl, in her frantic phone call to her father back home, had said the woman with the shotgun had a real or imagined complaint against the United States. The woman had taken the girl hostage to force the US government to send a senior American official to come to her house, hear her out, and solve her problem.

I was on very friendly terms with Bordeaux's prefect of police due to an unusual circumstance: we both were having our frozen shoulders massaged by the same Bordeaux physical therapist. The French have a different idea about bodily modesty than Americans. For example, until recently, most public toilets in France were unisex. And to this day, on many ocean beaches in France people bathe nude next to swimmers in bathing suits, without eyebrows being raised. So my Bordeaux physiotherapist had not hesitated in placing the prefect of police and me on side-by-side mattresses while he pummeled first one, then the other of us, both of us in a state of relative undress. The therapist was the best in town; the police prefect and I could choose to be embarrassed or we could laugh. We laughed and became friends.

I had his home phone number, and at my request he called around and found which police station was handling the hostage problem and gave me its phone number. I called the police station and told the policeman in charge of the case that I wanted to come and help, given that the woman wanted to see an American official. The policeman was afraid my arrival might provoke the woman to violence. He said that even he was hesitant to get too close to her door for fear she might do something we would all later regret. I asked that he keep me informed, and hung up feeling somewhat frustrated.

Then I called the Frenchwoman's number, and, as I had hoped, the girl answered. She said she had seen an ad in the woman's window asking for a native English speaker to give her language lessons. Though a first lesson had gone all right, this was the second lesson and the woman was clearly not in her right mind. The girl confirmed what I had been told about the Frenchwoman wanting to see a senior American government official. I congratulated the girl on handling things so well thus far and gave her my number and urged her to phone me at any time if she thought I should come. I called the father in Iowa and said more or less the same thing.

A half hour later, the girl called. She said I needed to come now.

John had already checked out on our street map where the house was. He got our Jetta out of the garage while I phoned the police to say that I was coming now, that I would have no weapon, and that I hoped that the police would not carry weapons either. The police officer agreed that this operation would be best handled "with velvet gloves."

John was in the driver's seat with the engine running while I stood looking vaguely about me in my own front hallway. It had suddenly occurred to me that the woman would hardly recognize in a middle-aged woman the "senior American government official" that she was demanding to see in return for releasing her hostage. Then I saw on my wall a present from some France-America Club friends: a framed recent page two from *Sud Ouest* with a nearly full-page article featuring an enormous photo of me holding a little plaster Statue of Liberty in my hands. I unhooked it from the wall and carried it along with my handbag out to the car.

We got to the house, and John waited in the car. The policeman I had spoken to on the phone allowed me to walk up alone to the door of the house with my framed newspaper article in my hands. Speaking through the keyhole, I was glad for once that my accent in French was so unmistakably American. I said I was the American Consul General in Bordeaux and I had something to show her that might interest her. Could she please open the door?

When the door opened, the girl—thank heaven—was there on the doorsill, facing the woman who was holding up a shotgun. I put my arm around the girl's shoulder and gently drew her toward me, while thinking that this gesture, so natural between an older woman and a girl younger than my daughter, would have set off alarm bells if done by a man. I kept walking backward with the girl while the police moved forward past me, engaging the woman in conversation until they could gently disarm her.

The following week, the demented woman sent me a note of apology, saying that when she did not take her medicine "volcanic eruptions went off" inside her. I learned later that her illness was thought to be either manic bipolar disorder or schizophrenia, and, with its focus on getting attention from an important person, it was not unlike the illness John Hinckley Jr. was suffering from when he shot President Reagan, Press Secretary Brady, and a Secret Service guard.

Whenever I think back on that evening in Bordeaux, I remember John, driving me in complete silence to that woman's house. He knew I needed to psych myself up for whatever might be coming next and that the last thing I needed was somebody, even him, interrupting my train of thought. His whole being must have been anxious at that moment for my safety, but one of his greatest gifts to me was his willingness to let me run my own risks.

How lucky I was to have him in my life. How I miss him! And how I miss the honorable craft of diplomacy we were privileged to practice together!

Acknowledgments

· · · · · · · · · · ·

In what is written above, I relied almost entirely on my memory (often supported by letters home to my mother), which is why there are few footnotes and no bibliography. But my mother taught me to have a great respect for the truth, and I have tried my best to stick to it.

For helping me write this book, I must first thank my indefatigably generous friend/editor, Don Ediger, Richard Morris (my patient and knowledgeable agent at Janklow and Nesbit), book developer Paul De Angelis, and Margery Thompson, the heart, soul, and publishing director of the Association for Diplomatic Studies and Training (ADST), the organization that, luckily for me, adopted this book and helped it find a publisher. I also could not have been luckier in my acquiring editor, Gill Berchowitz of Ohio University Press, who understood immediately what I was trying to do and helped me rid my draft of the occasional barnacles that were defacing the surface of the text. I am also deeply grateful for the press's managing editor Nancy Basmajian, copyeditor Teresa Jesionowski, production manager Beth Pratt, the other talented people at Ohio University Press, and indexer Amron Gravett of Wild Clover Book Services.

I also owe thanks to the following friends and family members who read—and in some cases reread—various drafts and gave me useful comments and encouragement: the much-mourned late Jean-François Baré first of all, and other dear friends: Sven Biscop, Daniel Bobrow, Parker and Anna Borg, Michael Carowitz, Elinor Constable, Michele Crown, Charlotte De Groote, Chantal De Smet, Rob Faucher, David and Morwenna Goodall, Glen Harley, Carolee Heileman, Debra Heimann, Stephanie Kinney, Kirsten Lawford Davies, Joan Lindsay, Edward Marks, Douglas McElhaney,

Cornelia Montgomery, Sister Miriam Moscow, Michael A. Newman, Bob and Phyllis Oakley, Thomas and Carolyn Ouchterlony, Ioanna Paraskevopoulos, Harlan and Linda Robinson, Elizabeth Schell, Marilyn Slatnick, Alan Stevens, Gilbert Tauber, Jan Van Kerkhove, Michele Wagner, and Ken Wilson.

I offer my apologies to those I forgot to thank, and for any errors of fact and omissions I made due to misremembering.

Every effort has been made to locate the copyright holder of the first photo, of Judy at age twelve. We would appreciate any information leading to our being able to acknowledge the copyright holder.

The opinions and characterizations in my book are my own and do not necessarily represent official positions of the United States government.

Appendix

• • • • • •

Our Foreign Service Career

11/1958–7/1960	Jakarta, Indonesia: John, political officer
7/1960–11/1961	Surabaya, Indonesia: John, vice consul
1/1962–6/1964	The Hague, Netherlands: John, commercial officer
6/1964–6/1965	Yale University: John, graduate student
6/1965–6/1966	Kuala Lumpur, Malaysia: John, commercial officer
7/1966–10/1968	Kuching, Malaysia: John, consul for East Malaysia and Brunei
11/1968–9/1972	State Department: John, political officer on Southeast Asia desk
5/1972	Judy becomes a Foreign Service officer
9/1972–8/1975	Brussels, Belgium: John, economic officer at embassy
1/1973–8/1975	Brussels, Belgium: Judy, vice consul
8/1975–6/1978	Antwerp, Belgium: John, consul
8/1975–6/1978	Brussels, Belgium: Judy commercial officer at embassy
8/1978–5/1980	Kinshasa, Zaire: John, economic counselor
9/1978–11/1978	Nairobi, Kenya: Judy, consular officer
11/1978–6/1980	Kinshasa, Zaire: Judy, political officer
9/1980–6/1984	Brussels, Belgium: John, political counselor at embassy

10/1980–12/1981	Brussels, Belgium: Judy, state and local government officer, US Mission to the European Union
12/1981–5/1983	Brussels, Copenhagen, and Bonn: Judy, EU presidency rover
5/1983–6/1984	Brussels, Belgium: Judy, special assistant to ambassador to Belgium
8/1984–5/1986	State Department: John, Foreign Service inspector; Judy, political officer, European regional political-economic affairs
5/1986–10/1987	The Hague, Netherlands: John, deputy chief of mission and chargé d'affaires
8/1986–9/1986	Amsterdam, Netherlands: Judy, acting consular officer
7/1987–7/1991	Bordeaux, France: Judy, consul general
10/1987	John retires from the Foreign Service to join Judy in Bordeaux
9/1991–5/1992	Manila, Philippines: Judy, refugee coordinator
5/1992	Judy retires from the Foreign Service
1993–95	Zagreb, Croatia: John, acting refugee coordinator for months at a time
1/1997–4/1997	Luxembourg: John is ambassador's senior adviser; Judy, political-economic officer
6/1998–8/1998	Luxembourg: John is ambassador's senior adviser, Judy, political-economic officer
6/2000	John dies in Washington, DC
2001–2	Judy works on terrorist assets freeze at State Department
2003–10	Judy works parts of most years on the Political-Military Action Team at the State Department
2001–11	Brussels, Belgium: Judy works parts of most years as senior adviser to embassy political section

Index

• • • •

Note: Page numbers in *italics* refer to illustrations.

dental care, 46, 79
De Schrijver, Adrien, 140–41
Desmond (Heimanns' butler), 180, 182
diamond trade, 203–4
diplomat, definition of, 206. *See also* Foreign
  Service work
diplomatic spouses. *See* gender and diplomacy
disease, 3, 21; asbestos and, 184; cancer, 172–
  73, 176, 178, 199; HIV/AIDS, 3, 160–62;
  in Indonesia, 17, 21, 56; malaria, 21, 56,
  79, 141; sleeping sickness, 70
domestic servants: in Bordeaux, 188, 191; for
  children, 43–44, 46–49, 67, 72, 84; in The
  Hague, 180, 182; in Indonesia, 21, 31–33,
  37–39, 43–49, 52, 115; security protection,
  183–85, 188
drug trade, 88, 89
Duemling, Bob, 46, 66
Dulles, Allen, 27–28
Dulles, John Foster, 27–28
Dumas, Roland, 191–92
Dutch language, 87, 107–8, 165, 167–68, 178
dysentery, 21

East Germany, 169, 191, 216. *See also* Germany
East Malaysia: description of, 70; languages in,
  64; oil interests, 81, 85; political history
  of, 64–66, 67, 71, 74; Sukarno's policy
  in, 75, 76, 81; US policy in, 66, 74–75.
  See also Kuching, Sarawak, East Malaysia;
  Malaysia
Ebola virus, 3
education: of Bremer, 181–82; of John
  Heimann, 1, 17, 114; of Judith Heimann,
  1, 17, 89, 115, 131–32, 134. *See also*
  language(s)
Eeckels, Guido, 107–8
Eisenhower, Dwight D., 27–28
elder housing programs, 167
Eleanor (pet), 191, 202
encephalitis, 70
Esther (pet), 191, 202
Ethiopian princess imprisonments, 169–70
etiquette in international diplomacy: in
  conversation, 50, 182, 209; at formal
  events, 50, 61–62; as host and hostess, 11,
  13, 29, 31–33, 50, 52–55; in Indonesia, 22,
  24–26, 30, 79–81, 84. *See also* clothing
European Union (EU), 133, 164, 167–69, 171.
  See also Council of Europe (COE); NATO;
  specific countries

Fabiola, Queen of the Belgians, 132–33
Federation of Malaysia. *See* Malaysia
Figaro (newspaper), 189
films on war, 23, 196
Fitzpatrick, Mike, 202–3
flour, 38, 51–52
food and supplies: in Bordeaux, 54–55; in
  Indonesia, 33, 39–41, 45, 51–52, 56,
  58–60, 62; in Kinshasa, 157; in Malaysia,
  61–62, 79; in Zaire, 152–53, 160
Ford, Gerald and Betty, 130
foreign currency exhange in Indonesia, 40–41
Foreign Service work: demarche procedures,
  8–9, 208; Foreign Service exam, 16, 86,
  127, 213, 214; language training for, 4,
  17, 37, 61, 87; management of, summary,
  214–17; policies on women in, 16, 26, 214;
  qualities for, 2, 206–8; Rogers Act, 215;
  timeline of Heimanns', 223–24; training for,
  4, 16, 37. *See also* communications; gender
  and diplomacy
formal attire, 28, 52, 62, 174
Fourth of July celebrations, 31–33, 64, 66
France: aeronautics industry in southwest, 190,
  195; communications in, 192; confidential
  communication capability in, 189; as EU
  member, 168, 169; Hundred Years' War,
  187; on Turkish human rights, 177; US
  relations with, 177–78, 189–90, 195–96;
  wine industries of, 55. *See also* Bordeaux,
  France
Franklin, Benjamin, 206
French language, 87, 91, 107, 138, 153
Frost, Robert, 152
Fugit, Ed, 167–68

Gaullist Party (France), 123, 190, 194
Geertz, Clifford, 33
gender and diplomacy: advantages to being
  a woman, 7, 54, 61–64, 200; challenges
  to being a female diplomat, 2, 10–11, 14,
  147–48; diplomatic spouse's role, 10, 22,
  24–26, 30, 38–39, 182–83; Foreign Service
  policies on, 16, 26, 37, 214. *See also* Foreign
  Service work; women
German language, 153
Germany, 166, 169, 191, 216
Gisenyi mercenary incident, Rwanda, 138–45
Goma missionaries, Zaire, 135, 136, 137–43
Goodall, David, 28–29
Gould, David, 6

as refugee coordinator in Manila, *125*, 199–200
retirement of, 199, 200
security protection of, 60 156, 188, 217–18
as senior advisor to political section, Embassy Brussels, 201, 202, 206–12
as State and Local Officer at US Mission to the EU, 166–67
at State Dept., worked on developing a list of terrorists for assets freeze, 203–5
at State's European Bureau, covered political relations with COE and EU, 173–79
as vice consul in Brussels, 87–100
Zaire border crossing incident, 148–51
Heimann, Judith, personal life
biography of Harrisson by, 183, 185, 200, 201
childhood nanny of, 44–45, 83, 101
childhood of, 101, *111*, 131–32
dancing by, 28, 79, 80–81
daughter of, 70, 75–77, 86, 128, 187, 201
education of, 1, 17, 89, *115*, 131–32, 134
father of, 1, 101
health of, 70, 218–19
images of, *111*, *115*, *118*, *126*
kong-si and, 46, 48–49
low morale of, 128–32
Makanda and, 157–62, 185
meeting John, 1, 17
memory of, 1–2, 151–52, 221
mothers of, 1–2, 44–45, 83, 101, *111*, 131, 137, 199
musical interests of, 154, 175–76, 184
pets of, 41–42, 156, 191, 202
son of (*see* Heimann, Paul)
street incidents of, 101–7
as teacher, 30, 43
Thanksgiving dinners, 83, 153–54
Heimann, Paul
adult life of, 184, 195, 201
birth and childhood of, 43–44, 52, 70
education of, 86, 128
Henderson, Hester, 20, 22, 24–25, 30
Henderson, John, 20, 22–24, 209
Hindu-Buddhism, 34
Hinson-Jones, Robyn, 202
Hinton, Dean, 8
HIV/AIDS, 3, 160–62
hoarding, Sukarno's measures against, 40–41
Holland. *See* Netherlands
hostess etiquette, 11, 13, 29, 31–33, 50, 52–55
housing: in Antwerp, 129; in Bordeaux, 187;

elderly refitting program, 167; in The Hague, 180; in Jakarta, 20–21, *105*; in Kinshasa, 3–4, 102–3, *120*; in Kuching, 71–73; of refugees, 97–98, 200
Hughes, Rusty, 192
human rights: in Brussels, 87–89, 96–100; in Copenhagen, 169–70; in Philippines, 199–200; in Turkey, 177; US policies on, 159–60; in Zaire, 14–15, 159
Hundred Years' War, France, 187
Hunter College High School, 131
Hussein, Saddam, 196. *See also under* Iraq

Iam (Heimanns' laundress), 43–44
Iban language, 68, 77
Iban tribespeople, 74; backyard incident with, 84; Dayak Day celebration with, 78–81; intercultural married life of Heidi and Sidi, 72, 76–77; paramount chief of, 66–68, 75, 77–78; women and clothing of, 79, *119*. *See also* Dayak tribes
IMF (International Monetary Fund), 5
immigration policies, US, 92–95
India, 35–36, 169
Indian population in Malaysia, 65
Indonesia: anti-American sentiment in, 16, 43, 60; *becaks*, 19, 58, 63, *118*; censorship in, 57; communications in, 37; Communist Party of, 23, 56–57; disease in, 17, 21, 56; food and supplies in, 33, 39–41, 45, 51–52, 56, 58–60, 62; languages in, 4, 33, 35–38, 44, 61; monetary exchange in, 40–41; religion in, 33–35; war and, 24, 27–28, 39, 56, 75, 84–85. *See also* Sukarno; *specific regions*
International Court of Justice, The Hague, 208
International Herald Tribune, 189
International Visitor Program, 82, 158, 160
Iraq, 181n1, 208. *See also* Hussein, Saddam
Iraq War (1990–91), 196–98
Iraq War (2003–11), 207, 208–11
Ireland, 168
Is Paris Burning? (film), 196
Israel, 211
Italy, 168, 169

Jakarta, Indonesia: description of, 16–17, 19–21; domestic servants in, 21, 37–39, 43–44, *115*; formal events in, 28–29; housing in, 20–21, *105*; Judith walks around the corner at night, 101–2; US Embassy in, 16, 27, 31, 56. *See also* Indonesia

Java, Indonesia, 33–35, 39, *116, 118*. *See also* Indonesia; Jakarta, Indonesia
Javanese language, 44
jeruks (fruit), 59–60
Johnson, Lyndon B., 47–48
Johnson, Samuel, 10
Jones, Howard P., 24–25, 28, 56, 57, *116*
Jones, Mary Lou, 24–25, 32

kasar behavioral style, 63
Kennan, George, 166
Kenya, 4, 146, 216
Kikongo language, 138
Kimberley Process, 204
Kinshasa, Zaire (now Democratic Republic of Congo): description of, 5, 12; food and supplies in, 157; housing in, 3–4, 102–3, 120; John's work in, 4–5, 11, 102–3, 178; Judith's work in, 4–15, 102–4, 135–36; languages in, 103, 138, 144; street incidents in, 102–4; US Embassy in, 10, 109, 135. *See also* Mobutu Sese Seko; Zaire
Kiswahili language, 11, 138, 144
Kivu, Lake (Zaire), travels by Judith, 136–43
kleptocracy, 6
Kolwezi massacre, Zaire, 3, 11
konfrontasi (armed confrontation) in Sarawak, 75, 76, 81
kong-si (organization), 46, 48–49
Kuala Lumpur, Malaysia: description of, 104–5; diplomatic life in, 61–64; housing in, 105; John's work in, 61; *kong-si* and, 46, 48–49; street incident in, 105–7. *See also* Malaysia
Kuching, Sarawak, East Malaysia, *119*; description of, 70–71; domestic servants in, 46–49; housing in, 71–73; Judith's first dinner at the Governor's Palace, 66–69. *See also* East Malaysia; Malaysia
kucing hutan (jungle cat), 41–42
Kuwait, 196

language(s): of Anita Cunningham, 51; bartering and, 58–60; in Belgium, 87, 107–8, 133–34; domestic servants and, 35–36, 44; Dutch, 87, 107–8, 165, 167–68, 178; in East Malaysia and Brunei, 64; French, 87, 91, 107, 138, 153; German, 153; importance of knowing several, 26, 35, 61, 87, 206, 213; in Indonesia, 4, 33, 35–38, 44, 61–64; John's skills with, 4, 35, 87, 107, 165; Judith's skills with, 4,

33, 35, 62, 68, 87, 107–8, 131–32, 134, 167–68; in Kinshasa, 103; Latin, 131–32, 134; training, 4, 17, 37, 61, 87; in Zaire, 11, 103, 138, 144. *See also specific languages*
Latin language, 131–32, 134
laundering clothes, 22, 38
Law of Universal Competence (Belgium), 210–12
Le Monde (newspaper), 189
Lingala language, 103, 138
loan repayment program, 214
Longequeue, Louis, 123
longhouses of Borneo, 75, 78, 79
Louise (Judith Heimann's nanny), 44–45, 83, 101
Luxembourg, 168, 201
Lyon, France, 191

macan tutul (spotted panther), 41–42
MacDonald, Malcolm, 65
Majid, Rugayah, 79–80
Makanda, 157–62, 185
malaria, 21, 56, 79, 141
Malay language, 4, 44, 61
Malaysia, 17; behavioral styles in, 63; Chinese population in, 65–66, 81–82; political history of, 64–66; weddings in, 61–64. *See also* East Malaysia; *specific regions*
Manila, Philippines, 125, 199–200
marijuana trade, 88, 89
Marks, Edward, 201–2
marriage: in Belgium, 91–92; in Java, 34; in Malaysia, 62–64
Martin, Joan, 52
Martin, Peter, 52
Mathew (pet), 41–42
McDonald's, 127–28
McDonnell Douglas, 195
memcons, 194
milk, 40, 42, 51
Millay, Edna St. Vincent, 20, 151
Mina (Heimanns' baby *amah*), 44, 45
missionary community, Kivu, Zaire, 135, 136, 137–43
Mitterrand, François, 190, 196–97
Mobutu Sese Seko: corruption by, 8–9, 14, 158; dissidents of, 13–14, 135, 138–39, 159–60; economic policy of, 6, 148; lunch with, 152–53; men's national attire instituted by, 143; naming of Zaire by, 3, 109;

surveillance by, 7, 11, 15, 156; US support of, 8, 10. *See also* Zaire (now Democratic Republic of Congo)

monetary exchange, 40–41

Moscow, Esther, 1, 101, *111*, 131, 199

Moscow, Warren, 1, 101

multiculturalism, 65–66, 76–77

Munan family, 72, 76–77

Muslim practices: in East Malaysia, 62, 63; in Java, 33–34; women and, 26–27. *See also* religion

M.V. Kinabalu, 70

Nairobi, Kenya, 4, 216

NATO, 56, 133, 164, 168–69, 177, 209. *See also* European Union (EU); *specific countries*

Netherlands, 166, 168, 182–84. *See also* The Hague, Netherlands

ngajat (Iban dance), 79, 80–81

Nixon, Pat, 130, 174

Nixon, Richard, 130

nonpaper, defined, 86, 207

Norway, 177

nuclear missile basing issues, 163–66, 182

Oakley, Robert, 15, 155, 178

Obama, Barack, 169

oil interests in Borneo, 81, 85

Olsen, Doris. *See* Heimann, Doris Olsen

Organization for Economic Cooperation and Development (OECD), 177

Orwell, George, 216

Pachelbel's Canon, 154

pacifism, 163–64, 165, 210

Palmer, Billy, 22–24

Pandit, Vijaya, 131

Paris Club, 5

Peace Corps: in Borneo, 68, 77; in Bukavu, 138, 140, 142

pets, 41–42, 156, 191

Pfeffer, Franz, 170

Philippines, 125, 199–200

Pierson, Jean, 195

poetry, 20, 151–52

polio, 21

Political-Military Action Team (PMAT), 205

Pope, Larry, 215–16

Porson, Sophie, 153–54

Portugal, 169

Powell, Colin, 211

POW experience, 152

Price, Carol, 173

Price, Charles, 167, 172, 173

prisoners' rights and assistance, 14–15, 87–89, 159–60, 169–70

protocol calls, 22, 24–27, 30, 51, 86–87

Puncak, West Java, Indonesia, 22–23

Queen's Birthday Ball, Jakarta, 28–29

Radcliffe College, 17, 20, *115*

radio communications: at US consulate in Bukavu, 37, 139–41. *See also* communications

rain prevention, 31–33

Reagan, Ronald, 159, 165, 220

rebel warfare. *See* war

refugee assistance, 96–100, 125, 199–200

religion, 33–35, 65–66. *See also* Muslim practices

Religion of Java, The (Geertz), 33

Remole, Bob, 5, 6, 8–10, 135, 145–46

Richardson, Cy, 87, 88, 92

Robinson, Harlan "Robby," 6, 10, 11, 14, 153

Robinson, Linda, 153

Rocard, Michel, 196

Rodgers, Joe M., *123*

Rogers Act (1924), 215

Roosevelt, Eleanor, 131

Rubber Research Institute, 48

Rwanda, 138–45, 211

Sabah, East Malaysia, 65, 66, 72, 81, 83

Sarawak, East Malaysia, *119*; description of, 70; political history of, 64–66, 75, 76, 81. *See also* East Malaysia; Kuching, Sarawak, East Malaysia

Sarawak United People's Party (SUPP), 82

Sayers, Dorothy, 145

Schell, Betsy, 172

Schmidt, Helmut, 166

security protection, 35, 60, 183–85, 188, 198, 216–18

selamatan (animist communal feast to appease local spirits), 31, 34

Sergeant York (film), 23

Shad, John, 122

shamans, 34, 76, 77

Shanghai, China, 17

Shapiro, David and Sharon, 153, 156

West Germany, 164, 166, 168, 169, 170, 191, 216. *See also* Germany

West Malaysia, 64–66. *See also* East Malaysia; Malaysia

White Rajahs, 64–66, 67, 71, 74. *See also* East Malaysia

WikiLeaks, 171n1

wine, 55

women: 1930s sexism in US, 18; Foreign Service policies regarding, 16, 26, 37, 214; Iban longhouse women's dispute with their men, 79–80; Muslim practices of, 26–27. *See also* gender and diplomacy

Women's Institute, Kuching Branch, 78

Women's International Club, Indonesia, 30, 57, 116

Wooten, Henry, 206

Yao, 18, *112*

Yong, Stephen, 82–83

Young, Bob and Margaret, 64

Zagreb, Croatia, 200–201

Zaire (now Democratic Republic of Congo): Air Zaire incident, 145–47; border crossing incident, 148–51; Bukavu, 135–45, 151–54; confidential communications in, 139–41; inflation in, 148, 156–57; Kolwezi massacre, 3, 11; languages in, 103, 138, 144; naming of, 3, 109; political dissidents in, 4–15, 102–3, 135, 158; prisoners' human rights in, 14–15, 159–60. *See also* Kinshasa, Zaire (now Democratic Republic of Congo); Mobutu Sese Seko

Zimbabwe, 204